Hadrat Abu Bakr Siddiq

by

Professor Masudul Hasan

KITAB BHAVAN
NEW DELHI-110002

KITAB BHAVAN
Publishers, Distributors, Exporters & Importers
1784, Kalan Mahal, Darya Ganj,
New Delhi - 1100 02 (India)

Mob. ✆ : +91-11-9953098606
Website : www.kitabbhavan.net
E-mail : info@kitabbhavan.net
: nasri@vsnl.com

Reprint : 2023

ISBN-10 : 81-7151-228-3
ISBN-13 : 978-81-7151-228-7

Book Code No. : H00178

Batch ID : SPRFN181123

Printed & Published in India by :

Moonis Ali Nasri for KITAB BHAVAN
1784, Kalan Mahal, Darya Ganj,
New Delhi - 1100 02 [India]

Preface

Next to the Holy Prophet, Hadrat Abu Bakr is the most outstanding figure of Islam. During the life time of the Holy Prophet, Hadrat Abu Bakr was in the words of the Holy Qur'an "the second of the two". He played a supporting role, and as "witness to the truth" corroborated all that the Holy Prophet said or did.

After the death of the Holy Prophet, Hadrat Abu Bakr rose to his full stature of greatness. When he came to office, many crises threatened to overwhelm Islam. Through his dynamic leadership he overcame all such crises. He suppressed apostasy and unified Arabia under Islam. Thereafter the Muslims marched to Iraq and Syria, and won outstanding victories. Hadrat Abu Bakr set the pace for making Islam a world force.

Inspite of the outstanding personality of Hadrat Abu Bakr, it is a matter of some regret that we do not have many books on him. In English there are hardly three or four books about his biography. That provides the justification for producing this book on Hadrat Abu Bakr.

The book is divided into twenty chapters and about a hundred sections. I am conscious of my limitations, and although I have not been able to make full justice to the greatness of Hadrat Abu Bakr, I have the consolation that profiting from the existing works on the biography of Hadrat Abu Bakr, I have produced a work which is an improvement on the existing works. It will be for the following writers to make further improvements.

I have tried to present the biography of Hadrat Abu Bakr in a scientific way. I have analysed the causes responsible for the success of Hadrat Abu Bakr. I have made an assessment of the various aspects of the greatness of Hadrat Abu Bakr. His effulgence is too dazzling, and one is apt not to have a full vision. For this disability I seek the indulgence of the readers. I, however, feel that I have provided the framework whereunder the learned readers can ponder and discover the greatness of Hadrat Abu Bakr for themselves.

The story of Hadrat Abu Bakr is the story of faith that moved mountains. I am, therefore, sure that a study of his life story will not only inspire the readers, but will fortify their faith as well.

May God bless my effort. May God help the readers in having a better understanding of Hadrat Abu Bakr.

Professor Masudul Hasan

CONTENTS

1

BEFORE AND AFTER CONVERSION TO ISLAM

Pre-Islamic Period

Date of birth. The exact date of birth of Hadrat Abu Bakr is not known. According to traditions he was younger than the Holy Prophet of Islam by two years and a few months. As the Holy Prophet was born in 571 C.E., we can safely hold that Hadrat Abu Bakr was born at Makkah some time in the year 573 C.E.

The family. Hadrat Abu Bakr's father was Othman surnamed Abu Qahafa, and his mother was Salma surnamed Umm-ul-Khair. They belonged to the Bani Taim branch of the Quraish.

The genealogy of Hadrat Abu Bakr joined with that of the Holy Prophet, eight generations back in their common ancestor Murrah.

The Holy Prophet was the son of Abdullah, who was the son of Abdul Muttalib, who was the son of Hashim, who was the son of Abd Manaf, who was the son of Qussayi, who was the son of Kulab, who was the son of Murrah.

Hadrat Abu Bakr was the son of Othman, who was the son of 'Amar, who was the son of 'Amr, who was the son of Ka'ab, who was the son of Sa'ad, who was the son of Taim, who was the son of Murrah.

Name. The original name of Hadrat Abu Bakr was Abdul

Ka'aba—the servant of Ka'aba. Some children were born to his parents before him, but they did not survive. When he was born, he was taken to the Ka'aba, dedicated to the gods of Ka'aba, and named Abdul Ka'aba.

Childhood. Hadrat Abu Bakr's family enjoyed affluence, and he was born with the proverbial silver spoon in his mouth. No detailed accounts are available about the life of Hadrat Abu Bakr during the period of childhood. Like other Arab children, he spent early years in the open air of the desert. He grew as a typical son of the soil. The leanness and barenness of the land around him was reflected in his phsyique. He was lean and thin with a slender constitution, but was otherwise very hardy and had a strong mind. He had the tenacity and the strength of the rocks around him. Like the golden sand of the desert, his face glowed with a white and red complexion. By all standards he was beautiful, and for his beauty he earned the surname of 'Atiq'.

Abu Bakr. Having been bred up in the early years in the midst of the bedouins who called themselves 'Ahl-i-Ba'eer'—the people of the camel, he developed particular fondness for camels. In the early years he played with the young ones of the camels, and his love for the camels earned him the surname of "Abu Bakr—the father of the foal of the camel."

Hadrat Abu Bakr's encounter with the idols of the Ka'aba. A story is preserved that once when Hadrat Abu Bakr was a child, his father took him to the Ka'aba, and asked him to pray before the idols. His father went away to attend to some other business, and Hadrat Abu Bakr was left alone with the idols. Addressing an idol, Hadrat Abu Bakr said, "O my God, I am in need of beautiful clothes; bestow them on me." The idol remained indifferent. Then Hadrat Abu Bakr addressing another idol said, "O God, give me some delicious food. I am so hungry." The idol remained cold to the prayer. That exhausted the patience of young Abu Bakr. He lifted a stone, and addressing an idol said, "Here I am aiming a stone; if you are a God protect yourself." "Hadrat Abu Bakr hurled the stone at the idol, which broke into pieces. Hadrat Abu Bakr left the Ka'aba." Thereafter Hadrat Abu Bakr never prayed to the idols in the Ka'aba. This Abraham style of encounter with the idols made Hadrat Abu Bakr a Muslim at heart long before his formal profession of Islam.

The monk Bahira. Jalal-ud-Din Syuti has preserved an account that when at the age of twelve, the Holy Prophet accompanied his uncle Abu Talib along with a trade caravan, Hadrat Abu Bakr was also with the caravan. The Holy Prophet reclined under a lote tree. The monk Bahira asked Hadrat Abu Bakr as to who was the person who was reclining under the lote tree. Hadrat Abu Bakr told the monk that he was Muhammad the son of Abdullah. Thereupon the monk said, "Then, by Allah he is the prophet for none has taken shelter under this tree since the time of Jesus, the son of Mary".

The war of Fijar. During the eightees of the sixth century, there was the war of Fijar between the Hawazin and the Quraish. We know that the Holy Prophet participated in this war, and his role lay in picking up the stray arrows thrown by the enemy, and handing them to his uncle Abu Talib. The sources are silent about the participation of Hadrat Abu Bakr. We can, however, safely presume that Hadrat Abu Bakr would have also participated in this war and played some peripheral role.

Hilf-ul-Fudul. After the war of Fijar, the "Hilf-ul-Fudul" was set up at Makkah. Its avowed object was to help all wronged persons in the redressing of their wrongs. The Holy Prophet often said that he was proud of the oath that he had taken about the fulfilment of the objectives of the "Hilf-ul-Fudul". The sources make no reference to Hadrat Abu Bakr in this respect. The organization was set up at the house of Abdullah b. Jad'aan who belonged to the same clan of the Quraish as Hadrat Abu Bakr, we have thus reason to presume that Hadrat Abu Bakr was also a member of the league, and subscribed to its objective.

Disciplined life. Though bred and brought up in an aristocratic family in the midst of an idolatrous society, conspicuous for indulgence in wine, women, and gambling, Hadrat Abu Bakr resisted these temptations, and led a disciplined life avoiding the frolics, frivolities, and dissipations that characterised the life of the contemporary youth of Makkah. Once Hadrat Abu Bakr was asked whether he ever drank wine during the days of ignorance. He replied, "God forbid, I never touched wine even in the days of ignorance." He was asked, "why", and he said, "I sought to preserve my reputation and retain my decorum, and verily he who drinks wine destroys his reputation and his decorum". This shows that Hadrat Abu Bakr enjoyed a good reputation, and was known for his decorum.

Education. As in the case of other Arab children, he did not receive any formal education. He was, however, a keen observer and observed things around him with a keen sense of perception. Even at an early age, he developed an eloquent way of expression. He even composed verses. He used to attend the annual fair at 'Ukaz, and participate in poetical symposia. He had a very good memory, and could recite verses after he had heard them only once.

Occupation. At the age of eighteen, Hadrat Abu Bakr went into trade and adopted the profession of a cloth merchant which was the family's business. Makkah was a commercial centre at the crossing of the caravan routes from Yemen to Syria and Iraq to Abyssinia, and the Quraish of Makkah sponsored trade caravans to Yemen, Syria, Iraq, and Abyssinia. Hadrat Abu Bakr travelled extensively with such caravans. Business trips took him to Yemen, Syria, and elsewhere. These travels brought him wealth, added to his experience, and broadened his outlook. He was honest, hardworking, steadfast, generous, hospitable, and diligent. These qualities paid rich dividends. His business flourished and he rose in the scale of social importance. He came to be recognised as one of the richest merchants of Mecca.

Political office. While still a young man, Hadrat Abu Bakr came to be recognised as the chief of the Bani Taim section in spite of the fact that his father was alive. Hadrat Abu Bakr was assigned the office of awarding blood money in cases of murder. His office was something like the office of an Honorary Magistrate. His judgments and awards were always fair and just which satisfied the parties.

His marriages and children. Hadrat Abu Bakr's first wife was Qutaila. She belonged to the Bani Amar. She was the mother of Asma and Abdullah. Some time later, Hadrat Abu Bakr married another wife Umm Ruman. She was a widow and belonged to the Bani Kinana section. She was the mother of Abdur Rahman and Ayesha.

Character of Hadrat Abu Bakr. In spite of being a rich man, Hadrat Abu Bakr was of a meditative cast of mind. As a trader he did not indulge in trade tricks. He stood for fair deals, and above board transactions. He came to enjoy reputation for honesty, and integrity. He had a wide circle of friends, and commanded considerable influence in the contemporary society of Makkah. He had a flair for social work. He delighted in attending to the sick, and looking after the poor. He gave rich bounties to the poor, and felt pleasure in helping those in distress.

Genealogical lore. Hadrat Abu Bakr was expert in genealogical lore. He knew intimately who was who in Makkah, and what was his ancestry. He carried in his head minutest details about the genealogies of various families in Makkah. He raised genealogy to the dignity of a science. Hadrat Abu Bakr had all the elements that make a historian or a scientist.

Hadrat Abu Bakr and the Holy Prophet. When Hadrat Muhammad (peace be on him) married Hadrat Khadija and shifted to her house, he became a neighbour of Hadrat Abu Bakr who lived in the same locality. That was the quarter of Makkan aristocracy. Like the house of Hadrat Khadija, the house of Hadrat Abu Bakr was double storeyed and palatial in structure.

As neighbours Hadrat Muhammad (peace be on him), and Hadrat Abu Bakr came in contact with each other, and were mutually attracted. Both of them were of the same age. Both of them were traders and good managers. Both of them were kind hearted and tender hearted gentlemen who felt for others. Both of them were men of strong and sterling character. They were men of strong convictions, and when they came to hold a particular view they knew no wavering. They never minced matters and always called a spade a spade. Both of them were critical of the evils that honeycombed the idolatrous society of Makkah. They had an identity of views on various matters. They felt themselves to be kindred spirits, and that set the base for life-long attachment between the two men who were destined to make history.

Conversion to Islam

Birth of Islam. One day in the year 610 C.E. when Hadrat Muhammad (peace be on him) was praying in the cave of Hira outside Makkah, the angel Gabriel appeared to him, and conveyed to him the tidings that Allah had chosen him as His Messenger, and he was to convey to the people the message of Islam. That was a novel sensation. As the Holy Prophet came home, he felt agitated. Hadrat Khadija comforted him, and was the first person to be converted to Islam. Hadrat Khadija consulted her cousin Waraqa who was proficient in religious lore. He gave Hadrat Khadija the glad tidings that her husband was the Prophet of God, about whose advent there were references in the scriptures of the Jews and the Christians. After Hadrat Khadija, Hadrat Ali, then a young boy living with the Holy Prophet, accepted Islam. Thereafter Zaid b. Harith a slave whom the Holy Prophet had adopted as his son became a Muslim.

Abu Bakr's conversion to Islam. When the Holy Prophet gave the call of Islam, Hadrat Abu Bakr was out of Makkah. He had gone on a business trip to Yemen. When Hadrat Abu Bakr returned to Makkah, he was informed by some of his friends that in his absence Hadrat Muh ımmad (peace be on him) had declared himself as the Messenger of God, and proclaimed a new religion. On hearing this, Hadrat Abu Bakr lost no time in calling on the Holy Prophet.

The Holy Prophet told Hadrat Abu Bakr full details of his experience in the cave of Hira, the visitation of the angel Gabriel, and the command of Allah to call the people to Him. On hearing the account, Hadrat Abu Bakr felt inspired. He felt convinced that what the Holy Prophet had said was the truth. Overwhelmed with emotion, and elated with joy at the discovery of the truth, Hadrat Abu Bakr said, "I believe in you and your mission from the depths of my heart. I testify and confirm that what you say is the truth. Call me to your religion, for verily you are the Prophet of God and that is a great honour".

The Holy Prophet stretched his hand, and Hadrat Abu Bakr grasped it reverently as a mark of faith and allegiance. He declared with great solemnity, "There is no god but Allah, and Muhammad is His prophet and messenger." This declaration forged new bonds between the Holy Prophet and Hadrat Abu Bakr. Heretofore only three family members of the Holy Prophet, namely Hadrat Khadija, Hazrat Ali, and Zaid bin Harith had accepted Islam. Hadrat Abu Bakr was the first person outside the family of the Holy Prophet to become a Muslim.

Significance of the conversion of Hadrat Abu Bakr. In the annals of Islam, the conversion of Hadrat Abu Bakr was an event of great significance. Hadrat Abu Bakr was a rich merchant, and his business depended on the goodwill of the people around him. He knew that his conversion to the new faith would make him unpopular with people around him, and that would adversely affect his business. He was well aware that by such conversion he would be inviting the wrath and hostility of the Quraish. But his mind was made up. He felt convinced that Hadrat Muhammad (peace be on him) had discovered the truth, and was required of him was to support the cause of the truth, whatever the cost.

Prior to his conversion, Hadrat Abu Bakr asked no questions; he did not enter into any argument; he laid down no conditions; and he wanted no assurances. He did not hesitate even for a moment; no doubts assailed him; and there was no wavering in his mind. His declaration of faith in Islam was spontaneous as if he had been waiting for such a declaration all his life.

Years later, the Holy Prophet recalling the conversion of

Hadrat Abu Bakr said, "Whenever I offered Islam to any one, he always showed some reluctance and hesitation and tried to enter into an argument. Abu Bakr was the only person who accepted Islam without any reluctance or hesitation, and without any argument."

Reasons for the ready acceptance of Islam by Hadrat Abu Bakr. Apart from Hadrat Abu Bakr, Hadrat Khadija was the other person who had accepted Islam readily and without any hesitation. In the case of Hadrat Khadija we know that she had already a premonition that Hadrat Muhammad (peace be on him) was destined to be a prophet. Indeed she had been prompted to marry Hadrat Muhammad (peace be on him) because she had an inner conviction that a great destiny awaited Hadrat Muhammad.

It appears that Hadrat Abu Bakr had a similar inner conviction that a great destiny awaited Hadrat Muhammad (peace be on him). There is a story that when Hadrat Muhammad at the age of twelve accompanied his uncle Abu Talib along with a trade caravan to Syria, and the monk Bahira on seeing Hadrat Muhammad (peace be on him) had foretold prophethood for him, Abu Bakr was also with the caravan, and since that day Hadrat Abu Bakr had harboured the conviction that Hadrat Muhammad (peace be on him) was going to be a prophet. Hadrat Abu Bakr travelled extensively, and in the course of such travels he had the occasion to learn from the Jewish rabbis and the Christian monks that the advent of a prophet was expected. This implies that Hadrat Abu Bakr was already expecting the advent of a prophet, and when Hadrat Muhammad (peace be on him) proclaimed his prophethood, and by first hand knowledge, Hadrat Abu Bakr knew of the stainless character of Hadrat Muhammad (peace be on him), he felt certain that Hadrat Muhammad (peace be on him) was the prophet whose advent was expected, and as such there was no hesitation on his part in accepting the new faith.

As-Suyuti's account of the premonition of Hadrat Abu Bakr about the advent of the Holy Prophet. In As-Suyuti's book *History of the Caliphs*, there is an account which corroborates the conclusion that Hadrat Abu Bakr had a premonition about the advent of the Prophet. It is related that before Hadrat Muhammad (peace be on him) had declared his mission, Hadrat Abu Bakr had visited Waraqa bin Naufal, who was expert in Scriptures, and Waraqa had told Hadrat Abu Bakr of the advent of the Prophet. According to As-Suyuti, Hadrat Abu Bakr is reported to have declared:

> "I had a premonition about the advent of the Prophet. Therefore when the Apostle of God was sent, I believed in him and testified to him."

According to Al-Bayhaqi as quoted by As-Suyuti, Hadrat Abu Bakr accepted Islam readily because he had been accustomed to behold the proofs of the prophetic mission. Al-Bayhaqi also states on the authority of Abu Maysarah, the freed man of Hadrat Abbas an uncle of the Holy Prophet, that when before the call, the Holy Prophet went forth, he used to hear some invisible person calling him, "O Muhammad". The Holy Prophet used to tell of these voices to Hadrat Abu Bakr who was his intimate friend.

Impact of Islam on Hadrat Abu Bakr. Islam changed the course of the life of Hadrat Abu Bakr. Before conversion he was known as Abdul Ka'aba. The name was indicative of paganism, and after conversion the Holy Prophet changed his name to Abdullah. The change in name marked a change in the purpose of life for Hadrat Abu Bakr. He was no longer the servant of the Ka'aba; henceforward he was to be the servant of Allah.

Change in family relationship. Islam brought a change in the family relationship of Hadrat Abu Bakr. His wife Qutaila did not accept Islam and he divorced her. His other wife Umm Ruman became a Muslim at his instance. All his children except Abdur Rahman accepted Islam, and Hadrat Abu Bakr separated from his son Abdur Rahman.

Hadrat Abu Bakr's services to Islam. Hadrat Abu Bakr was a man of shrewd judgement. He was highly intelligent and was endowed with the sense to discern the truth. When Hadrat Abu Bakr accepted the new faith without any hesitation that was indicative of the fact that Islam was the truth. The conversion of Hadrat Abu Bakr in fact set the pace for the extension of Islam. Hadrat Abu Bakr commanded considerable social influence, and he pressed such influence into service for promoting Islam. He made no secret of his conversion to Islam. Indeed he felt proud and honoured that he had been blessed with Islam. In fact he became the messenger of the Messenger of God. He persuaded his intimate friends to accept Islam. He presented Islam to others in such a way that many of his friends opted for Islam.

Hadrat Abu Bakr's missionary efforts. Those who accepted Islam at the instance of Hadrat Abu Bakr were:

(1) Othman bin Affan;
(2) Zubair bin Awam;
(3) Talhah bin Ubaidullah;
(4) Abdur Rahman b. 'Auf;
(5) Sa'ad b. Abi Waqas;
(6) Umar b. Masoan;
(7) Abu Ubaidah b. Al-Jarrah;
(8) Abdullah b. Abdul Asad;
(9) Abu Salma;
(10) Khalid b. Saeed; and
(11) Abu Hudhaifah.

All of them were men of status and high social standing and they proved to be great assets for Islam.

After conversion. Before conversion to Islam, Hadrat Abu Bakr used to meet Hadrat Muhammad (peace be on him) occasionally. After becoming a Muslim, Hadrat Abu Bakr made it a point to spend most of his time every day in the company of the Holy Prophet. Conversion to Islam made a phenomenal change in the life of Hadrat Abu Bakr. He was little more than thirty seven years at the time of conversion to Islam. He lived thereafter for twenty six years, and during all these years, Islam was for him the end all and be all of existence.

Significance of the conversion of Hadrat Abu Bakr. According to Gibbon *(Decline and Fall of the Roman Empire)*—

"the moderation, and the veracity of Abu Bakr confirmed the new religion, and furnished an example for invitation". Muir has observed *(Life of Muhammad):*

> "Abu Bakr's judgment was sound and impartial; his conversation agreeable and his demeanour affable and much sought after by the Quraish and he was popular throughout the city.... The faith of Abu Bakr was the greatest guarantee of the sincerity of Muhammad in the beginning of his career, and indeed, in a modified sense, throughout his life. To have such a person as a staunch adherent of his claim, was for Muhammad a most important step."

NOTES

This Chapter is entitled "Before and after conversion to Islam." The Chapter has been divided into two sections. The first section deals with the pre-Islamic period, and the second section tells the story of the conversion of Hadrat Abu Bakr to Islam.

In the sources ordinarily available there is hardly any information about the life of Hadrat Abu Bakr during the pre-Islamic period. As a matter of fact the real life of Hadrat Abu Bakr began when he became a Muslim. His life during the pre-Islamic period, the so-called period of Ignorance was obscure and uneventfull. The Muslim historians were not much interested in the details about this period. Here and there we come across fragments of information, which throw some light on the various aspects of the life of Hadrat Abu Bakr. Based on the fragments of all available information. I have made an attempt to project the salient features of the life of Hadrat Abu Bakr during the period.

The particulars about the names of the father and mother of Hadrat Abu Bakr are generally available in all books about Hadrat Abu Bakr. In his book *Hadrat Abu Bakr* Nawab Sadr Yar Jung Bahadur has given the genealogy of Hadrat Abu Bakr, according to which the genealogy of Hadrat Abu Bakr and the Holy Prophet joined in their common ancestor Murrah eight generations back. The genealogical table given in other sources, including the book *Hadrat Abu Bakr by* Muhammad Hussain Haikal, are identical.

Apart from the names of parents of Hadrat Abu Bakr, the sources do not tell about the other members of the family. We are told that the brothers of Hadrat Abu Bakr born before him died in childhood. We do not know whether any brothers were born after the birth of Hadrat Abu Bakr. Hadrat Abu Bakr had some sisters, but particulars about them are not available.

After considering the various sources I have arrived at the conclusion that Hadrat Abu Bakr was born some time in

573 C.E. This date has a great element of probability and is very nearly correct.

We find that Hadrat Abu Bakr was a man of many names. He was originally named Abdul Ka'aba. On conversion to Islam he was named Abdullah. He, however, became popular by the name of Abu Bakr. He was also named "Ateeq", and "Siddiq". According to my research, he came to be known as Abu Bakr because of his fondness for camels. "Attiq" was his surname. One account is that he was called "Attiq" because of his beauty. According to another account, as narrated by Hadrat Ayesha, the Holy Prophet called him "Attiq", because of his immunity to hell fire. "Sidiq" was also his surname which he earned because of his truth, veracity and discernment in judgment.

The story of Hadrat Abu Bakr's encounter with the idols is told by S. A. Salik in his book *The Early Heroes of Islam.* There is a reference to this story in Suyuti's *History of the Caliphs* as well. This encounter was more or less of the same style as the encounter of the Prophet Ibrahim with the idols. If we study the life of Hadrat Abu Bakr, we find that he was a proto-type of Hadrat lbrahim. Like Hadrat Ibrahim, Hadrat Abu Bakr used to sigh very often, and the companions called him "Awwah", the epithet by which Hadrat Ibrahim was known. Like Hadrat Ibrahim, Hadrat Abu Bakr was most generous and liberal.

In Suyuti's *History of Caliphs,* it is related that Hadrat Abu Bakr was with the caravan with which the Holy Prophet went as a boy of twelve. According to this narrative the monk Bahira at Busra talked to Hadrat Abu Bakr, and told him that the boy Muhammad (peace be on him) was destined to be a prophet. This is an important piece of information which is genuine, but is not found in other books. I have adopted this story and analysed its significance. This shows that the Holy Prophet and Hadrat Abu Bakr were companions even in childhood.

We know that the Holy Prophet played a peripheral role in the war of Fijar. We also know that he was associated with

Hilf-ul-Fudul. The sources are silent about the association of Hadrat Abu Bakr with these events. Judging by the general character of Hadrat Abu Bakr I am inclined to presume that Hadrat Abu Bakr was associated in some way with these events. Hadrat Abu Bakr's association with "Hilf-ul-Fudul" is most likely firstly because its objects were the ideals for which Hadrat Abu Bakr stood all his life, and secondly because the association was set up in the house of a noble of the Bani Taim, who must be related to Hadrat Abu Bakr.

While talking of the disciplined life of Hadrat Abu Bakr, I have referred to Hadrat Abu Bakr's own account according to which he never drank wine even in the days of Ignorance. This anecdote is given in Suyuti's *History of the Caliphs*, and highlights an important aspect of the life of Hadrat Abu Bakr.

The particulars which I have given with regard to the political office held by Hadrat Abu Bakr, his marriages and children, his expertise in genealogical lore, and his character are based on the accounts which are found in almost every biography of Hadrat Abu Bakr.

The Holy Prophet married Hadrat Khadija some time around 596 C.E, and shifted to her house. In my book *Hadrat Khadija* I have shown that Hadrat Abu Bakr was a neighbour. As such companionship developed between the Holy Prophet some fifteen years before the Holy Prophet declared his prophetic mission.

In the second section of this Chapter I have given an account of the conversion of Hadrat Abu Bakr. These are the well known facts found in every biography of Hadrat Abu Bakr. I have tried to examine how was it that Hadrat Abu Bakr accepted Islam readily without any argument. My finding is that this was due to the premonition of Hadrat Abu Bakr that Hadrat Muhammad (peace be on him) was destined to be the Prophet. Hadrat Khadija had a similar premonition and she too accepted Islam without any hesitation.

In most of the biographies of Hadrat Abu Bakr there is some controversy on the point whether Hadrat Abu Bakr was the first to accept Islam or whether Hadrat Ali was the first.

When the Holy Prophet declared his call, Hadrat Abu Bakr was out of Makkah. Hadrat Ali who resided with the Holy Prophet lost no time in accepting the new faith. As a matter of fact this question whether Hadrat Ali was the first to accept Islam or whether Hadrat Abu Bakr was the first is not material. The basic issue is: what was the significance of the conversion of Hadrat Abu Bakr? Hadrat Abu Bakr proved to be "the second of the two" even at the outset, and he virtually became the messenger of the Messenger of God. According to Muir, *The Life of Muhammad*, the faith of Hadrat Abu Bakr was the greatest proof of the sincerity of Muhammad (peace be on him).

I have also tried to indicate what was the impact of Islam on Hadrat Abu Bakr. Some western writers have expressed their views on the point. I have quoted them and analysed their viewpoints. There are apt references to Hadrat Abu Bakr in Gibbon's *Decline and Fall of the Roman Empire* and Muir's *Life of Muhammad.*

2
WITNESS TO TRUTH

Liberation of the Slaves

Slavery. During the times of Hadrat Abu Bakr, slavery was a deep rooted institution, and was a conspicuous feature of Makkah. Most of the Quraish were slave owners and thus in the society of Makkah there was a considerable sprinkling of slaves. These slaves were the victims of exploitation, and were treated in an inhuman way by their masters. Many of the slaves were attracted by Islam, for in its teachings lay a charter of freedom for the distressed humanity. Islam preached the cult of equality. It stipulated that all persons were the slaves of God, and no person could be the slave of another person. When many slaves accepted Islam, the slave owners of Makkah felt much concerned, and considered such conversions as a threat to their economic interests.

Persecution of the slaves. Of all the persons who became Muslims, the slaves were the most vulnerable. Those men of the Quraish who were converted to Islam continued to enjoy the protection of their respective tribes. The slaves enjoyed no such protection. In order to arrest the progress of Islam among the slaves, the Quraish accordingly resorted to a campaign of persecution and torture against the slaves who professed to be Muslims.

Bilal. Bilal, an Abyssinian who later became the 'Muadhdhin' of Islam was a slave of Umayyah bin Khalaf. Bilal accepted Islam and thereupon his master subjected him to great torture. Umayyah would make Bilal lie down on the burning sand, and would place a huge block of stone on his chest. Umayyah would then ask Bilal to give up Islam, or he would be tortured to death. Umayyah would sometimes tie a rope round the neck of Bilal, and had him dragged in the streets. Sometimes Bilal was made to put on steel armour, and stand in the hot sun for hours. In spite of these tortures and threats, Bilal remained firm and steadfast in his faith in Islam. The condition of Bilal excited the pity of Hadrat Abu Bakr. He purchased him from his master and set him free.

Abu Fakih. Abu Fakih was a slave of Safwan bin Umayyah. Abu Fakih accepted Islam, and when Safwan came to know that Abu Fakih had become a Muslim, he subjected him to great torture. He would bind him with a rope, and drag him on the burning sand. Abu Fakih was asked to worship the idols, but he said that he would worship Allah alone. His master put a very heavy stone on his chest which brought out his tongue. In spite of these persecutions, the faith of Abu Faith in Islam did not waver. When Hadrat Abu Bakr came to know of the pitiable condition of Abu Fakih, he purchased him from his master and set him free.

Lubaynah. Lubaynah was a slave girl of Umar. She accepted Islam, and Umar who had not accepted Islam by that time would beat her mercilessly until he was tired. He would then say, "I have only stopped beating you, because I am tired." She would say. "May God treat you in the same way". He asked her to renounce Islam, but she stuck to her faith. When Hadrat Abu Bakr came to know of her sad state, he paid for her, and set her free.

Al-Nahdiah. Al-Nahdiah and her daughter who became Muslims were the slaves of a lady of Bani Abdul Dar. Their mistress subjected them to great torture when she came to know that they had accepted Islam. Hadrat Abu Bakr remonstrated with the lady at the treatment she meted out to her slaves. The mistress said, "You have corrupted them; you may free them if you are so sympathetic to them." Hadrat Abu Bakr paid the price asked for, and liberated the women.

Umm Ubays and Zinnira. Hadrat Abu Bakr also

liberated two women slaves, Umm Ubays and Zinnira. Abu Jahl beat Zinnira on her conversion to Islam to such an extent that she lost her eye sight. When she lost her eye sight the Quraish said that she had lost her sight because of the curse of Al-Lat and Al-Uzzah. She was asked to recant, but she remained steadfast in her faith in Islam. She prayed to God, and miraculously her eye sight was restored. Hadrat Abu Bakr paid for these women and set them free.

Slaves liberated by Hadrat Abu Bakr. Hadrat Abu Bakr purchased the freedom of eight slaves—four men and four women. The men were: Bilal, Abu Fakih, Ammar, and Abu Fuhayra. The women were: Lubaynah, Nahdiya, Umm Ubays, and Zinnira.

Hadrat Abu Bakr's father's reaction to the liberation of slaves. Most of the slaves liberated by Hadrat Abu Bakr were either women or old and frail men. The father of Hadrat Abu Bakr said to him, "Son, I hear you are freeing old and weak persons; why don't you free healthy and strong persons who could be a source of strength to you?" Hadrat Abu Bakr replied that he was freeing the slaves for the sake of God, and not for his own sake.

Divine approval. The Holy Prophet of Islam was all praise for Hadrat Abu Bakr for his generosity in purchasing the freedom of slaves who were tortured on the ground that they had accepted Islam.

The conduct of Hadrat Abu Bakr was approved by God in the following verses of the Holy Qur'an:

> "He who gives in charity and fears Allah
> And in all sincerity testifies to the Truth;
> We shall indeed make smooth for him the path
> of Bliss" XCll: 5-7

> "Those who spend their wealth for increase in
> self-purification;
> And have in their minds no favour from any
> one
> For which a reward is expected in return,

> But only the desire to seek the Countenance,
> Of their Lord, Most High;
> And soon they shall attain complete
> satisfaction." XCII: 18-21.

Persecutions of the Quraish

The first public address about Islam. For three years the Muslims kept a secret of their faith, and prayed in secret. Hadrat Abu Bakr always urged on the Holy Prophet that as Islam was the Truth, it should be declared publicly. The Holy Prophet assured Hadrat Abu Bakr that Islam would be proclaimed publicly when Allah so commanded. Some time in 613 C.E. the Holy Prophet received the Divine Command to make an open declaration of faith. At the first public meeting held to call the people to God, the first public address in the history of Islam, inviting the people to offer allegiance to the Holy Prophet was delivered by Hadrat Abu Bakr. The Quraish were exasperated at this daring of the Muslims. In a fit of fury the Quraish young men rushed at Abu Bakr, and beat him mercilessly till he lost consciousness.

Conversion of the mother of Hadrat Abu Bakr to Islam. Hadrat Abu Bakr was carried to his home. When he regained consciousness, he did not care for his own wounds: he wanted to know how was the Holy Prophet. When Hadrat Abu Bakr felt some relief, he insisted that he should be taken to the Holy Prophet. His mother agreed to take him to the Holy Prophet. When the Holy Prophet saw Hadrat Abu Bakr coming to enquire about him when his own wounds had not healed, he was much impressed with the loyalty and faith of Hadrat Abu Bakr. The Holy Prophet blessed Hadrat Abu Bakr and kissed him on the forehead. Overwhelmed with emotion, the mother of Hadrat Abu Bakr declared the article of faith and became a Muslim.

The Holy Prophet in the Ka'aba. One day the Holy Prophet went to the Ka'aba and circumambulated it. As he passed in front of the 'Black Stone', and kissed it, some of the Quraish assembled there used foul language against him. The Holy Prophet kept quiet and took another round of the Ka'aba. As he came to the 'Black Stone' for the second time, the Quraish abused him again. The Holy Prophet did not mind them, and went moving round the Ka'aba. As he completed the third round the Quraish abused him once again. This time he turned his face to them, and said, "Listen to me O Quraish; I bring you slaughter." This overawed the Quraish and they dispersed.

The following day the Quraish assembled in the Ka'aba, and vowed vengeance against the Holy Prophet. After some time, the Holy Prophet also came to the Ka'aba. The Quraish surrounded him and said, "Are you the one who has abused our gods ?" The Holy Prophet said that it was so. Thereupon the Quraish fell upon the Holy Prophet, and gave him a severe beating. When Hadrat Abu Bakr came to know of this he rushed to the spot. He interposed himself between the Holy Prophet and the Quraish weeping and saying, "Would you kill a man for saying that Allah is his Lord". Thereupon the Quraish fell on Hadrat Abu Bakr, and beat him. The beating was so severe that blood flowed from the head of Hadrat Abu Bakr and clotted his hair. He did not mind his own injuries, and even on the sick bed, he expressed his anxiety about the safety and welfare of the Holy Prophet.

Uqba b. Abi Mohit. Once when the Holy Prophet was saying prayers in the Ka'aba, Uqba b. Abi Mohit a Quraish young man threw his sheet round the neck of the Holy Prophet, and twisted it with a view to strangling him. Hadrat Abu Bakr who hovered close by fell on Uqba and rescued the Holy Prophet.

Abu Lahab. When the Holy Prophet invited the people to Islam, his uncle Abu Lahab and his wife Umm Jamil became hostile to him. Umm Jamil would carry thorns and place them in the way of the Holy Prophet. About Abu Lahab and his wife, the Holy Prophet received the following revelation from God:

"Abu Lahab and his hands God blast
His wealth and gains useless at the last
He shall roast in flames held fast

With his wife, the bearer of the wood aghast,
On her neck a rope of palm fibre cast."

Umm Jamil. One day Umm Jamil came to the Ka'aba where Hadrat Abu Bakr and the Holy Prophet were praying. She failed to see the Holy Prophet, and addressing Hadrat Abu Bakr she said:

"I hear that Muhammad is satirising me.
If I find him I will smash him.
We reject the reprobate.
His words we repudiate,
His religion, we loathe and hate."

When Hadrat Abu Bakr remonstrated with her, she abused him.

Persecutions of other Muslims. The persecutions of the Quraish were not confined to the Holy Prophet or Hadrat Abu Bakr. Almost every Muslim convert became a victim of the persecutions of the Quraish.

When Hadrat Usman b. Affan who later became the third Caliph of Islam, was converted to Islam, he was bound and beaten by his uncle Hakam b. Al-Aas.

When Zubair b. Awam accepted Islam his uncle wrapped him in a mat, and passed smoke through his nose.

When Abdullah bin Masud recited the Qur'an in the Ka'aba, he was mercilessly beaten by the Quraish.

Umm Shareek a lady who accepted Islam was made to stand under the hot sun for three days, and was not allowed to drink water.

Khabbab when converted to Islam was forced by the Quraish to lie on live cinders.

Ammar when converted to Islam was thrown on burning sand and severely beaten till he lost consciousness. His mother Sumaiyya was stabbed to death by Abu Jahl. His father Yasir was tortured to death.

Suhaib was beaten so mercilessly that he lost his mental balance.

Reaction of Hadrat Abu Bakr. Hadrat Abu Bakr felt distressed at the persecution of the Muslims. He did all he could to alleviate the sufferings of the Muslims. Hadrat Abu Bakr suffered along with other Muslims. He had a flourishing business, but as a result of his acceptance of Islam his business suffered a good deal. At the time of his conversion to Islam he had 40,000 dirhams with him. He spent a great part of this money for the relief of the Muslims in distress. Hadrat Abu Bakr did not mind these sufferings, and the more he suffered the deeper became his faith in Islam.

Protection of Ad-Dughna

Migration of the Muslims to Abyssinia. As more and more persons in Makkah became Muslims, the Quraish lost their nerve, and intensified their persecutions against the Muslims. Seeing the afflictions of his companions, the Holy Prophet advised them to migrate to Abyssinia, the ruler whereof was known for his tolerance. When the first batch of the Muslims migrated to Abyssinia, Hadrat Abu Bakr decided to stay in Makkah to be by the side of the Holy Prophet.

Boycott against the Banu Hashim. Some time in 617 C.E., the Quraish enforced a boycott against the Banu Hashim, and the Holy Prophet and whole of Banu Hashim, except Abu Lahab and his family, were shut up in a pass away from Makkah. All social relations with the Banu Hashim were cut off and their state was that of a sort of imprisonment.

Three groups of the Muslims. At this stage the Muslims came to be divided in three groups. One group comprised of the emigrants to Abyssinia. The other group comprised of the Banu Hashim who were ex-communicated. The rest of the Muslims formed the third group. They were not ex-communicated but there was no relaxation in their persecution by the unbelievers.

Hadrat Abu Bakr's migration. Hadrat Abu Bakr

belonged to the third group. He felt sad at the ex-communication of the Banu Hashim. As Hadrat Abu Bakr looked around him he felt much distressed. With a heavy heart, Hadrat Abu Bakr left Makkah one day with the intention to migrate to Abyssinia. He took the road to Yemen from where he was to sail for Abyssinia. When he had proceeded some five stages from Makkah, he met Ad-Dughna at Barka al Ghamaad. Ad-Dughna was an old friend of Hadrat Abu Bakr. He was the chief of the Qarah tribe, a section of the Quraish. The Qarah tribe was in alliance with the Bani Zuhra.

Ad-Dughna's offer of protection. Ad-Dughna enquired of Hadrat Abu Bakr as to where he was going, and he told him that he was going to seek refuge in Abyssinia as the Quraish of Makkah would allow him no peace. Ad-Dughna who had a high opinion about Hadrat Abu Bakr said: "O Abu Bakr, we cannot suffer you to go from Makkah. You are an asset to the city. You are always keen to fulfill the needs to others. You are so good and noble. I take you under my protection, and you should come back with me to Makkah. Rest assured no harm will come to you."

Back in Makkah. Back in Makkah, Ad-Dughna declared that Hadrat Abu Bakr was under his protection and that no one should molest him in any way. Hadrat Abu Bakr built a small mosque by the side of his house. This was indeed the first mosque built in the history of Islam. In this mosque Hadrat Abu Bakr would pray and recite the Holy Qur'an. Hadrat Abu Bakr was tender hearted and he was so overwhelmed with the depth of the Word of God that while reciting the verses he would burst into sobs and tears. He had a sweet melodious voice, and his recitation from the Holy Qur'an had a melody which appealed to the heart. Women and young men of the Quraish watched him pray and recite verses from the Holy Qur'an with particular interest, and they felt that if a man of the status and standing of Hadrat Abu Bakr could be so overwhelmed with these words, these must be the Word of God and should have a ring of truth about them.

Withdrawal of the protection of Ad-Dughna. The

Quraish felt nervous. They apprehended that if Hadrat Abu Bakr continued his prayers in the open, he might attract some persons to him. Some of the leading Quraish went to Ad-Dughna and said,

> "Have you given him this protection so that he may publicly injure our feelings ? He recites the Qur'an in a sweet voice, and we fear that he may seduce our women and youth to his faith. You should advise him to pray indoors."

Ad-Dughna saw Hadrat Abu Bakr and advised him that the most expedient course for him was to pray indoors and not to annoy the Quraish. To Hadrat Abu Bakr there could be no expediency in the matter of faith. He said to Ad-Dughna "You are advising me as I am under your protection. What if I renounce your protection?" "In that case I will have nothing to say" answered Ad-Dughna. Thereupon Hadrat Abu Bakr said, "Under these circumstances I renounce your protection. The protection of Allah is enough for me."

Ad-Dughna returned crest-fallen, and he told the Quraish that as Hadrat Abu Bakr was no longer under his protection, they could deal with him direct in any way they liked.

Holy Prophet's Engagement to Hadrat Ayesha

Deaths of Abu Talib and Hadrat Khadija. In 619 C.E. Abu Talib and Hadrat Khadija died. Among the Muslims the year 619 C.E. came to be known as 'The Year of Sorrow'. Abu Talib had been more than a father to the Holy Prophet. In spite of the strong pressure of the Quraish he had protected the Holy Prophet. Hadrat Khadija had been for the Holy Prophet more than a wife. She had placed all her wealth, which was considerable, at his disposal. She had given him love. She was the first person to be converted to Islam, and had been a pillar of strength for the Holy Prophet as well as the Muslims.

The passing away of Abu Talib and Hadrat Khadija

created a great vacuum in the life of the Holy Prophet, and he felt very lonely and disconsolate. In this hour of bereavement Hadrat Abu Bakr tried to console the Holy Prophet, and he spent most of his time in his company. It was the endeavour of Hadrat Abu Bakr that he should as far as possible fill the vacuum created by the deaths of Abu Talib and Hadrat Khadija.

Holy Prophet's marriage with Sauda. At the instance of Khawja bint Hakim the Holy Prophet married Sauda bint Zama'a. Sauda was an elderly lady and was among the early converts to Islam. She was a good housewife, and looked very well after the house and the children of the Holy Prophet.

Proposal for engagement to Hadrat Ayesha. Khawla bint Hakim suggested to the Holy Prophet that he should marry some young lady as well who could keep him company. Whom could he marry, enquired the Holy Prophet. Khawla suggested that Hadrat Ayesha the daughter of Hadrat Abu Bakr would be a good choice. The Holy Prophet left it to Khawla to pursue the matter with Hadrat Abu Bakr. Khawla approached Hadrat Abu Bakr, and his wife Umm Ruman and made the proposal for the engagement of Hadrat Ayesha to the Holy Prophet. Hadrat Abu Bakr felt honoured at the proposal, but his difficulty was that Hadrat Ayesha was already engaged to Jubayr son of Mut'im, and it was against Hadrat Abu Bakr's code of conduct to break his pledge. When this difficulty was brought to the notice of the Holy Prophet, he said that God would Himself provide a way out of the difficulty.

Mut'im. Hadrat Abu Bakr called at the house of Al-Mut'im. Al-Mut'im was still a disbeliever, and Mu'tim's wife said to Hadrat Abu Bakr "O son of Abu Qahafa, suppose we married our son to your daughter, you would turn him into an infidel, and convert him to your religion". Hadrat Abu Bakr made no reply, but turning to Mut'im said, "What does she mean ?" Mutim said indifferently, "She is saying what you have heard."

Hadrat Abu Bakr said, "This means that you repudiate the engagement."

"So let it be," said Al-Mut'im.

Hadrat Ayesha's engagement to the Holy Prophet. At the repudiation of the engagement by Al-Mut'im, Hadrat Abu Bakr felt happy, and returned home relieved of a great burden. God had Himself provided a way out of the difficulty. Hadrat Abu Bakr hastened with the good news to Khawla, and asked her to invite the Holy Prophet to his house. The Holy Prophet responded to the call, and formally asked for the hand of Hadrat Ayesha. Hadrat Abu Bakr was overwhelmed with joy and emotion and said, "O Prophet of God, all that I have is yours".

At a simple ceremony Hadrat Ayesha was engaged to the Holy Prophet. It was, however, decided that the actual marriage ceremony would be held later.

Age of Hadrat Ayesha. In most of the accounts that have come down to us, it is stated that at the time of her engagement to the Holy Prophet, Hadrat Ayesha was a girl of six or seven years only. This appears to be an understatement. We have it on record that when Hadrat Abu Bakr became a Muslim his children included Abdur Rahman, Abdullah, Asma, and Hadrat Ayesha. Hadrat Abu Bakr became a Muslim in 610 A.D. and Hadrat Ayesha must be at least eleven or twelve years of age at the time of her engagement, and not six or seven years.

Hadrat Abu Bakr's relationship with the Holy Prophet. After the engagement of Hadrat Ayesha to the Holy Prophet, the new relationship further strengthened the bonds between the Holy Prophet and Hadrat Abu Bakr. Hadrat Abu Bakr was now not merely a follower or a disciple; he was the Holy Prophet's father-in-law as well. That added to his stature, and Hadrat Abu Bakr felt elated at the honour.

Witness to Truth

Ascension. One night in 620 C.E., after the deaths of Abu Talib and Hadrat Khadija when the Holy Prophet felt sad and disconsolate, and things for Islam appeared to be dark, the Holy Prophet was uplifted to the Heavens, and there he was assured of the destiny of Islam. After this experience of ascension the Holy Prophet declared that the previous night he had been carried from Makkah to Masjid al-Aqsa at Jerusalem, and from there he had ascended to the heavens.

Reaction of the people. When the non-believing Quraish heard of this visitation to the heavens, they regarded it as an absurdity, and ridiculed the Holy Prophet for his declaration. They contended that a caravan took a month to reach Jerusalem, and another month to come back, and thus it was impossible for any one to go to Jerusalem and return in one night. They further held that it was fantastic that a man should ascend the heavens.

Reaction of Hadrat Abu Bakr. There were some Muslims as well who wavered in their belief in the truth about the ascension of the Holy Prophet to the heavens. Some persons went to Hadrat Abu Bakr, and told him of the news of the journey of the Holy Prophet to Jerusalem and ascension to the heavens. When some persons expressed doubts about the veracity of the ascension, Hadrat Abu Bakr silenced them with the remarks:

> "There are many things beyond one's comprehension, and if Muhammad (peace be on him) says that he went to Jerusalem and ascended the heavens, it must be true for he never tells a lie, and being a prophet he commands resources that are not available to others".

Witness to truth. On hearing the news, Hadrat Abu Bakr hastened to the mosque where the Holy Prophet was describing his nocturnal journey to the people who had assembled there. After hearing the account, Hadrat Abu Bakr stood up and said:

> "All this is true. Your description is faithful and correct. I believe in every word of what you have said, for you say nothing but the truth. I testify that you are the Messenger of God, and God has placed invisible forces at your disposal. As such there is nothing improbable in your ascension to the heavens."

Siddiq—the Veracious. The Holy Prophet felt happy at what Hadrat Abu Bakr had said. Addressing Hadrat Abu Bakr, the Holy Prophet said:

> "Verily, Abu Bakr you are the Siddiq. You have a penetrating vision and you can discern the truth which an ordinary person finds difficult to understand. Surely many things can be done under the command of Allah which ordinary human intellect may not be able to grasp."

That is how Hadrat Abu Bakr got the honorofic title of 'Siddiq' the Veracious (Witness to Truth), which hence forward became a part and parcel of his name.

Ar-Rum

Persian conquests. Four years after the proclamation of the mission of the Holy Prophet, war broke out between the Persians and the Byzantines. The sympathies of the Quraish of Makkah was with the Persians who were polytheists. The Muslims on the other hand had their sympathies for the Byzantines who were Christians and believed in one God. In the war the Persians overran the Byzantine territories. Syria and Jerusalem fell to Persians in 614 C.E. The Persians next marched to Egypt and annexed it 616 C.E. The Byzantines were defeated, and lost a good deal of territory. The Quraish of Makkah rejoiced at the victory of Persia. They took such victory to signify that their gods were superior to the God of the Christians and the Muslims.

Surah Ar-Rum. It was at this stage that the Surah Ar-Rum (Surah XXX) was revealed. It provided:

> "Alif, Lam Mim.
> The Greeks (Byzantines) have been defeated in
> a neighbouring land;
> But after their defeat, they will gain a victory
> within a few years
> Allah's is the command before and after.
> On the day that the Greeks win a victory,

The believers will rejoice.
Allah gives victory to whom He wills.
He is the Mighty One, the Merciful.
That is Allah's promise.
His promise can never be untrue;
yet most men do not know it."

Reaction of the Quraish. When the Holy Prophet informed his companions of the revelation, they felt very happy. When the revelation was made, the Byzantines lay low, and *prima facie* it appeared difficult that the Byzantines would defeat the Persians and regain their territories. Even among the Muslims there were some persons who felt sceptic. Hadrat Abu Bakr's faith know no wavering. He felt confident that the prophesy would be fulfilled. When the unbelievers came to know of this revelation they ridiculed it. They said, "By Lat and Uzza, the Byzantines can never defeat the Persians." Hadrat Abu Bakr had an altercation with some of the Quraish. He said "How can the revelation of God be false?"

The Wager. Ubaiy b. Khalf a Quraish leader said to Hadrat Abu Bakr, "If you are sure, let us have a wager. That will show where the truth lies." Hadrat Abu Bakr said "Agreed". The revealed verses did not specify any time limit about the fulfilment of the prophesy. Hadrat Abu Bakr consulted the Holy Prophet as to the time limit and he said that God willing the prophesy would be fulfilled within nine years. Hadrat Abu Bakr accordingly entered into a wager agreement with Ubaiy b. Khalf. According to the agreement it was stipulated that the party which lost the wager would pay one hundred camels to the other party. The time limit for the fulfilment of the prophesy was fixed at nine years. It was further laid down that the agreement would be binding on the heirs of the parties.

Fulfilment of the prophesy. Within a few years the Byzantines were strong enough to launch an attack against Persia. In the battle of Issus in 622 C.E. the Persians suffered the first defeat. Other battles were fought during 623-25 in which the Byzantines had the upper hand. The decisive battle was fought on the banks of the Tigris near the city of Mosul in 627 C.E. when Persia surrendered and asked for terms. As a result of this reverse there was a revolt against the Persian king Khosroes II who was killed by his own son Sherwayh. Sherwayh made peace with the Byzantines by abandoning all the conquests that Persia had made earlier. Thus the promise of God as made in Surah Ar-Rum was literally fulfilled. By this time Ubaiy was dead, but his heirs honoured the agreement and gave a hundred camels to Hadrat Abu Bakr. They also accepted Islam, for the fulfilment of the prophesy was a proof positive of the truth of Islam. Hadrat Abu Bakr gave away all the hundred camels as *Sadaqa.*

NOTES

This Chapter covers the post-Islam Makkah period i.e. 610-622 C.E. This makes a period of twelve years. We have no detailed accounts about the life of Hadrat Abu Bakr during this period. In the biographies of the Holy Prophet there are references to Hadrat Abu Bakr here and there, and with such references as the base we can reconstruct the life story of Hadrat Abu Bakr to some extent.

At the outset of the career of Islam, the issue about the slaves became a matter of concern. Slavery was deep routed institution in Makkah, and most of Quraish of Makkah had slaves who did odd jobs for them. The slaves were attracted by Islam and many slaves accepted the new faith. Those who accepted Islam were tortured. Hadrat Abu Bakr purchased the slaves and liberated them. That adversely affected the interests of the Quraish of Makkah, in the economy whereof the slaves played an important part. That made the Quraish oppose Islam.

Hadrat Abu Bakr liberated eight slaves, four men and four women. References to these slaves exist in almost every biography of Hadrat Abu Bakr. The first section of this Chapter is based on these accounts. The conduct of Hadrat Abu Bakr in the matter of the liberation of slaves was approved by Allah, and we have some verses in Surah Al-Laif which refer to Hadrat Abu Bakr by implication. I have quoted these verses.

The second section of this Chapter deals with the persecution of the Quraish. References to such persecutions exist in almost every biography of the Holy Prophet. I have referred to such persecutions where under Hadrat Abu Bakr was involved somehow. During this period Hadrat Abu Bakr acted as the body guard of the Holy Prophet. Whenever the Holy Prophet appeared in the public, and there was an encounter with the Quraish, Hadrat Abu Bakr was always there to interpose himself between the Holy Prophet and the Quraish. In one of such encounters Hadrat Abu Bakr received some injuries. So great was his love for the Holy Prophet that he forgot his own wounds, and was anxious about the security of the Holy Prophet. According to traditions Hadrat Abu Bakr's mother became a Muslim at that stage. It is established that Hadrat Abu Bakr's father became a Muslim after the conquest of Makkah. At that stage, Muslim women were not enjoined to separate from non-Muslim husbands. As such, Hadrat Abu Bakr's mother did not separate from her husband who was still a non-Muslim. There is no mention about her in the later accounts. Presumably she died before the conquest of Makkah.

The third section deals with the protection of Ad-Dughna. It is not clear why Hadrat Abu Bakr had to seek the protection of Ad-Dughna when he had his own clan Bani Taim to protect him. In his book *Muhammad at Makkah*, Montgomery Watt has advanced the view:

> "Clansmen and confederates could be formally disowned by the clans. This seems to have happened to Abu Bakr since we find him accepting the protection of Ad-Dughna, and we also hear of Talha and him being bound together."

The position is obscure, and it is not clear whether the clan of Hadrat Abu Bakr disowned him at any stage. Ad-Dughna withdrew his protection later. This appears to indicate that the clan of Hadrat Abu Bakr did not disown him.

In the fourth section I have given an account of the engagement of Hadrat Ayesha to the Holy Prophet. This section is based on the account given in the book *Wives of the Holy Prophet* by Bint al-Shat (Translated in English by Matti Moosa and Nicholas Ranson). In most of the accounts that have come down to us, it is said that at the time of her engagement Hadrat Ayesha was six or seven years old only. According to my research she was eleven or twelve years old at the time of engagement, and was fourteen or fifteen years old at the time of marriage.

The fifth section deals with the ascension of the Holy Prophet and Hadrat Abu Bakr's complete faith in what the

Holy Prophet said. That earned for Hadrat Abu Bakr the surname of "Siddiq."

During the years 619-622 C.E., the Holy Prophet was very disconsolate. It can safely be presumed that during this period, Hadrat Abu Bakr consoled the Holy Prophet and looked after him affectionately. After the engagement of Hadrat Ayesha this attachment obviously gained in depth. With reference to the main events in the life of the Holy Prophet during this period, the sources make no mention of Hadrat Abu Bakr.

The sixth section narrates how Hadrat Abu Bakr wagered with a Quraish leader about the truth of the prophesy made in Surah "Ar-Rum" of the Holy Qur'an. In writing this section I have derived help from:

(1) *Commentary of the Holy Qur'an* by Allama Yusuf Ali.
(2) *Commentary of the Holy Qur'an* by Maulana Maududi.
(3) *Dictionary of Islam.*
(4) My book *Digest of the Holy Qur'an.*

This episode establishes the truth of Islam. It is also indicative of the great depth and dimensions of the faith of Hadrat Abu Bakr.

3

MIGRATION TO MADINA

Second of the two

Hijrat. In 622 C.E. at the invitation of the people of Yathrib, it was decided by the Holy Prophet that the Muslims should migrate from Makkah to Yathrib. In the name of religion the Muslims were to leave their homes and hearths, and begin a new life in another city. The Muslims were to leave for Yathrib in batches.

Hadrat Abu Bakr's preparations. Hadrat Abu Bakr sought permission to migrate to Yathrib, but the Holy Prophet bade him wait, for it was possible that he might have a companion. Hadrat Abu Bakr took this hint to imply that he was to accompany the Holy Prophet. Hadrat Abu Bakr felt happy and honoured at the prospect of being a companion of the Holy Prophet on the journey to Yathrib. He bought two camels, and made other preparations for the journey.

The call to migrate. The Quraish of Makkah made a plot to murder the Holy Prophet. Allah frustrated their design. One hot afternoon, the Holy Prophet called at the house of Hadrat Abu Bakr, and gave him the tidings that the time for their migration had arrived. Allah had given the order:

> Make war on the persecutors
> Till persecution is no more,
> And religion is for Allah only.

At night in the cover of darkness, the Holy Prophet and Hadrat Abu Bakr left Makkah, but they did not take the road to Yathrib. They moved in the opposite direction, and took refuge in a cave in Mount Thaur some five miles south of Makkah.

In the cave of Mt. Thaur. When the Quraish came to know that the Holy Prophet had left Makkah they were much disturbed. They offered a reward of a hundred she camels to any one who found the Holy Prophet, and brought him back to Makkah. During the day, Abdullah the son of Hadrat Abu Bakr would listen to the plans and talks of the Quraish, and at night he would carry the news to the fugitives in the cave. Asma the daughter of Hadrat Abu Bakr brought them meals every day. Aamir a servant of Hadrat Abu Bakr would bring a flock of goats to the mouth of the cave every night where they were milked.

Second of the two. The Quraish sent search parties in all directions. One party came dangerously close to the entrance to the cave. Hadrat Abu Bakr had a feeling of great uneasiness at the impending danger. The Holy Prophet consoled him, and said "Fear not, for Allah is with us." And verily Allah was with them. Miraculously a spider wove its nest at the entrance to the cave, and seeing the nest the search party turned away after it had reached the very mouth of the cave. This event is referred to in the Holy Qur'an in the following terms:

> "He being the second of the two
> When they were in the cave,
> And when Muhammad said to his companion,
> 'Grieve not, surely God is with us'.
> Then God came to their help.
> And protected them with an army
> Which they saw not." (IX: 40)

Journey to Yathrib. The Holy Prophet and Hadrat Abu Bakr remained in the cave for three days and three nights. By this time the Quraish gave up the search in despair, and the Holy Prophet and Hadrat Abu Bakr decided to proceed to Yathrib. The servant of Hadrat Abu Bakr brought two camels for them to ride upon for the journey. Asma the daughter of

Hadrat Abu Bakr brought a bag of provisions. She had forgotten to bring a string to tie the bag. She tore her girdle and tied the bag with it. For this ingenuity, the Holy Prophet conferred on her the title 'She of the Girdle". The party consisting of the Holy Prophet, Hadrat Abu Bakr, a servant of Hadrat Abu Bakr, and a guide set off by a circuitous route to Yathrib by way of Tihama on the coast of the Red Sea.

Account of Asma. Asma has related that when the Holy Prophet and her father left for Yathrib and she returned to Makkah, a party of the Quraish headed by Abu Jahl called at their house and made enquiries regarding the whereabouts of Hadrat Abu Bakr. When Asma told them that she was unaware of the whereabouts of her father, Abu Jahl slapped her so violently on the face that her earing flew off. She has also related that Hadrat Abu Bakr took all the available money with him. Abu Qahafa the father of Hadrat Abu Bakr who had lost his eye sight said that Hadrat Abu Bakr had not done well in taking with him all the money, and not leaving anything for the family. Asma took some pebbles, and put them in a niche where Hadrat Abu Bakr used to keep money. She covered the pebbles with a piece of cloth, and leading her grandfather to the niche said, "Put your hand on the money, grandfather." Abu Qahafa did so, and felt satisfied that Hadrat Abu Bakr had left ample money for the family.

The Road to Yathrib

The party. The party that book the road to Yathrib consisted of four persons The Holy Prophet and the guide Abdullah b. Ariqat rode on one camel. Hadrat Abu Bakr and his servant Ibn Fuhayra rode on another camel. The party struck off by a track considerably to the left of the common road. Hurrying westward, the party soon gained the vicinity of the sea shore. The party travelled during the night, and spent the day resting in some sheltered place. They travelled through unfrequented ways. It was an arduous, and nerve racking journey. They were haunted by the fear of the pursuit of the Quraish, but they were upheld by the faith that God would protect them.

Suraqah b. Malik. The Quraish had offered a reward of one hundred she camels to anyone who could pursue and apprehend the Holy Prophet and his companion. Suraqah b. Malik an expert horseman scoured the country side in search of the Holy Prophet and Hadrat Abu Bakr. It was reported to him that four men had been seen moving to the west along the sea shore. Suraqah felt convinced that these four men must be the Holy Prophet and his party. He pursued the party. After some fast riding he came to within seeing distance. He felt happy that these were the men he was in search of. At this stage his horse stumbled and he fell on the ground. He resorted to divination through arrows, and the oracle did not favour his advance. Ignoring the oracle he remounted the horse and galloped fast until he came within talking distance of the Holy Prophet and his party. Seeing Suraqah, Hadrat Abu Bakr felt uneasy. The Holy Prophet counselled him not to worry, for God was with them. At this stage the horse of Suraqah stumbled again. He resorted to divination, and once again the verdict was unfavourable. Suraqah now felt that some supernatural power protected the Holy Prophet and his party and it would be futile to contend against supernatural powers. He remounted the horse and galloped again. When he came close to the party, he shouted that he was not coming as a pursuer; he was coming as a friend. He said that he wanted that a certificate of immunity should be granted to him. Suraqah approached the party and the Holy Prophet asked Hadrat Abu Bakr to write for Suraqah a document of immunity. With this document, Suraqah returned to Makkah. In the way he met some other persons who were in pursuit of the Holy Prophet and his party. He made them turn back saying that the party had not gone that way. Suraqah presented this document at the time of the conquest of Makkah, and he was duly rewarded. He was also converted to Islam, and he regarded this conversion as the greatest reward.

Umm Ma'bad. After the encounter with Suraqah the party reached the encampment of Umm Ma'bad. Umm Ma'bad was a gracious old lady. She welcomed the party. Her flock was in the pasture, and with her was a goat which was dry. She therefore regretted that she was not in a position to offer them any milk. Taking the name of Allah, the Holy Prophet touched the udders of the goat, and plenty of milk flowed therefrom which was not only sufficient for the guests, but considerable quantity was left for the hostess as well. Umm Ma'bad wondered at the miracle. She wanted the party to stay for the night with her, but they thanked her saying that they had a long way to go and they had to travel during the night.

Zubayr. When the party were two or three stages from Madina, they came to the main road. Now they were out of the danger of pursuit. Here they met a caravan from Syria led by Zubayr. Zubayr presented the Holy Prophet and Hadrat Abu Bakr some garments that he had brought with them to Syria. He told them that the people of Yathrib were keenly awaiting their arrival.

Life at Madina

Quba. When the Holy Prophet and Hadrat Abu Bakr reached in the neighbourhood of Madina their first stop was at Quba, a suburb of Madina. As they arrived at Quba the people crowded round them. As the people had not seen them before, it was difficult for them to know as to who out of the two was the Holy Prophet. Seeing this predicament of the people, Hadrat Abu Bakr stood up and shielded the Holy Prophet with his mantle. Thereupon the people came to know who was the Holy Prophet. The Holy Prophet and Hadrat Abu Bakr stayed at Quba for a few days, and then they proceeded to Yathrib which was named Madinat-un-Nabi or Madina in the honour of the arrival of the Holy Prophet.

Reception at Madina. At Madina the Holy Prophet and Hadrat Abu Bakr were given a royal welcome. The maidens of Madina mounted on the roof tops of their houses and sang:

"From the hill tops of the south,
The full moon doth arise,
With what a lovely call,
Unto God doth he call,
And we thank him for it all.

O you sent by Allah the Rahman
We bow to thy demand."

The change. The world of Madina was quite different from the world of Makkah. At Makkah the Muslims were a persecuted people, at Madina they were the masters of their destiny. The life at Madina was a great break with the past. The days of trial, tribulations and tortures were now over, the Muslims were now set on the path of fulfilment. They were now poised to build a new commonwealth and a new ideal society.

Construction of the mosque. The first thing that the Holy Prophet called upon the Muslims to do at Madina was to build a mosque which was to be the prayer house as well as the community centre. The owner of the plot of land selected for the purpose of building the mosque insisted on donating the land free. The Holy Prophet, however, paid the price at the market rate, and this price was paid by Hadrat Abu Bakr. All the Muslims including the Holy Prophet and Hadrat Abu Bakr participated in the construction of the mosque. As the Muslims laboured, they chanted:

"There is no life, but the life of the next world,
O God have mercy on the Muhajreen and the Ansar."

Within a few months the mosque was completed. It was square in form each side measuring fifty yards. It faced towards the north, and had three gates on each of the remaining three sides. Adjoining the mosque, apartments were constructed for the household of the Holy Prophet, and for some of the companions, including Hadrat Abu Bakr. The mosque was a monument of simplicity. The walls were made of mud bricks, and the roofs were supported by trunks of palm trees. The apartments for the houses of the Holy Prophet and Hadrat Abu Bakr were simple structures, and blankets of camel hair were hung at the doors. The courtyard in each case was hardly six to seven paces in length, and the length of the rooms did not extend beyond ten paces.

Rehabilitation of the Muhajireen. To rehabilitate the migrants from Makkah in the society of Madina, the Holy

Prophet established a fraternity among the Muslims of Makkah and those of Madina whereunder each migrant was paired with an Ansar of corresponding status. The brotherhood thus established was unique in the annals of mankind. So strong and cordial were these bonds that they even surpassed the relationship of blood. In this roll of brotherhood, Hadrat Abu Bakr was paired with Khaarijah bin Zaid Ansari. Hadrat Abu Bakr's relationship with his brother-in-Islam was most cordial which was further strengthened when Hadrat Abu Bakr married Habiba, a daughter of Khaarijah.

Sukh. Khaarijah had his house at Sukh, a suburb of Madina. Hadrat Abu Bakr also settled at Sukh. When the family of Hadrat Abu Bakr came from Makkah they were lodged in the apartments adjoining the Prophet's mosque at Madina. Hadrat Abu Bakr visited them frequently but he continued to have his personal residence at Sukh. He usually walked from Sukh to Madina on foot. Sometimes he rode on a horse.

Change in climate. The climate of Makkah was dry, but the climate of Madina was damp. That adversely affected the health of the emigrants. On arrival at Madina most of the emigrants fell sick. Hadrat Abu Bakr also suffered from fever for several days. During his sickness he was attended to by Khaarijah and his family.

Trade in Madina. At Makkah, Hadrat Abu Bakr was a trader in cloth. He started the same business at Madina. He was a wholesaler. He had his store at Sukh, and from there cloth was supplied to the market at Madina. Hadrat Abu Bakr was a shrewd businessman, and we have reasons to hold that his business flourished at Madina in the same way as it did at Makkah. From the accounts, that have come down to us, it appears that at the time of his conversion to Islam Hadrat Abu Bakr had an amount of 40,000 Dirhams, and that at the time of his death he left no money. These accounts tend to give the impression that after conversion to Islam, Hadrat Abu Bakr did not attend to business, and subsisted all the years from 610 to 634 C.E. on the original amount of 40,000 Dirhams. That is not the correct position. As a matter of fact, Hadrat

Abu Bakr remained active in business throughout his life. It is related that even after he had been elected as a Caliph he took the cloth to the market for disposal. At the insistence of Hadrat Umar, and Hadrat Abu Ubaida he suspended his business activities and accepted a meagre allowance from the treasury. This shows that upto the time of his election as the Caliph, Hadrat Abu Bakr remained active in business.

Hadrat Abu Bakr as the Chief Counsellor. After attending to business it was the wont of Hadrat Abu Bakr to spend his spare time in the company of the Holy Prophet. Hadrat Abu Bakr always acted as the 'Second of the Two'. He was the Chief Counsellor of the Holy Prophet. The Holy Prophet consulted Hadrat Abu Bakr on all important matters, and the advice tendered by him was usually accepted. The Holy Prophet used to say that Hadrat Abu Bakr was the best counsellor. At meetings Hadrat Abu Bakr was always assigned a special place to the right of the Holy Prophet.

Hadrat Abu Bakr and Finhas the Jew

The Jews of Madina. In Madina there was a considerable number of Jews. They were wealthy, controlled the trade, and commanded great influence. The Holy Prophet followed the policy of 'live and let live'. He accordingly entered into a treaty with the Jews. According to the terms of the treaty the Jews were to enjoy religious freedom and there was to be no interference in religious affairs. The Muslims and the Jews were to be on friendly terms, and were to help each other in the promotion of objects of mutual interest. It was stipulated that Muslims and the Jews would help each other in case of an attack by an enemy. No party was to give protection to the Quraish, and in case the Quraish invaded Madina, both the Muslims and the Jews were to join hands in the defence of the city.

Betrayal of the Jews. The Jews knew that in their holy books there were references to the advent of a prophet in Arabia. They were however under the impression that the prophet would rise from their midst. When the Holy Prophet rose from the ranks of the Quraish in Makkah, the Jews recognised in him all the signs of prophethood foretold in their sacred books. When the Holy Prophet came to Madina the Jews thought that he would be subservient to them and would acknowledge their supremacy. When the Holy Prophet followed an independent policy, the Jews followed the policy of betrayal and embarked on a campaign of ridicule.

Hadrat Abu Bakr and Finhas the Jew. One day Hadrat Abu Bakr came across Finhas, one of the Jewish rabbis. Hadrat Abu Bakr invited him to Islam, but Finhas ridiculed the offer. The Holy Prophet had enjoined on the Muslims to spend in the way of Allah, and according to the Holy Qur'an this was to be a loan against God repayable manifold the original amount. The Muslims were forbidden to charge interest. According to the religion of the Jews, interest was permissible. In this context Finhas argued:

> "We are rich, but your Allah is poor for He asks loan of us. Had He been independent of us He would not have given us interest, which He has denied to you."

The blasphemy. Hadrat Abu Bakr felt outraged at this blasphemy. In a fit of anger Hadrat Abu Bakr slapped in the face and said: "Were it not for the treaty between the Muslims and the Jews, I would have cut off your head, you enemy of Allah." Finhas went to the Holy Prophet and complained that Hadrat Abu Bakr had struck him on the face. When put to explanation, Hadrat Abu Bakr said, "This enemy of Allah spoke blasphemy. He alleged that Allah was poor and they were rich. At such insolence against Allah I could not control myself, and I hit him."

Revelation of the Holy Qur'an. Finhas denied the charge levelled against him by Hadrat Abu Bakr. A revelation, however, confirmed what Hadrat Abu Bakr had alleged. According to the revelation it was said that Allah had heard the speech of those who had said that Allah was poor and they were rich. About Hadrat Abu Bakr's anger, the following verses were revealed:

> "And you will certainly hear from those

Who received the Book before you
And from the polytheists much that is wrong,
But if you preserve and fear God
That is the steadfastness of things."

Expedition of Ubayda Bin Al-Harith

Expedition of Ubayda bin al-Harith. In 622 C.E., the first year of the Hegira the Holy Prophet sent an expedition against the Quraish under Ubayda bin al-Harith. The Muslim force consisted of eighty persons including Hadrat Abu Bakr. The Muslim force encountered the Quraish led by 'Ikrama bin Abu Jahl at some distance from Madina on the way to Makkah. Sa'd bin Abi Waqqas from the Muslim ranks fired an arrow shot against the Quraish. It was the first arrow shot in the cause of Islam. The Quraish did not choose to fight. They increased their speed, and escaped to Makkah.

Verses composed by Hadrat Abu Bakr. The following verses composed by Hadrat Abu Bakr on the occasion of the raid are on record:

"Could you not sleep because of the spectre of Salma in sandy valleys,

And the important event that happened in the tribe?
You see that neither admonition nor a prophet's call
Can save some of Lu'ayy from unbelief;
A truthful prophet came to them,
And they gave him the lie,
And said 'You shall not live among us'.
When we called them to the truth they turned their backs,
They howled like bitches driven back panting to their lairs;
With how many of them have we ties of kinship,
Yet to abandon piety did not weigh upon them;
If they turn back from their unbelief and disobedience
(For the good and lawful is not like the abominable);
If they follow their idolatry and error

God's punishment on them will not tarry.
We are men of Ghalib's highest stock
From which nobility comes through many branches;
I swear by the lord of camels urged on at even by singing.
Their feet protected by old leather thongs,
Like the red-backed deer that haunt Makkah
Going down to the well's slimy cistern;
I swear and I am no perjuror,
If they do not quickly repent of their error,
A valiant band will descend on them,
Which will leave women husbandless,
It will leave dead men, with vultures wheeling round.
It will not spare the infidels as Ibn Harith did.
Give the Banu Sahm with you a message
And every infidel who is trying to do evil;
If you assail my honour in your evil opinion
I will not assail yours."

Hadrat Ayesha's Marriage to the Holy Prophet

Marriage of Hadrat Ayesha. When the Muslims were duly settled in Madina, and the families of the Holy Prophet and Hadrat Abu Bakr had come to Madina, it was decided that the formal ceremony of the marriage of Hadrat Ayesha the daughter of Hadrat Abu Bakr to the Holy Prophet should be performed. Hadrat Ayesha was now of age. The crisis of Islam was over. The Holy Prophet was no longer a persecuted person; he was now the ruler of Madina. The Holy Prophet needed a young lady by his side whom he could love. One day early in 623 C.E., the Holy Prophet accompanied by his companions went to the house of Hadrat Abu Bakr at Sukh to seek hand of Hadrat Ayesha in marriage.

Hadrat Ayesha's account of marriage. Hadrat Ayesha has left an account of the wedding day in the following terms:

"The Prophet of Allah came to our house where many of

the companions were waiting. My mother brought me sitting in a litter on two poles. She made me descend; then she smoothened my hair, and washed my face with water. Then she led me to the door of the house where she stopped until I regained my composure. Then she took me to where the Prophet of God was sitting in our house, and made me sit near him saying, 'These are your people. May God bless them through you, and you through them'. The people then left, and the Prophet consummated the marriage while in our house."

After the marriage. After the marriage, Hadrat Ayesha was assigned a separate quarter adjoining the mosque. Hadrat Ayesha was handsome, intelligent and eloquent, and the Holy Prophet loved her intensely. The marriage brought Hadrat Abu Bakr still closer to the Holy Prophet. There is a tradition that once a companion asked the Holy Prophet whom did he love most, and he said 'Ayesha'. 'And whom do you love next' asked the companion, and the Holy Prophet said 'Her father Abu Bakr'.

Jealousy against Hadrat Ayesha. On account of the Holy Prophets's love for Ayesha many persons got jealous of her. One day one of the other wives of the Holy Prophet complained in strong terms against the favour shown to Hadrat Ayesha. The Holy Prophet wanted Hadrat Ayesha to hear the complaint and reply thereto. Hadrat Ayesha replied with such force and eloquence that she won her case. Thereupon the Holy Prophet said "Do you see how eloquent Ayesha is, and what great force is in her arguments. She is after all the daughter of Abu Bakr. No wonder for her qualities she deserves to be loved."

Hadrat Fatima and Hadrat Ayesha. One day Hadrat Fatima the daughter of the Holy Prophet at the instance of the other wives of the Holy Prophet complained against the preferential treatment accorded to Hadrat Ayesha. The Holy Prophet merely smiled and said, "My dear, wont you love the person whom your father loves ?"

NOTES

This Chapter gives an account of Hadrat Abu Bakr's migration from Makkah and settlement in Madina. Abu Bakr reached the summit of fulfilment when he accompanied the Holy Prophet on migration to Makkah. For this consummation Hadrat Abu Bakr had the distinction of being referred to in the Holy Qur'an as the "Second of the Two".

The first section of this Chapter is based on the accounts given in all the biographies of the Holy Prophet. I have profited from the biographies of the Holy Prophet by Hafiz Ghulam Sarwar, and Abdul Hamid Sidiqi.

The second section gives an account of the actual journey to Yathrib. This was the occasion of two miracles, firstly the penitence of Suraqa who came to pursue, but returned with a letter of immunity, and secondly the milking of the dry goat of Umm Ma'bad. The migration or 'Hijrat' is by itself a great miracle. How a band of believers persecuted by their people and driven from their homeland, reconquered their home town within ten years, and the new faith was accepted by all the people of Arabia is a miracle of history. Surely the Will of God manifested itself through the Holy Prophet and his companions. Indeed the Hijrat marks the beginning of the Islamic calender. The journey of the Holy Prophet from Makkah to Yathrib is thus a landmark in the history of Islam in general and Islam in particular.

The third section deals with Hadrat Abu Bakr's settlement at Madina. It is based on the accounts given in the biographies of the Holy Prophet. The sources indicate that at Madina, Hadrat Abu Bakr followed the profession of a cloth merchant. It is repeatedly said that at the time of conversion to Islam, Hadrat Abu Bakr had 40,000 Dirhams with him, and at the time of his death he left nothing. Hadrat Abu Bakr was a shrewd and expert businessman and he must have earned a good deal of income. It appears that the scholars who wrote early accounts were not interested in such material things, and we are therefore deprived of any knowledge as to the income of Hadrat Abu Bakr and the sources from which it was derived.

The sources give no idea of the financially condition of the Holy Prophet. An impression is generally created that whenever any funds were needed these were provided by Hadrat Abu Bakr or some other companion. After marriage with Hadrat Khadija, the Holy Prophet became the owner of a big business concern, and considerable income would have accrued therefrom. Hadrat Muhammad (peace be on him) married Hadrat Khadija in 596 and the call came in 610 C.E. During these fourteen years, the Holy Prophet would have earned considerable income. It is not known what happened to this wealth. Our early historians in their enthusiasm for poverty take pride to write that the Holy Prophet had to starve on many occasions. It is difficult to accept this statement at its face value. The Holy Prophet was the head of Government at Madina, and if he had to starve on occasions this implies that there was something wrong with the Government. It is true that the Holy Prophet lived a simple life, and avoided luxurious living, but it cannot be true that he had to starve on occasions. I wish some study could be undertaken to assess the financial resources available to the Holy Prophet, Hadrat Abu Bakr and other distinguished companions. In the fourth section I give an account of Hadrat Abu Bakr's encounter with Finhas the Jew. When the Jew uttered blasphemy against Allah, Hadrat Abu Bakr felt outraged, and he slapped the Jew on the face. This brings out a special aspect of the character of Hadrat Abu Bakr. He was a soft spoken tender hearted man, but when anything was said against Allah, or the Holy Prophet, he could become very hard and go to any length against the slanderer. The account in this section based on the account contained in Guillame's *The Life of Muhammad.*

The account of the expedition of Ubayda b. Al-Harith given in the fifth section is also based on the account given in Guillaume's book *Life of Muhammad.* Herein certain verses are quoted which are attributed to Hadrat Abu Bakr. There is some controversy on the point whether Hadrat Abu Bakr was a poet or not. Hadrat Ayesha is reported to have said that

Hadrat Abu Bakr never wrote poetry. On the other hand there is evidence that Hadrat Abu Bakr could quote apt verses. Even on death bed he quoted some verses. It may be safely presumed that in the early years, Hadrat Abu Bakr did write poetry, but on becoming a Muslim he was so charmed with the excellence of the Holy Qur'an that instead of quoting verses of poetry he would quote verses from the Holy Qur'an.

In the sixth section I have given an account of Hadrat Ayesha's marriage. This account is based on the account given in Bint al Shaati's book *The Wives of the Prophet.* As we read the life story of Hadrat Ayesha we are struck by the deplorable fact that there was some jealousy between Hadrat Ayesha and Hadrat Fatima. When Hadrat Fatima complained to the Holy Prophet against the preference given to Hadrat Ayesha, the Holy Prophet very wisely said, "My dear, wont you love the person your father loves".

4

THE NEW WORLD OF MADINA

Battle of Badr

The battle of Badr. In 624 C.E. the Quraish of Makkah mustered a strong force, and decided to give the Muslims a battle with a view to crushing them. When the Holy Prophet came to know of the intentions of the Quraish he held a council of war at Madina. At this council, Hadrat Abu Bakr was the first to rise and make an offer to sacrifice his life in the defence of Islam. The Muslims could muster a force of 313 men only to fight against the Quraish. With this meagre force the Holy Prophet marched from Madina to Badr, some eighty miles away.

Bravest Muslim. At Badr a pavilion was constructed for the Holy Prophet where he prayed. Here Hadrat Abu Bakr stood as a guard with a drawn sword. It is related that once Hadrat Ali asked his associates as to whom they considered to be the bravest among the Muslims. All of them said that Hadrat Ali was the bravest. Hadrat Ali said:

> "No. Hadrat Abu Bakr is the bravest of men. At the battle of Badr we had prepared a pavilion for the Holy Prophet, but when we were asked to offer ourselves for the task of guarding it, none came forward except Hadrat Abu Bakr. With a drawn sword he took his stand by the sidė of the Prophet of Allah and guarded him from the infidels by attacking those who dared to proceed in that direction. He was, therefore, the bravest of men."

Prayer of the Holy Prophet. At the battle of Badr the force of the Quraish was three times as large as the force of the Muslims. The Muslims were poorly equipped, but the Quraish were well armed. All the advantages lay with the Quraish. There was the danger that if the Muslims were defeated that would be the end of Islam. In this crisis the Holy Prophet prostrated himself before God and prayed:

> "O Lord ! I beseech You to fulfil the promise that You have given to me. O Lord ! if You allow this band of Muslims to perish, there will be none to worship you on the earth."

As the Holy Prophet beseeched God overwhelmed with emotion, his mantle fell on the ground. Hadrat Abu Bakr covered him with the mantle and said, "Holy Prophet, rest assured, God will fulfil His promise." Allah assured the Holy Prophet of His help. Thereupon the Holy Prophet concluded his prayers, and joined his companions to lead the attack. He gave the Muslims the glad tidings that soon the enemy would be routed. The Holy Qur'an refers to this incident in the following terms:

> "When you sought aid from your Lord He answered you I will assist you with a thousand angels." (VIII:9)

The battle. In the battle the Holy Prophet led the centre, while Hadrat Abu Bakr held the charge of the right wing. In the battle Hadrat Abu Bakr's son Abdur Rahman who was still a non-Muslim fought on the side of the Quraish. When after the pact of Hudaibiya Abdur Rahman became a Muslim, he told his father that on the day of Badr he had got a chance when he could have easily struck him, but then he had turned in another direction. Hadrat Abu Bakr replied, "If I had such an opportunity, I would not have spared you".

Victory for the Muslims. In the battle of Badr, God gave victory to the Muslims. Seventy men from the Quraish were killed, and seventy of them were taken captive and brought to Madina. At Madina the Holy Prophet consulted his companions as to how the captives should be treated. Hadrat Umar was of the view that they should be killed. Hadrat Abu Bakr said, "All of them are our kinsmen and relatives. They may be set free on ransom." The Holy Prophet accepted the advice of Hadrat Abu Bakr, and set the captives free on ransom.

Banu Qainuqa'

Hostility of the Jews. When the Holy Prophet came to Madina, a few Jews accepted Islam and they were sincere in their faith in Islam. Some other Jews accepted Islam, but they were not sincere in their faith. They were hypocrites, and their object in accepting Islam was to disrupt it from within. The rest of the Jews were hostile to Islam. They ridiculed Islam and slandered the Holy Prophet and the Muslims. Ka'ab b. Ashraf, Abu Afak, and Asma bint Marwan composed filthy songs satirising the Holy Prophet and the Muslims.

Molestation of a Muslim woman by the Jews. Some time after the battle of Badr, a Muslim woman went to the street in the quarter of Banu Qainuqa', and gave an order to a goldsmith in the street for the making of some ornaments. One of the Jews came behind her, and opened the fastenings of her dress while she was talking to the goldsmith. She remained unaware of the rascality of the Jew, and when she stood up to depart, her trouser slipped exposing her nakedness. The Jews had a hearty laugh at her exposure. She shrieked and cried for help. A Muslim who passed that way came to her help and he killed the rascal who had done the mischief. The Jews in turn fell upon the Muslim and killed him.

The Holy Prophet's ultimatum. In this sad episode the Jews were the aggressors. The Holy Prophet, therefore, asked the Jews to make amends failing which punitive action would be taken against them. The Jews accepted the challenge and replied as follows:

> "O Muhammad, let not the victory at Badr over a people who did not know how to fight deceive you. By God if you fight us, you will know that we are men who know to fight."

The fight. The Holy Prophet mustered a force, and ordered an attack on the quarter of Banu Qainuqa'. The Holy

Prophet gave the standard to Hadrat Abu Bakr. Banu Qainuqa' did not dare fight in the open. They shut themselves in their strongholds. The Muslims besieged these strongholds. The Quraish of Makkah had promised to help Banu Qainuqa', but no help came. The siege lasted for a fortnight by which time the Jews were brought to bay and they surrendered. The Holy Prophet and his companions were of the view that the treacherous Jews should be killed. Abdullah b. Ubayy interceded for them, and the Holy Prophet ultimately agreed to spare their lives provided they migrated from Madina. They were allowed to carry such movable property except arms as they could. They emigrated to Wadi al-Qara, north of Arabia, and finally to Syria. Their property left at Madina was distributed among the Muslims. That was the first victory of the Muslims against the Jews. It showed that the Muslims were strong enough to take action against those who fomented treason.

Battle of Uhud

Battle of Uhud. The battle of Uhud was an extension of the battle of Badr. In 625 C.E. the Quraish came with a force of 3,000 men to avenge their defeat at Badr. The Muslims could muster a force of 1,000 persons only, and out of these three hundred persons under Abdullah b. Ubbay, a hypocrite, withdrew at the last moment thus leaving only 700 persons to face the hostile Quraish.

Hadrat Abu Bakr and his son Abdur Rahman. Hadrat Abu Bakr marched to the battlefield of Uhud a few miles outside Madina by the side of the Holy Prophet. Abdur Rahman the son of Hadrat Abu Bakr fought on the side of the Quraish. Before the battle began, Abdur Rahman stepped forward, and threw a challenge to the Muslims to send some one to fight with him. Hadrat Abu Bakr decided to accept the challenge. The Holy Prophet, however, stopped him saying, "Sheath your sword, and let us continue to profit by your wise counsels."

Battle array. The Holy Prophet arranged his force in battle array and posted a small contingent of archers to guard a vulnerable passage in the rear. The archers were instructed that they were not to leave their positions without the instructions of the Holy Prophet.

The Quraish women. With the Quraish was a contingent of women. They beat drums and sang songs to excite the soldiers to action. They sang:

> "We are the daughters of the morning star;
> We tread on carpets;
> If you advance we embrace you;
> If you turn back we leave you."

The course of the battle. The Quraish charged with full force, but the Muslims held fast. Then in the counter attack the Muslims broke the enemy's line, and the Quraish fell back. At this stage the contingent of the Muslim archers, contrary to instructions, left their position in order to plunder the camp of the retreating Quraish. Khalid b. Walid who was still a non-Muslim and was fighting on the side of the Quraish rushed with his contingent, and occupied the position vacated by the Muslim archers. The Quraish rallied and launched an attack on the Muslims both from the front as well as the rear. In the confusion that followed many Muslims were martyred. Even the Holy Prophet was wounded, and he fell in a pit where many of his followers lay dead.

The Holy Prophet. When ths Holy Prophet could no longer be seen at the battlefield a cry rose from the ranks of the Quraish that he was dead. That demoralised the Muslims. Hadrat Abu Bakr was the first person to find the Holy Prophet lying wounded in a pit. With the help of other companions, Hadrat Abu Bakr led the Holy Prophet to a place of safety.

The call of the Quraish. Abu Sufyan the leader of the Quraish climbed a hillock and shouted, "Is Muhammad there?" The Prophet asked his companions to remain quiet. Abu Sufyan then called for Hadrat Abu Bakr and Hadrat Umar. No reply was made, and thereupon Abu Sufyan shouted, "All of them have been killed". At this Hadrat Umar could not restrain himself, and said, "O enemy of Allah, we are all alive" Abu Sufyan in a mood of exultation cried "O Hubbal, glory to thee."

Hadrat Abu Bakr replied, "Only Allah is Most High and Great". Abu Sufyan said, "We have Uzza with us, and you have no lord". Hadrat Abu Bakr retorted, "Allah is our Lord, and you have no lord".

Drawn battle. When the two armies withdrew from the battlefield, seven Muslims lay dead on the battle field. In this battle the Quraish had the upper hand. They felt satisfied that they had avenged their defeat at Badr. It was really a drawn battle, for the Quraish were not in the position to press their advantage and march to Madina. They chose to return to Makkah. The Holy Prophet sent a contingent under Hadrat Abu Bakr to follow the Quraish. Hadrat Abu Bakr covered some distance, and when he saw that the Quraish were speeding to Makkah with all haste, he returned to Madina.

Banu Nadeer

Banu Nadeer. Banu Nadeer were Jews who resided at Madina. Hadrat Muhammad (peace be on him) entered into a pact of alliance with them. The Jews in spite of their pact with the Muslims resorted to intrigues. They opened secret negotiations with the Quraish against the Muslims. They deliberately mispronounced the sacred words of the Holy Qur'an in order to pervert their meanings. The Jewish poets wrote satirical poems against Islam and the Holy Prophet.

Tragedy of Bir Ma'una. On the invitation of certain tribes, the Holy Prophet sent them a party of seventy missionaries to teach them the precepts of Islam. Before these men could reach their destination they were waylaid, and martyred by the tribes of Banu Sulaym. Only one man Amr b. Umayya escaped the tragedy of Bir Ma'una. While returning to Madina, he met two men of Banu 'Amir, and thinking that they were enemies killed them. Banu 'Amir were however allied with the Muslims and Banu Nadeer, and the Muslims and the Jews had to pay the blood money of the two men who had been killed by 'Amr under a mistake.

Holy Prophet's visit to Banu Nadeer. The Holy Prophet decided to pay indemnity to Banu 'Amir. He along with his companions including Hadrat Abu Bakr went to the quarter of Banu Nadeer, and asked them to pay their share of the indemnity in accordance with the terms of their alliance. The Jews expressed their readiness to pay their share. They made the Holy Prophet and his companions sit under a high wall, and deputed a Jew to throw a big stone on the Holy Prophet from the top of the wall. It was revealed to the Holy Prophet that the Jews meant mischief. Immediately he rose from his seat and left for Madina.

Expulsion of Banu Nadeer. On this treachery of Banu Nadeer, the Holy Prophet served an ultimatum on them to leave Madina within ten days. Abdullah b. Ubayye, the leader of the hypocrites asked the Jews to put up a fight against the Muslims and assured them of his help. After the expiry of ten days, the Holy Prophet mustered a force including Hadrat Abu Bakr and marched to the quarter of Banu Nadeer. The Banu Nadeer shut themselves in their strongholds, and waited for help from the hypocrites. No help came and after a fortnight, the Banu Nadeer surrendered, and asked for terms. They were asked to leave Madina, and could take away whatever movable property, other than arms, they could carry. They pulled down their houses with their own hands and left for Khyber. Whatever property was left by them was distributed among the Muslims.

Banu Mustaliq

The Banu Mustaliq. The Banu Mustaliq, a branch of Banu Khuza'a occupied the territory of Qadid on the Red Sea shore between Jeddah and Rabigh. In 527 C.E. news was brought to Madina that the Banu Mustaliq in alliance with some other tribes were gathering to make a raid on Madina. The policy of the Holy Prophet was that the Muslims should not lose the initiative in such cases, and should take such tribes by surprise. Another aspect of the policy was that action against individual tribes should be taken before they could effect an alliance.

Expedition against Banu Mustaliq. In pursuance of

this policy, the Holy Prophet decided to lead an expedition to Banu Mustaliq secretly and immediately. In the Muslim force that was mustered, Hadrat Abu Bakr was the standard bearer of the Muhajreen. By forced marches the Muslim force reached Muraisi, where there was a spring from where Banu Mustaliq obtained their water supply. The Muslims cut off all communications by which other tribes could come to join Banu Mustaliq. Banu Mustaliq were taken by surprise. They offered some resistance, but they lost heart and surrendered. In order to placate the tribe the Holy Prophet married a daughter of their chief Harith b. Abi Dirar. Thereupon the entire tribe was converted to Islam.

Abdullah b. Ubayye. The success of Muslims against Banu Mustaliq was marred by an unfortunate incident which exposed the hypocrisy of certain persons who professed to be Muslim but were otherwise hypocrites. In the matter of the watering of animals there was a dispute between two persons one of whom was a Muhajir and the other was Ansar. The Muhajir invoked the help of the Muhajirs while the Ansar invoked the help of the Ansar. Thereupon Abdullah b. Ubayye a Muslim hypocrite said: "On reaching Madina we will drive away the Muhajreen from our city. By God our and their case is like the saying of old 'Fatten your dog and he will eat you."

Reaction of the Holy Prophet. On hearing of this outburst of Abdullah b. Ubayye, the Holy Prophet felt much annoyed but he suppressed his anger, and ordered an immediate return to Madina. Some of the companions volunteered to cut off the head of the hypocrite. The Holy Prophet, however, remained silent. The son of Abdullah b. Ubayye waited on the Holy Prophet and said, "I understand you are thinking of killing my father for his insolence. If some body else kills my father, it will be incumbent on me to take revenge and kill his murderer, and thus one Muslim will be killed. If you are annoyed with my father and want him to be killed, command me, and I will kill him myself". The Holy Prophet was impressed with the loyalty of the young man to Islam, and assured him that he contemplated no action against his father.

Ordeal of Falsehood

Ordeal of falsehood. In 628 C.E. the jealousy of vested interests against Hadrat Ayesha culminated in what came to be known as the 'ordeal of falsehood'. Hadrat Ayesha had accompanied the Holy Prophet on the expedition against Banu al-Mustaliq. On the way back the army camped for the night and early next morning departed without realising that Hadrat Ayesha was not in the litter on the camel. She had gone to answer the call of nature where her necklace dropped and it was with some difficulty that she was able to locate the lost necklace. When she returned, the caravan had left.

The scandal. Hadrat Ayesha wrapped herself and lay down. After some time a companion Safwan bin Mu'attal passed that way. He led his camel to Hadrat Ayesha which she mounted. Safwan walked on foot leading the camel. Hadrat Ayesha joined the camp at the next stop. The interested parties made this simple incident the subject of scandal and calumny. Hamna daughter of Jahsh, and a sister of Hadrat Zainab another wife of the Holy Prophet, Abdullah bin Ubayye the hypocrite, Mistah a relative of Hadrat Abu Bakr whom he supported, and Hassan bin Thabit, the poet, were active in spreading the calumny.

The crisis. The Holy Prophet became cool to Hadrat Ayesha and she shifted to her father's house. Her mother Umm Ruman said, "My daughter, take life calmly for it is seldom that a beautiful woman married to a loving husband, having rival wives, will not have problems for them and other people". This incident created a great crisis for Hadrat Abu Bakr and he was at a loss to understand what to do or not to do.

The revelation. One day the Holy Prophet called at the house of Hadrat Abu Bakr and said, "If Ayesha is guilty of what is said about her she should repent and ask for the forgiveness of God". Hadrat Ayesha said, "I swear I shall never ask forgiveness for the thing you speak of, for if I admit, that will be an admission of what I have never done, and if I do not admit you will not believe me." At this some verses of Surah

Nur were revealed to the Holy Prophet absoluing Hadrat Ayesha of the false accusation against her. The Holy Prophet recited the revealed verses and said, "Ayesha rejoice, for God has revealed to me your innocence."

Umm Ruman wanted Hadrat Ayesha to rise up and thank the Holy Prophet. Hadrat Ayesha said, "I will never get up, in gratitude to him for I have no one to thank except God Who has declared me innocent."

The predicament of Hadrat Abu Bakr. Hadrat Ayesha next turned to Hadrat Abu Bakr and said "Father would you not have pardoned me if there had been no revelation". Hadrat Abu Bakr kissed her on the forehead and said, "What heaven would cover me, and what earth would carry me if I judged that which I could not know."

Mistah. The Holy Prophet went to the mosque and told the people of the revelation. Those who had taken part in the calumny without any proof were punished. Mistah used to get an allowance from Hadrat Abu Bakr, and in view of the part played by Mistah in the ordeal of falsehood, Hadrat Abu Bakr decided to discont the allowance, and swore that he would no longer help Mistah. On this descended the verse:

> "And let not those who possess dignity and affluence among you,
> Swear not to give to kinsmen and the poor,
> And those who migrated for God's sake.
> Let them forgive and show forbearance.
> Do you wish that God should forgive you;
> And God is Forgiving, Merciful."

When this revelation was brought to the notice of Hadrat Abu Bakr he said, "Yes, by Allah, I want God to forgive me". Thereupon he restord the allowance to Mistah.

NOTES

Madina was a new world for the Muslims. That was the end of the persecution of the Muslims, but that was not the end of the struggle. Here the Muslims had to face a new set of problems. Although the Muslims had escaped from Makkah, the danger from the Quraish was still there. The Muslims had to face the hostility of the Jews. The Muslims had also to put up with the treachery of hypocrites who professed to be Muslims, but Islam sat lightly on them. The Muslims had also to contend against tribes inimically disposed to Islam.

This chapter covers a period of three years i.e. 624 to 627 C.E. During this period the Muslims had to face the Quraish in two battles, the battle of Badr and the battle of Uhud. In the battle of Badr which is described in the first section, the Muslims won an outstanding victory. In the battle of Uhud which is described in the third section, Muslims met a reverse though the Quraish could not take advantage of their victory.

During these years the Muslims had to take action against two tribes of the Jews the Banu Qainuqa‘ and the Banu Nadeer. Both these tribes were expelled from Madina. An account of the action against Banu Qainuqa‘ is given in the second section while an account of the action against Banu Nadeer is given in the fourth section.

The fifth section gives an account of the action taken against the tribe Banu Mustaliq. The Holy Prophet married a daughter of the chief of Banu Mustaliq and thereupon the whole tribe was converted to Islam. That shows that the marriages of the Holy Prophet were contracted not because of personal or physical considerations but because of political considerations dictated in the interests of Islam.

The sixth section gives an account of the ordeal of falsehood. It tells of the false accusation against Hadrat Ayesha, and gives an account how God established her innocence.

An account of the betrayal and treachery by hypocrites

may be read in the account of the battle of Uhud, in the campaign against Banu Mustaliq and in the ordeal of falsehood. It is a matter of relief to note that the Holy Prophet succeeded in overcoming all these problems one by one.

5

MAKKAH REVISITED

Battle of the Ditch

Combined opposition of the Quraish and other hostile tribes. In 627 C.E. the Muslims had to face the combined opposition of the Quraish and other tribes. The Quraish and their allies mustered a force ten thousand strong and marched to Madina. The Holy Prophet was advised that a face to face fight against such a large force was not possible for the Muslims, and the safest course for them was to remain on the defensive. It was accordingly decided that a french should be dug round Madina for protective purposes.

The ditch. The entire Muslim community in Madina was turned to dig the ditch. When the Muslims dug the ditch, the following war song was on their lips:

> "By God, had not Allah guided us,
> We would not have seen the right path,
> Or given Sadaqah nor offered the prayers;
> May Allah bestow on us confidence and calmness of mind;
> And make our steps firm to face the enemy.
> The enemy has risen against us, and he intends insurrection,
> But we refuse to submit.
> O God there is no welfare except that of the next world,
> Shower Thy Grace on the Ansars and the Muhajirs."

The site for the ditch was demarcated by the Holy Prophet. He allotted ten yards of ditch to be dug by each party of ten persons. One of such parties was led by Hadrat Abu Bakr. The ditch was dug in twenty days. It was five yards deep.

The siege. When the Quraish and their allies arrived they found that a ditch which could not be crossed lay between them and the Muslims. This was a mode of warfare with which the Quraish were not familiar. They camped beyond the ditch and decided to besiege the Muslims.

The Holy Prophet divided the ditch into a number of sectors and a contingent was posted to guard each sector. One of such contingents was under the command of Hadrat Abu Bakr. The enemy made frequent assaults in the attempt to cross the ditch. All such assaults were repulsed. Hadrat Abu Bakr showed great courage in guarding the belt of the ditch in his sector. To commemorate this event a mosque was later constructed at the site where Hadrat Abu Bakr had heroically repulsed the charge of the enemy. The mosque was known as 'Masjid-i-Siddiq'.

Victory of the Muslims. The siege prolonged for a month and the Muslims were subjected to great hardships. Food ran short, and subsistence became a problem. The Muslims nevertheless preserved and hoped that God would come to their relief.

And God did come to the relief of the Muslims. There were dissensions in the camp of the enemy. Provisions with them ran short. Above all a strong storm lashed the countryside. The Muslims were safe in their houses in Madina, but the Quraish and their allies who had to bear the brunt of the fury of the storm were unnerved. In a fit of desperation Abu Sufyan ordered that the siege should be withdrawn and the Quraish should return to Makkah. Their allies also dispersed. The Muslims won the day due to the Grace of God, and on account of their unusual perseverance against heavy odds.

Banu Quraiza

Treachery of Banu Quraiza. After the expulsion of the

Jews of the Banu Qainuqa' and Bani Nadeer, the Jews of Banu Quraiza alone remained in Madina. They assured the Holy Prophet of their loyalty. In the battle of the Ditch, the Banu Nadeer Jews who had been expelled by the Muslims to Khyber were in the forefront in the matter of hostility to the Muslims. Huyayy b. Akhtab the leader of the Banu Nadeer opened negotiations with Banu Quraiza to attack the Muslims from behind. Ka'ab b. Asad the leader of the Banu Quraiza at first hesitated, but when it was brought to him that in view of the overwhelming strength of the coalition against the Muslims, the Muslims were apt to be destroyed, the Banu Quraiza agreed to throw in their lot with the coalition against the Muslims.

Holy Prophet's emissary to Banu Quraiza. Banu Quraiza were an ally of the Aus. When the Holy Prophet came to know of the intended treachery of Banu Quraiza, he sent Sa'ad b. Ma'aadh, the leader of the Aus, as an emissary to Banu Quraiza. He tried to prevail upon Banu Quraiza the desirability of remaining faithful to their pact with the Holy Prophet. In a fit of arrogance Ka'ab b. Asad said, " Who is the Prophet of God ? There is no agreement between us and Muhammad." The mission of Sa'ad b Ma'aadh failed, and the position of the Muslims exposed to attack from within as well as without seemed to be precarious. The Holy Prophet, however, did not lose heart. He felt confident that God would help the Muslims. And God did help the Muslims. Before Quraiza would attack the Muslims, the coalition against the Muslims withdrew and the siege was lifted.

Action against Banu Quraiza. With the disintegration of the forged united front against the Muslims, the initiative once again came to rest with the Muslims. Immediately the battle of the ditch was over, the Holy Prophet moved with his force against Banu Quraiza to chastise them for their treachery. Huyayy b. Akhtab the leader of Banu Nadeer promised the Banu Quraiza every possible help, and to assure them of Banu Nadeer help he came to reside with Banu Quraiza. When the Muslims marched against Banu Quraiza, the latter shut themselves in their forts. Ka'ab b. Asad the leader of Banu Quraiza advised his tribe to be converted to Islam or acknowledge the suzerainty of the Muslims. Under the influence of Huyayy b. Akhtab, the Banu Quraiza did not accept the advice of their leader, and said that they would fight to the bitter end.

Fate of Banu Quraiza. The Muslims tightened the siege, and took steps to ensure that no outside help could reach Banu Quraiza. The siege lasted for a fortnight, and ultimately brought to bay, Banu Quraiza surrendered, and pleaded that the same terms should be allowed to them as had been offered to Banu Qainuqa' and Banu Nadeer before them. This was not agreed to by the Holy Prophet as he had enough of the treachery of Banu Nadeer. After further negotiations it was decided that an arbitrator should be appointed who should decide the fate of Banu Quraiza. As Banu Quraiza were allied with the Aus, they named Sa'ad b. Ma'aadh, the leader of the Aus, as the arbitrator. The Holy Prophet accordingly appointed Sa'ad b. Ma'adh as the arbitrator. On his appointment as arbitrator, Sa'ad b. Ma'aadh took a pledge from both the parties that whatever decision was given by him would be binding on both the parties. After the pledge had been given, Sa'ad asked the Jews as to what was the penalty of traitors under Jewish law. It was discovered that the penalty in such cases was death. Sa'ad next posed the question whether the Jews had any pact with the Muslims. It was brought to light that there was originally such an agreement. Sa'ad then asked whether it was a fact that they had repudiated that agreement on the occasion of the battle of the Ditch. This could not be denied by the Jews as Sa'ad had come to them as an emissary and they had told him at that time that they had no agreement with the Muslims. Sa'ad accordingly gave the award that as the Jews had acted as traitors, all the adult male Jews deserved to be killed under the Jewish law. The sentence was duly executed and that was the end of Banu Quraiza.

Treaty of Hudaibiya

Journey to Makkah. Early in 628 C.E. the Holy Prophet along with his companions including Hadrat Abu

Bakr started for Makkah with a view to performing the Haj. When the Quraish of Makkah came to know that the Muslims were coming to Makkah they sent Khalid bin Walid and Ikramah bin Abu Jahl with two hundred horsemen to intercept the Muslims and prevent their advance to Makkah. Finding the way to Makkah barred, the Holy Prophet consulted his companions as to what course of action they should adopt. Hadrat Abu Bakr advised:

> "O Prophet of Allah, we have come to perform the Haj. We have no intention of fighting with the Quraish. Let us go ahead. If they stop us we shall fight, otherwise not."

This advice was accepted by the Holy Prophet. The Holy Prophet enquired of his companions whether anyone out of them could lead the Muslims to Makkah by a path other than the main route which had been barred by the enemy. One of the companions volunteered to show an alternative way. He accordingly led the Muslims on a way full of rough rocks through the ravines of Mudniya.

Camp at Hudaibiya. After a weary march the Muslims reached Hudaibiya on the lower side of Makkah and within the sacred territory. The Muslims encamped at Hudaibiya and here Urwa b. Masud came to see the Holy Prophet on behalf of the Quraish. He talked in diplomatic language, and tried to impress the Muslims that the Quraish were strong, and would not allow the Muslims to visit Makkah. He also insinuated that at the time of crisis the followers of the Holy Prophet were likely to abandon him. Thereupon Hadrat Abu Bakr flared up and said, "May God curse you, how dare you think that we will abandon the Holy Prophet. Rest assured we will fight to the last for him." While talking, Urwa in the usual Arab way pushed his hand too close to the beard of the Holy Prophet. Mughira, a companion who stood near, warned him, "Keep your hands away from the beard of the Holy Prophet, for the hand that touches the sacred beard will be cut."

Hudaibiya pact. When Urwa returned to the Quraish he gave his impressions about the Holy Prophet and the Muslims in the following terms:

> "O people of the Quraish. I have seen kings but by God I have never seen any king as I have seen Muhammad amongst his companions. If he makes his ablutions they would not let the water fall on the ground; if a hair from his body falls they pick it up. They will not surrender him for anything in any case, do what you please."

After some further negotiations a pact was executed between the Quraish and the Muslims. According to the treaty of Hudaibiya, truce was declared between the Quraish and the Muslims for a period of ten years. It was stipulated that if any tribe wished to enter into treaty with the Muslims it could do so, and whoever wished to enter into a covenant with the Quraish was likewise free to do so. It was provided that if any one from the Quraish came to the Muslims without the permission of his guardian he was to be returned to the Quraish. On the other hand if a Muslim sought refuge with the Quraish. He was not to be delivered to the Muslims. It was further agreed that the Muslims would withdraw that year without performing the pilgrimage, and that they would be free to perform the Haj the following year when they could stay in Makkah for three days.

Hadrat Abu Bakr on the treaty of Hudaibiya. *Prima facie* the Hudaibiya pact favoured the Quraish, and some of the Muslims were critical of the terms of the treaty. Hadrat Umar regarded the treaty as humiliating to the Muslims. He saw Hadrat Abu Bakr, and wanted him to persuade the Holy Prophet to withdraw from the pact. Hadrat Abu Bakr said:

> "The Holy Prophet knows things more than we do. What the Holy Prophet has done is in the interest of the Muslims. Do not be critical, but hold fast to the stirrup of the Holy Prophet."

Hadrat Umar waited on the Holy Prophet, and gave expression to his discontentment with the terms of the treaty. The Holy Prophet assured him that whatever he had done was under the command of God, and the terms which appeared to be against the interests of the Muslims would turn out to their advantage.

Hadrat Abu Bakr expressed his views about the treaty of Hudaibiya in the following words:

> "No victory of Islam has more importance than the treaty of Hudaibiya. Men are always for hurrying things on, but God lets them ripen. Previously there had subsisted a wall of partition between the Muslims and the rest of men; they never spoke to each other, and wherever they met they began to fight. Subsequently hostility died down and security and mutual confidence took its place. Every man of even moderate intelligence who heard of Islam joined us and in the twenty-two months in which the truce subsisted the number of conversions was greater than throughout the whole of the previous period, and the faith of Islam diffused itself in all directions among the people."

Battle of Khyber

The Jews. After having been driven away from Madina the Jews settled at Khyber. The Jews were a cunning and crafty people, and they involved themselves in intrigues against the Muslims. The pact of Hudaibiya brought for the Muslims truce with the Quraish for a period of ten years. This meant that the Quraish could no longer openly aid the Jews against the Muslims. In spite of this situation there was no diminution in the hostility of the Jews against the Muslims, and they began to work for the formation of another coalition against the Muslims.

Battle of Khyber. To forestall the evil designs of the Jews, the Holy Prophet marched to Khyber in 629 C.E. with a force of 1,400 Muslims. The Jews shut themselves in their forts. Some of these forts were very formidable with frowning walls built of the living rock. The Jews had ample provisions, and there was no shortage of arms with them. On the first day the Muslims led the attack against the Jews under the command of Hadrat Abu Bakr. The Jews remained locked up in their forts, and there was no confrontation. The following day Hadrat Umar commanded the Muslim forces. The Jews remained shut in their forts and there was no fight. On the third day Hadrat Ali commanded the Muslim forces. Surprisingly the Jews came out of the forts that day and fought in the open. In a hand to hand fight that followed the Jews were overpowered and they sought terms. The Jews agreed to submit to the suzerainty of the Muslims, and to pay them one half of the land produce.

Consequences of the battle of Khyber. The battle of Khyber had far reaching consequences. It established the paramountcy of the Muslims in the Arabian peninsula. The Jews now became the subjects of the Muslim State. As the Quraish lost the support of the Jews, the battle of Khyber paved the way for the conquest of Makkah.

Zainab bin Harith. At Khyber, Zainab bin Harith a Jewish lady invited the Holy Prophet and his principal companions to a feast. Hadrat Abu Bakr sat by the side of the Holy Prophet. The Holy Prophet first took a morsel of meat, and after chewing it threw it out saying, "The meat is poisoned." Hadrat Abu Bakr had so far held his hand but Bishr bin Bra' who sat next to the Holy Prophet on the other side ate a good deal of meat, and after a few moments he was dead. The feast ended in confusion. Zainab was put to explanation, and she admitted her guilt. She pleaded that she had poisoned the meat thinking that if Muhammad (peace be on him) was a prophet he would find that it was poisoned, and if he was not a prophet the world would get rid of him. Accounts of subsequent proceedings differ. According to one account, Zainab became a Muslim and was forgiven. According to another account she was beheaded.

Makkah Revisited

Journey to Makkah. Early in 629 C.E. on the occasion of the Hajj the Holy Prophet at the head of 2,000 Muslims including Hadrat Abu Bakr proceeded to Makkah to perform the Hajj, in accordance with the terms of the Hudaibiya pact. As the Muslims reached Makkah, most of the Quraish left their houses, and climbed the neighbouring hills. In view of the Hudaibiya pact, the Quraish had no option but to permit the Muslims visit Makkah, but they were loath to welcome the Muslims. Their general view was that if their young men and women came in contact with the Muslims, they were apt to be attracted by the new faith, and as such any contact with the Muslims was to be avoided.

Reaction of the Muslims. In contrast to the Quraish the Muslims felt very happy on their visit to the sacred city of Makkah. The Muhajreen were in particular happy to revisit the city of their birth. They were visiting the city after seven years. Much had happened during these years. The Muslims were no longer a small group of hapless people exposed to the persecution of the Quraish, they were now a power in Arabia. It was a proof positive of the truth of Islam. The Muslims offered their prayers in the Kaaba. The "Adhaan" resounded in the valleys of Makkah, and the Quraish felt very much irritated at the call. They felt that they had made a mistake in making the Hudaibiyya pact, and allowing the Muslims access to Makkah. Some of the Muslims felt that as the city was practically deserted they could very well occupy it. The Holy Prophet vetoed the suggestion. Islam enjoined the Muslims to honour their pledge, and they could not resort to any treachery. The Holy Prophet said that the day was not distant when the Muslims would return to Makkah as victors, and that might be sooner than what they could think of.

Hadrat Abu Bakr. Hadrat Abu Bakr visited his father and other family members in Makkah. It was a happy reunion, but as his father and other family members were still pagans, Hadrat Abu Bakr prayed to God that He may show them His Light. Hadrat Abu Bakr met some of his old friends among the Quraish. In spite of their hostility to Islam his Quraish friends could not fail to notice that under the impact of Islam, Hadrat Abu Bakr was a changed man, and this change was definitely a change for the better.

Consequences of the Muslim visit to Makkah. The visit of the Muslims to Makkah was very short and did not extend beyond three days but it led to some far reaching consequences. Maimuna a young Quraish lady of twenty-six years was so much impressed with the general behaviour of the Holy Prophet and the Muslims that she professed her faith in Islam. She was a sister-in-law of Hadrat Abbas, an uncle of the Holy Prophet. Hadrat Abbas advised the Holy Prophet to marry the young lady in recognition of her conversion. The Holy Prophet agreed and was married to Maimuna in Makkah. As a result of the Muslim visit to Makkah, it was not Maimuna alone who realised the truth of Islam. Even men like Khalid bin Walid the hero of the Quraish victory at Uhud realised the truth of Islam, and was converted to Islam soon after the return of the Muslims from Makkah. Another great warrior Amr b. Al-'A'as also hastened to accept Islam.

Return to Madina. When the three days were over, Suhail b. Amr and Hwitab b. Abdul Uzza came to the Holy Prophet as emissaries of the Quraish and desired that the Muslims should leave Makkah. The Holy Prophet desired that as he had been married to Maimuna he should be allowed to hold the marriage feast in Makkah and the Quraish should share the feast with the Muslims. The Quraish emissaries said, "We are not in need of your meals." The Muslims were strong enough to stay in Makkah in spite of the refusal of the Quraish, but the Holy Prophet said that he would remain faithful to his pledge. He accordingly left Makkah along with his followers.

NOTES

The events narrated in this Chapter cover a period of two years only namely 627 to 629 C E.

In 627 C.E. when the Quraish, the Jews, and the other tribes made a coalition against the Muslims and invaded Madina with a force of 10,000, things for the Muslims appeared to be very dark. The Muslims had not merely to face an attack from without, they had to face the treachery of the Banu Quraiza, a Jewish tribe from within as well. Miraculously enough the coalition disintegrated and the invaders had to withdraw discomfited by the natural forces.

After the withdrawal of the invaders the Muslims took the Banu Quraiza to task, and the treacherous Jews had to suffer the punishment for their treachery.

After the elimination of the Jews in Madina, the Muslims turned to the Quraish. The contact with the Quraish led to the Hudaibiya. This pact though apparently loaded in favour of the Quraish ultimately turned out to be a victory for the Muslims. Among the companions of the Holy Prophet, Hadrat Abu Bakr was the first to realise the significance of the Hudaibiya pact.

After having arrived at a truce with the Quraish, the Muslims were able to turn to the Jews of Khyber who had played a leading role in the battle of the Trench in their hostility to the Muslims.

After having vanquished the Jews of Khyber, the Muslims visited Kaaba and performed the Hajj. This visit did not merely mean the fulfilment of a religious obligation; it had a political significance as well. It showed that the Muslims were now a power who could not be ignored.

In 627 C.E. the situation for the Muslims was very grave and precarious. By 629 C.E. the Muslims were strong enough to visit Makkah and thus beard the lion in its cave. In all these events crowded in a short space of two years, one cannot help noticing the Hand of God working in aid of the Muslims. The

Muslims had staked their everything for the cause of Allah, and Allah in His Mercy helped them in a miraculous way.

In all these events the Holy Prophet played the leading role but Hadrat Abu Bakr was the "second of the two." He was always by the side of the Holy Prophet, offered him his advice, and faithfully carried out his commands.

In writing this Chapter I have depended on the biographies of the Holy Prophet, particularly the books by Hafiz Ghulam Sarwar and Guillaume.

6
CONQUEST OF MAKKAH AND AFTER

Conquest of Makkah

Betrayal of the Quraish. According to the terms of the treaty of Hudaibiya the Arab tribes had the option to be allied with the Quraish or the Muslims. As a consequence the Banu Bakr joined the Quraish, and Banu Khuza'ah joined the Muslims. In disregard of the treaty, Banu Bakr attacked the Banu Khuza'ah, and even when the Banu Khuza'ah sought the sanctuary of the Ka'aba, many persons of the Banu Khuza'ah were chased and put to death. The Banu Khuza'ah appealed to the Muslims to come to their aid in accordance with the terms of the treaty. The Holy Prophet admitted the obligation of the Muslims to come to the aid of the Banu Khuza'ah. He accordingly gave an ultimatum to the Quraish making three alternative demands, i.e. to pay the blood money for the victims, or terminate their alliance with Banu Bakr, or consider the Hudaibiya pact to be abrogated. In a fit of arrogance the Quraish replied that they would neither pay blood money, nor terminate their alliance with Banu Bakr, and that they were prepared to consider the Hudaibiya pact as having been abrogated. The Holy Prophet welcomed this stand, and he decided to take action. The Quraish soon realised that they had imprudently abrogated the treaty. Abu Sufyan the leader of the Quraish visited Madina to arrive at some amicable settlement with the Muslims, but his efforts proved futile.

March to Makkah. After Abu Sufyan had left Madina, the Holy Prophet ordered preparations to be made for a foray. As Hadrat Abu Bakr came to see his daughter Hadrat Ayesha he saw that she was packing some goods. He enquired whether the Holy Prophet had ordered her to get things packed up, and she said that he had. Hadrat, Ayesha wanted her father to get ready as well. Later the Holy Prophet took Hadrat Abu Bakr into confidence and told him that he was leading an expedition to Makkah. The Holy Prophet mustered a force over ten thousand strong and marched to Makkah. Having reached in the neighbourhood of Makkah the Muslim army encamped at Marr al-Zahran. The Quraish realised they were no match for this force. Abu Sufyan visited the Muslim camp and became a Muslim. That was the end of the Quraish opposition. The next day the Muslim army marched triumphantly into Makkah.

Occupation of Makkah. The triumphant entry of the Muslims in Makkah marked the vindication of the truth of Islam. One of the contingents of the Muslims which entered Makkah was led by Hadrat Abu Bakr. The city which ten years ago had treated the Muslims cruelly, and had driven them to take refuge with strangers now lay at their foot. In the hour of triumph the Holy Prophet forgot every evil suffered, and forgave every injury that had been inflicted on him. He granted amnesty to the people of Makkah. Having entered Makkah the Holy Prophet along with his companions offered prayer of thanks to Allah. Then the Holy Prophet along with Hadrat Abu Bakr visited the Ka'aba. The idols were broken, and as one by one the stone gods were destroyed the Holy Prophet recited the verse from the Holy Qur'an:

> "Say the Truth is come and falsehood gone;
> Verily, falsehood is ever vanishing."

The Holy Prophet's address at the Ka'aba. The people assembled at the Ka'aba, and the Holy Prophet delivered the following address:

> "There is no God but Allah. He has no associate. He has made good His promise that He held to His bondman and helped him and defeated all his confederates. Bear

in mind that every claim of privilege, whether that of blood or property is abolished except that of the custody of the Ka'aba and of supplying water to the pilgrims. Bear in mind that for anyone who is slain the bloodwit is hundred camels. O people of Quraish, surely God has abolished from you all pride of the time of ignorance and all pride in your ancestry, because all men are descended from Adam, and Adam was made of clay."

Then the Holy Prophet turning to the people said: "O ye Quraish, what do you think of treatment that I should accord you". And they said, " Mercy, O Prophet of Allah. We expect nothing but good from you." Thereupon the Holy Prophet said: " I speak to you in the same words as Joseph spoke to his brothers. This day, there is no reproof against you: Go your way, for you are free". This announcement was received with great joy and applause.

Conversion of the father of Hadrat Abu Bakr. Hadrat Abu Bakr went to his home in Makkah and the other members of his family. It was happy reunion. Then Hadrat Abu Bakr took his father to the Holy Prophet. On seeing him the Holy Prophet said, "Why did you trouble the respected old man; I would have come to him in your house". Hadrat Abu Bakr said that it was but meet that he should have come to the Holy Prophet to accept Islam. The Holy Prophet made Abu Qahafa the father of Abu Bakr sit before him and stroke his chest, and asked him to accept Islam which he did by declaring the article of faith.

The locket of the sister of Hadrat Abu Bakr. When the Muslim army had marched to Makkah some one had deprived the sister of Hadrat Aba Bakr of her silver locket. Hadrat Abu Bakr stood up before an assembly and addressed the people. He said, "I ask in the name of God for my sister's necklace". No one answered him, and thereupon turning to his sister he said, "Sister, regard your necklace as taken by God, and look to Him to requite you."

Battles of Hunain and Taif

Tribes of Hawazin and Thaqeef. After the fall of

Makkah the neighbouring tribes of Hawazin and Thaqeef had to choose between Islam and war against the Muslims. They chose the war path, and the two tribes along with their allies mustered in considerable strength at Autas to the east of Makkah. The coalition was led by Malik bin Auf a fiery commander of considerable skill.

The Muslim Force. When the Holy Prophet came to know of the hostile intention of the tribes, he decided to take action against them. On a cold day in January 630 C.E. the Muslim force set out from Makkah. The force comprised 12,000 persons fully armed. Of these 10,000 were from Madina who had attacked Makkah, and 2,000 were the newly converted Muslims from Makkah. It was a large army, and as Hadrat Abu Bakr saw it, he is reported to have said in some unguarded moment "It is a splendid army; who can defeat it".

Battle of Hunain. This boast was not liked by God, and later things happened which made Hadrat Abu Bakr regret such a boast. As on the way to Autas the Muslim army passed through the valley of Hunain some eleven miles north east of Makkah, a rain of arrows fell on it let loose by a group of archers of the hostile tribes that lay hid in the mountain pass. Taken unaware the advance guard of the Muslim army fled in panic. There was considerable confusion, and camels, horses and men ran into one another to seek cover.

The Holy Prophet stood firm. There were only nine companions around him including Hadrat Abu Bakr. All the rest had fled. Under the instructions of the Holy Prophet, Hadrat Abbas shouted at the top of his voice, "O Muslims come to the Prophet of Allah". The call was heard by the Muslim soldiers and they gathered by the side of the Holy Prophet. When the Muslims had gathered in sufficient number, the Holy Prophet ordered a charge against the enemy. In the hand to hand fight that followed, the tribes were routed and they fled to Autas.

Confrontation at Autas. The Holy Prophet posted a contingent to guard the Hunain pass, and led the main army to Autas. In the confrontation at Autas the tribes could not withstand the Muslim onslaught. Finding the resistance useless the tribes broke the camp and retired to Taif. Hadrat Abu Bakr thanked God for the victory, but he was in a chastened mood. He humbly prayed before God, and asked for forgiveness for having boasted about the invincibility of the Muslim army.

Battle of Taif. Hadrat Abu Bakr was commissioned by the Holy Prophet to lead the attack against Taif. From Autas the Muslim force marched to Taif. The tribes shut themselves in the fort and refused to come out in the open. The Muslims employed catapults to throw stones in the town, but this did not lead to any tangible results. The Muslims tried the testudo device whereunder a group of soldiers shielded by a cover of cowhide advanced to set fire to the gate. The enemy threw red hot scraps of iron on the testudo which made it ineffective. The siege dragged on for two weeks and still there was no sign of the fall of the fort. The Holy Prophet held a council of war. Hadrat Abu Bakr advised that the siege might be raised and that God would Himself make arrangements for the fall of the fort. The advice was accepted, and in February 630 C.E. the siege of Taif was raised and the Muslim army withdrew to Makkah. A few days later, Malik bin Auf the chief of Taif came to Makkah and became a Muslim. Thereafter all the people of Taif accepted Islam. Thus the forecast of Hadrat Abu Bakr came to be fulfilled, and God Himself arranged for the surrender of Taif to Islam.

Expedition to Tabuk

Financing the expedition to Tabuk. In 630 C.E., after return from Makkah the Holy Prophet decided to lead an expedition to Tabuk on the Syrian border. In order to finance the expedition the Holy Prophet invited contributions and donations from his followers. Hadrat Othman provided ten thousand camels. Hadrat Umar made a liberal contribution. When the Holy Prophet asked him what he had left for himself and his family he said that he had given one half of his wealth for the cause of Allah, and had left one half for himself and his family. Then Hadrat Abu Bakr came loaded with his contribution and the Holy Prophet put him the same question as to what had he left for himself and his family. Hadrat Abu Bakr said, "I have brought all that I had. I have left Allah and His Prophet for myself and my family". This episode has formed the theme of one of the poems of Allama Iqbal. The last verse of the poem reads:

> "For the moth the lamp; for the nightingale the flower,
> For Siddiq God and His Prophet alone suffice."

The call to arms. The call to arms was given at a very critical time. The weather was burning hot. Crops were ripe and ready for harvesting. The journey was long and arduous. Many persons preferred to stay back. In spite of these obstacles and difficulties, an army of thirty thousand persons was raised. The army assembled at Al-Jorf outside Madina. The Holy Prophet remained at Madina for some time to attend to other affairs and at Al-Jorf, Hadrat Abu Bakr deputised for the Holy Prophet and led the prayers.

The march to Tabuk. The Muslim army led by the Holy Prophet reached Tabuk after a weary march. At Tabuk the standard of the army was entrusted to Hadrat Abu Bakr. There was no Byzantine force at Tabuk to meet the Muslims. On coming to know of the Muslims the Byzantines had withdrawn their army well within Syria. The Muslims achieved their object without firing a shot. The Byzantines who had at one time threatened to invade Arabia were no longer in the mood to measure swords with the Muslims. The tribes in the region which were under the suzerainty of the Byzantines transferred their allegiance to the Muslims.

The Holy Prophet's address at Tabuk. At Tabuk, the Prophet delivered a classical address which has passed into history. He said:

> "Verily, the most veracious discourse is the Book of Allah. The most trusty stronghold is the word of piety. The best of religions is the religion of Islam. The best of precedents is the precedent of Muhammad. The noblest speech is the invocation of Allah. The finest of the narratives is the Qur'an. The best of the affairs is that which has been firmly resolved upon. The worst in

religion are those things which are created without sanction. The best of the ways is the one trodden by the prophets. The noblest death is the death of a martyr. The most miserable blindness is waywardness after guidance. The best of the actions is that which is beneficent. The best guidance is that which is put into practice. The worst blindness is the blindness of the heart."

Hadrat Abu Bakr as Amir-ul-Haj

The first Amir-ul-Haj. In 631 C.E., the Holy Prophet sent from Madina a delegation of three hundred Muslims to perform the Haj according to the new Islamic way. Hadrat Abu Bakr was appointed as the leader of the delegates. Hadrat Abu Bakr had thus the honour of being the first Amir-ul-Haj in the history of Islam.

Hadrat Ali. Some time after Hadrat Abu Bakr and his party had left for the Haj, the Holy Prophet received revelation about the regulation of the Haj, and the ordering of relationship with the infidels. It is related that when the revelation came, some one suggested to the Holy Prophet that he should send news of it to Hadrat Abu Bakr. The Holy Prophet said that a man of his own house was to proclaim the revelation. The Holy Prophet summoned Hadrat Ali, and commissioned him to proclaim the revealed verses to the people on the day of sacrifice when they were assembled at Mina. Hadrat Ali went forth on the Holy Prophet's slit-eared camel, and overtook Hadrat Abu Bakr and his party. When Hadrat Ali joined the party, Hadrat Abu Bakr wanted to know whether he had come to give orders or to convey them. Hadrat Ali said that he had not come to replace Hadrat Abu Bakr as Amir-ul-Haj, and that his only mission was to convey a special message to the people on behalf of the Holy Prophet.

The proclamation. At Makkah, Hadrat Abu Bakr presided at the Haj ceremony, and Hadrat Ali read the proclamation on behalf of the Holy Prophet. The main points of the proclamation were:

(1) Henceforward the non-Muslims were not to be allowed to visit the Ka'aba or perform the pilgrimage.

(2) No one was to be allowed to circumambulate the Ka'aba naked.

(3) Polytheism was not to be tolerated. Where the Muslims had any agreements with the polyaheists such agreements were to be honoured for the stipulated periods. Where there were no agreements, a grace period of four months was to be given, and thereafter no quarter was to be given to the polytheists.

The new era. From the day this proclamation was made a new era dawned in Arabia. Henceforward Islam alone was to be supreme in Arabia. In some quartres an argument is advanced that as on this occasion the proclamation was read by Hadrat Ali on behalf of the Holy Prophet that established the precedence of Hadrat Ali over Hadrat Abu Bakr, and that therefore when after the death of the Holy Prophet, Hadrat Abu Bakr became the Caliph in disregard of the claims of Hadrat Ali, he was a usurper. It will be seen that on this occasion Ali did not replace Hadrat Abu Bakr as Amir-ul-Haj. Hadrat Ali was merely assigned a special mission to read the proclamation as according to the Holy Prophet only a man from his own house had to communicate the revelation. We can thus say that on that occasion Hadrat Abu Bakr represented the temporal side while Hadrat Ali represented the spiritual side. After the death of the Holy Prophet there was no longer the question of any spiritual representation; the issue was only temporal representation, and for this Hadrat Abu Bakr was the best choice as he had represented the Holy Prophet even in his life-time.

Dhat-ul-Salasil

Raid on Dhat-ul-Salasil. In 631 C.E. the Holy Prophet sent a party under Amr b. Al-A'as to conduct a raid on Dhat-ul-Salasil, the country of Banu 'Adhra on the Syrian border.

When Amr came to Salasil he felt that the contingent at his disposal was inadequate to meet the challenge of the tribe. He accordingly appealed to the Holy Prophet for reinforcement. The Holy Prophet sent a contingent under the command of Hadrat Abu Ubaida bin al-Jarrah. The contingent included Hadrat Abu Bakr and Hadrat Umar.

Hadrat Abu Bakr's advice to Hadrat Umar. It is recorded by Al-Bayhaqi that when the Muslim troops arrived at the battlefield, Amr commanded that they should not light fire. Hadrat Umar felt worth at this command, and wanted to remonstrate with Amr b. Al-A'as. Hadrat Abu Bakr counselled Hadrat Umar to keep quiet, for the Holy Prophet had appointed Amr as the Commander for his knowledge of the strategy of wars, and there must be some justification for his order.

Raaf'i b. Umayera. On this occasion, Raaf'i b. Umayera was a companion of Hadrat Abu Bakr. He was formerly a Christian and was known as Serjis. He acted as a guide in the sandy desert. During the pagan period he used to bury water in ostrich shells in various places in the desert and then raid men's camels. Then he became a Muslim, and abandoned the profession of brigandage. In the raid against Dhat-ul-Salasil, he joined the Muslim force under Amr b. Al-A'as. On this occasion, he chose Hadrat Abu Bakr as his companion. According to the account of Raaf'i b. Umayera, Hadrat Abu Bakr wore a Fadak cloak, and whenever they halted he would spread it out, and put it on when they rose. For this, Hadrat Abu Bakr came to be called "the man with the cloak".

Hadrat Abu Bakr's advice. On the return journey, Raaf'i b. Umayera asked Hadrat Abu Bakr to give him some advice. Hadrat Abu Bakr advised him to proclaim the unity of God, and not to associate anything with him to perform prayer, to pay the poor tax, to fast in the Ramadhan, to wash after impurity, and never to assume authority over two Muslims. According to Raaf'i when the Holy Prophet died, and Hadrat Abu Bakr became the Caliph, he went to see Hadrat Abu Bakr and reminded him that he had forbidden him to assume authority over two Muslims, and yet he had become the Caliph. Hadrat Abu Bakr said that he was still of the same view, but he had accepted the caliphate as he was afraid that if he did not accept the responsibility, the unity of the Muslim community was at stake.

'Auf b. Malik al-Ashja'i. In this raid on Dhat-ul-Salasil, 'Auf b. Malik was also among the party. He has related that he passed by some people who were butchering a camel they had slaughtered. They could not dismember it, and as he was a skilled butcher, they asked him to do the work of dismembering for them. He did so, and they gave him a share of the meat. He cooked it and gave it to Hadrat Umar and Hadrat Abu Bakr to eat as well. After they had eaten, he told them how he had got the meat. When he told them as to how he had got the meat, Hadrat Abu Bakr said that he had done wrong in giving it to them to eat. Thereafter both Hadrat Abu Bakr and Hadrat Umar vomited what they had swallowed.

The Farewell Pilgrimage

The Holy Prophet's last pilgrimage. In 632 C.E. the Holy Prophet decided to proceed to Makkah for performing the pilgrimage. The pilgrimage was planned on a large scale. Messengers were sent to all parts of Arabia asking the Muslims to collect at Madina for the purpose of the pilgrimage. In response to this call over one lakh Muslims from all parts of Arabia assembled at Madina.

The caravan. After all arrangements had been completed, a caravan of over one lakh Muslims, fired with their enthusiasm for Islam, started for Makkah in submission to the call of Allah. It was a remarkable sight the like of which the people of Arabia had not seen before. The Holy Prophet rode at the head of the caravan. All his wives accompanied him. By the side of the Holy Prophet rode Hadrat Abu Bakr. He too was accompanied by his wives.

Dhul Hulaifa. At Dhul Hulaifa on the outskirts of Makkah, the Holy Prophet and all his followers put on the *Ihram*—the pilgrim's garb. The Holy Prophet gave the signal call *Labbayk Allahumma Labbayk*—here I am at your service O Lord, and this was repeated by all the one lakh persons in the congregation. The entire valley came to ring with this sound—the resolve of the Muslims to place themselves at the disposal of God.

Makkah and Mina. The party reached Makkah on the 4th of Zul Haj, after a journey of nineteen days. After a stay of four days in Makkah the party left Makkah for Mina on the 8th of Zul Hajj, and passed the night there. The following day the pilgrims proceeded to Arafat.

Farewell address. After mid-day prayers on the 9th of Zul Haj at Arafat, the Holy Prophet delivered his historic farewell address. After giving praise to God, the Holy Prophet said:

> "O people, listen carefully to my words for I may not be among you next year, nor ever address you again from this spot. O people just as you regard this month as sacred, so regard the life and property of every Muslim as sacred. Return the goods entrusted to you to their rightful owners. Hurt no one that none may hurt you. Usury is forbidden. Satan has despaired in leading you astray in big things, so beware of obeying him in small things. Women have rights over you and you have rights over them. Be good to them. You may soon have to appear before Allah and answer for your deeds. So beware. Do not go astray after I am gone. O people, no prophet will come after me, and no new faith will be born. Worship your Allah, say your prayers, fast during the month of Ramadan, and give of your wealth in charity. All Muslims, free or enslaved have the same rights and the same responsibilities. None is higher than the other unless he is higher in virtue. Feed your slaves as you feed yourselves. Do not oppress them, nor usurp their rights......"

Having spoken thus the Holy Prophet turned his face to the Heavens and said "Be my witness O Allah, that I have conveyed Your message to Your people". Thereupon the people corroborated saying "Yes, you Prophet of Allah you have done so".

The revelation. After the Prophet had delivered his address. God revealed to him the verses:

> "This day have I perfected for you your faith,
> And completed My blessing upon you
> And have chosen for you Islam as religion."

Reaction of Hadrat Abu Bakr. As Hadrat Abu Bakr heard the verses about the faith having been perfected he wept because he realised that the mission having been completed, the day when the Holy Prophet was to depart to meet his Lord was imminent.

Return to Madina. After the farewell address, the party left Arafat in the evening and passed the night at Muzdalifa. The following day they went to Mina and sacrificed the animals. The Holy Prophet sacrificed 63 animals, one for each year of his life. Hadrat Abu Bakr sacrificed 61 animals, one for each year of his life. The men then shaved their heads and the ceremony of the Haj was completed. Thereafter the pilgrims returned to Madina. On the return journey. Hadrat Abu Bakr was overwhelmed with the feeling that one epoch was coming to close and another epoch was about to begin which would be fraught with difficulties for the Muslims.

NOTES

This Chapter covers the period 630-632 C.E. The main events of this period are:

(1) the conquest of Makkah;
(2) the battles of Hunain and Taif;
(3) expedition to Tabuk;
(4) appointment of Hadrat Abu Bakr as Amir-ul-Hajj;
(5) expedition to Dhat-ul-Salasil; and
(6) the farewell pilgrimage.

Hadrat Abu Bakr played his part in all these events.

The conquest of Makkah was a turning point in the history of Islam. In 622 C.E. a hapless band of Muslims was driven away from Makkah and it had to seek refuge in the city of Yathrib. Eight years later, the Muslims marched to Makkah as victors. The Makkans who had been so hostile to Islam were now converted to Islam. That was a great spiritual victory for Islam. It was on this occasion that the father of Hadrat Abu Bakr was converted to Islam.

The battles of Hunain and Taif bring out the lesson that if the Muslims rely on God they are apt to succeed, but if they feel elated they are apt to meet a reverse.

The expedition to Tabuk is significant as Hadrat Abu Bakr donated his entire wealth to the financing of the expedition holding that for him and his family Allah and His Apostle were enough.

Hadrat Abu Bakr had the honour of being the first Amir ul-Hajj in the history of Islam. This Hajj marks the unification of Arabia under Islam, and non-Muslims were henceforward not to be allowed to visit the Ka'aba.

In the expedition to Dhatul Salasil, Hadrat Abu Bakr did not play the leading role, but two episodes stand out prominently. Amr b. ul-A'as the commander prohibited the lighting of fire in the Muslim camp. Hadrat Umar was critical of the order, but Hadrat Abu Bakr advised him that the

Commander knew best as to what was to be done or not. Raaf'i a companion of Hadrat Abu Bakr asked for the advice of Hadrat Abu Bakr and Hadrat Abu Bakr advised that one should never be a ruler over two Muslims.

The farewell pilgrimage marked the perfection of the faith of Islam. While other companions felt happy at such consummation, Hadrat Abu Bakr alone felt unhappy, for he realised that such consummation implied that the Holy Prophet having completed his mission was to return to God.

In writing this Chapter I have derived help from the biographies of the Holy Prophet, particularly the books by Muir, Guillaume, and Abdul Hameed Siddiqi. I have also profited from:

(1) *Abu Bakr* by Muhammad Husain Haykal;
(2) *Abu Bakr the Caliph* by A. A., Aziz, and
(3) *Hadrat Abu Bakr* by Syed Moinul Haq.

7

SUCCESSOR TO THE HOLY PROPHET

Appointment of Hadrat Abu Bakr as the Imam

Illness of the Holy Prophet. A short time after returning from the farewell pilgrimage, the Holy Prophet fell sick. The poison which a Jewess had given to him at Khyber had slowly penetrated into his system, and had begun to show its fatal effects. The Holy Prophet felt that having fulfilled his mission, his earthly life was to end, and he was to be summoned to his Master.

One night the Holy Prophet went to the graveyard and there prayed for the soul of his companions who had fallen in the battle of Uhud. The Holy Prophet felt that he was soon going to meet his dead companions. After the visit to the graveyard the Holy Prophet came home and visited the apartment of his wife Maimuna. There the fever became violent. The Holy Prophet assembled all his wives, and told them that on account of his sickness it would not be possible for him to visit the apartment of each wife according to her turn. He wanted their permission to stay in the apartment of Hadrat Ayesha till he recovered. All the wives agreed to the proposal, and the Holy Prophet supported by Hadrat Ali and Hadrat Abbas moved to the apartment of Hadrat Ayesha.

The Imamate of Hadrat Abu Bakr. The Holy Prophet directed Hadrat Abu Bakr to lead the prayers in the Prophet's mosque during his illness. Hadrat Ayesha intervened to suggest that her father be not entrusted with this responsibility. She said that her father had a tender heart, and he would burst into tears while reciting the Holy Qur'an in the course of the prayer. The Holy Prophet overruled the objection and insisted that Hadrat Abu Bakr alone should lead the prayers.

Holy Prophet's tribute to Hadrat Abu Bakr. After shifting to the apartment of Hadrat Ayesha the Holy Prophet felt some relief. A day later he took a bath. Refreshed by the bath, he felt some relief and went to the mosque to offer the noon day prayer. At the conclusion of the prayer the Holy Prophet took his seat on the pulpit, and addressing the congregation said:

> "There is a servant whose Lord has given him the option between this life, and the life in the next world close to the Lord, and the servant has chosen the latter."

Out of the congregation, Hadrat Abu Bakr alone understood the implication of the address. Tears trickled down from his eyes, and with a heavy heart he said, "Holy Prophet, how can we live without you?" Thereupon the Holy Prophet continued:

> "O people, it has reached me that you are afraid of the approaching death of your Prophet. Has any previous prophet lived for ever among those to whom he was sent so that I would live for ever among you? Behold, I am about to go to my Lord. You too will go sooner or later."

The Holy Prophet paid a glowing tribute to Hadrat Abu Bakr when he said:

> "There has been none more bountiful to me for his unwavering loyalty, devotion and sacrifice of wealth than Abu Bakr. If I were to choose a bosom friend it would be he; but Islam has made a closer brotherhood among us all".

The Holy Prophet also directed:

> "Let every door that leads into the mosque be closed, except the door of Abu Bakr."

Thereafter the Holy Prophet returned to the apartment of Hadrat Ayesha.

The last address of the Holy Prophet. The malady of the Holy Prophet increased, and his condition grew worse. The night following the seventh of June 632 lay heavy upon him. He was overheard praying constantly to Allah for His blessings. The morning of the 8th June brought some relief. Fever and pain somewhat abated. Moving the curtain of his apartment he saw the faithful offering their prayers under the Imamate of Hadrat Abu Bakr. The Holy Prophet supported by Hadrat Ali walked to the mosque. The people made way for him, opening their ranks as he stepped forward. Hadrat Abu Bakr stepped backward to vacate his seat for the Holy Prophet. The Holy Prophet told Hadrat Abu Bakr by a motion of his hand to continue to lead the prayers.

After the conclusion of the prayer, the Holy Prophet took his seat on the pulpit, and addressed the faithful thus:

> "By the Lord ! As for myself, I have not made lawful anything excepting that which God has declared lawful; nor have I prohibited naught but that which God has forbidden."

The Muslims felt happy to see the Holy Prophet in their midst. They felt that the Holy Prophet had recovered, and that there was no danger to his life. Hadrat Abu Bakr greeted the Holy Prophet on his recovery, and got his permission to go out of Madina to visit his family at Al-Sukh. Thereafter the Holy Prophet returned to the apartment of Hadrat Ayesha and Hadrat Abu Bakr left for Al-Sukh.

Death of the Holy Prophet

Passing away of the Holy Prophet. After Hadrat Abu Bakr had left for Al-Sukh, the condition of the Holy Prophet grew worse, and within a few hours he passed away.

When the sad news of the death of the Holy Prophet was conveyed to Hadrat Abu Bakr at Al-Sukh, he burst into sobs. Without the Holy Prophet, there appeared to be no charm of life for Hadrat Abu Bakr. Everything around him appeared to be dark. The passing away of the Holy Prophet was a great tragedy, and the grief of Hadrat Abu Bakr was too poignant to be told in words. But then Hadrat Abu Bakr felt that that was not the occasion to give way to personal grief, in spite of the stupendousness of the shock. The death of the Holy Prophet was verily the end of an epoch, but that was not the end of his mission. His mission had to be carried forward.

Hadrat Abu Bakr in Madina. Hadrat Abu Bakr wiped his tears and hastened to Madina. Entering the apartment where the dead body of the Holy Prophet lay, Hadrat Abu Bakr removed the sheet that covered the face of the Holy Prophet. Hadrat Abu Bakr felt the pulse and then touched the body of the Holy Prophet. There was no sign of life, and the soul had departed from the body. In spite of the paleness of death the face of the Holy Prophet shone with divine radiance. Bending low, Hadrat Abu Bakr kissed the auspicious forehead of the Master, and choking with grief said:

> "Master, sacred you were in life, and sacred you are in death. Since you have tasted of death ordained by God, henceforth you will be immune from its clutches. Your abode will now be in the Paradise close to Allah. From Allah you came, and to Allah you have returned."

The faithful assembled in the mosque. The faithful were assembled in the mosque. They sat in groups here and there. There was an air of uneasiness in the atmosphere. There was a whispering that the Holy Prophet of Islam was dead. There were suppressed sobs and sighs. Many persons were weeping. What would happen to the Muslims when the great Prophet was to be no more in their midst was the thought that disturbed every body.

All eyes were turned to the quarter of Hadrat Ayesha. The faithful had the fond hope that the door of the chamber would open any moment, and the Holy Prophet would emerge therefrom with his face radiating divine light.

In the courtyard of the mosque, Hadrat Umar moved among people and said:

> "Who says that the Holy Prophet is dead ? I testify that he is alive, and has gone to Allah like Moses, and would return to us after some time."

Hadrat Abu Bakr's address to the Muslims. The door of the chamber of Hadrat Ayesha opened; and a thin frail old man walking stoopingly moved towards the courtyard of the mosque. He was dressed in a long loose toga with a shawl spread over his shoulders. His complexion was fair; his beard was dyed red; and he had the look of a patriarch. He was Hadrat Abu Bakr.

As he stood among the people, his furrowed face and tear stained eyes betrayed the grief within him. In measured words he said:

> "Listen to me, ye people. Those of you who worshipped Muhammad know that he is dead like any other mortal. But those of you who worship the God of Muhammad (SAW) know that
> He is alive and would live for ever."

A hushed silence fell on the assembly. They were stunned and bewildered with the poignancy of grief. Hadrat Abu Bakr wiped the tears from his eyes, and turning to the people recited the following verses from the Qur'an:

> "Muhammad is but a messenger,
> Messengers of God have passed away before him,
> What, if he dies or is killed ?
> Will you turn back upon your heels ?
> And whosoever turns back upon his heels
> Will by no means do harm to Allah,
> And Allah will reward the thankful."

Hadrat Abu Bakr added:

"Verily Muhammad the great Prophet of Allah was a mortal. Having fulfilled his mission he has gone back to his Master. From God he came, and to God he has returned."

Effect of Hadrat Abu Bakr's address. The effect of Hadrat Abu Bakr's address was electrical in character. It appeared as though the people did not know that the verses of the Holy Qur'an had come down until Hadrat Abu Bakr had recited them that day. Hadrat Umar said:

> "By God when I heard Abu Bakr recite these words I was dumb-founded so that my legs would not bear me, and I fell to the ground knowing that the Holy Prophet was indeed dead."

Election of Hadrat Abu Bakr as the Caliph

Crisis in the affairs of the Muslims. The death of the Holy Prophet led to an immediate crisis in the affairs of the Muslims over the question as to who was to be the leader of the Muslims after the Holy Prophet.

While the dead body of the Holy Prophet of Islam was being prepared for burial the Ansar of Madina assembled at their meeting place 'Saqeefa Bani Sa'dah' to discuss the question of succession to the Holy Prophet. The Holy Prophet was the last of the prophets, and there was to be no prophet after him. He was also the leader of the Muslims, and it was therefore necessary that after him there should be some one who should be the head of the Muslim community.

The Ansars. At the meeting of the Ansars at *Saqifa Bani Sa'idah'*, Sa'd bin Ubadah, a leader of the Ansars made a passionate plea that the successor to the Holy Prophet for managing the temporal affairs of the Muslims should be chosen from the Ansars. He argued that as they were the people who had protected Islam and offered a home for the Holy Prophet and his companions when they were persecuted by their own people, the Ansars had right to the leadership of the Muslims. It was through the efforts of the Ansars that Islam had grown and spread; their city was capital of the Muslim state, and it was but meet that an Ansar should be the head of the State after the Holy Prophet. When Sa'd concluded his speech, he was applauded by the Ansars. The arguments advanced by him appealed to them, and it appeared that they were poised to choose him as their leader in succession to the Holy Prophet.

Reaction of the emigrants. When the meeting was being held at *Saqeefa Bani Sa'idah* it was reported to the emigrants assembled in the Prophet's mosque that the Ansars had assembled to choose a successor to the Holy Prophet. It was a critical situation. The burial of the Holy Prophet was a matter that needed priority, but the question of choosing a successor to the Holy Prophet was a question of life and death for the Muslim community, and if any wrong decision was taken at that stage, the future of Islam itself was likely to be jeopardised. Hadrat Abu Bakr, Hadrat Umar and Hadrat Abu Ubaidah accordingly decided among themselves to proceed to *Saqeefa Bani Sa'idah'* to negotiate the matter with the Ansars before it was too late.

Hadrat Abu Bakr's appeal to the Ansar. When Hadrat Abu Bakr, Hadrat Umar and Hadrat Abu Ubaidah reached *Saqeefa Bani Sa'idah* the Ansars were on the verge of electing Sa'id bin Ubadah, the Ansar leader, as the successor to the Holy Prophet. Hadrat Abu Bakr took the stage and brought home to the people assembled, the gravity of the problem. He pointed out that the matter did not concern the citizens of Madina alone; it was a matter of concern for all the Arabs who had become Muslims. All the Arab tribes were not likely to accept the leadership of the Ansars, particularly when there were differences among the two principal tribes of the Ansars themselves. Hadrat Abu Bakr pointed out that under the circumstances the Quraish who were the custodians of the Kaaba could alone provide the leadership for the Muslim community. Addressing his appeal to the Ansar he said:

> "O Ansar, none can deny the superiority of your position in religion or the greatness of your eminence in Islam. You were chosen by Allah as the helpers of His religion and His Apostle. To you the Prophet was sent on his emigration from Makkah and from you come the majority of his companions and his wives. Indeed in position you are next only to the earliest companions. Therefore it would be fair if we take the Amirate and you accept the ministry. You should not be obstinate in your stand. We

assure you that we will do nothing without consulting you."

The Debate. After the address of Hadrat Abu Bakr, Habab bin Mandhar an Ansar leader rose to say that the Amirate was the right of the Ansars and they could not forego their right. He added that the utmost concession that they could make in favour of the emigrants was that they could have two Amirs, one from the Ansars and the other from the emigrants.

Hadrat Umar said that Islam stood for unity—one God, one Prophet, and one Qur'an. It followed as a necessary corollary that the Muslim community should have one Amir. If the proposal of having two Amirs was once accepted, other people would later lay claim to the election of an Amir from them. Such multiple Amirate would lead to the disintegration of the Islamic polity. Hadrat Umar emphasized that in the interest of the solidarity of Islam they could not have more than one Amir, and it was imperative that such Amir should be from the Quraish, the tribe of the Holy Prophet.

There was some exchange of hot words between Habab and Hadrat Umar. Then Abu Ubaida appealed to the Ansars saying:

> "O Ansars you were the first to help Islam: do not now be the first to take steps towards the disintegration of Islam".

That appeared to have some effect on the Ansars, and they seemed to hesitate to press their demand. Thereupon Hadrat Abu Bakr took the stage again and said:

> "God is our witness that we are not pressing the claim of the Quraish because of any selfish interest. The proposal is based solely on the interest and solidarity of Islam. To give you a proof positive of our sincerity I declare before you that I do not covet the office. Here are Umar and Abu Ubaida. You may choose any one out of these two."

That softened the attitude of the Ansars. Zaid bin Thabit

an eminent Ansar leader rose to say:

> "In fact the Holy Prophet was among the Quraish. There is considerable force in the proposal that after him his successor should also be selected from among the Quraish. God chose the 'Ansars' as helpers, and it is but meet that they should continue to play the role of helpers."
>
> Supporting him another Ansar leader Bashir bin Sa'd said:
>
> "O Ansars, if we have secured a position of superiority in holy wars against the polytheists and gained precedence in the matter of religion it was with the object of pleasing our Allah and obeying the Holy Prophet. It is not proper for us to make this a ground for self-aggrandisement. We should leave our reward to Allah. We must realise that the Holy Prophet came from the Quraish, and that the Quraish have the strongest claim for his succession. We should not quarrel with the Quraish on this issue."

That turned the tables, and the Ansars now appeared to be inclined to choose the leader from among the Quraish. Taking advantage of this situation, Hadrat Abu Bakr repeated his proposal that they might choose anyone out of Hadrat Umar, or Abu Ubaida.

Election of Hadrat Abu Bakr. At the offer of Hadrat Abu Bakr, Hadrat Umar rose quickly to say:

> "O Abu Bakr, how can I or Abu Ubaida be preferred to you ? You are undoubtedly the most excellent of the Muslims. You were the 'Second of the Two' in the Cave. You were appointed as 'Amir-ul-Haj'. During his illness the Holy Prophet appointed you as the Imam to lead the prayers. Of all the companions you were the closest and the dearest to the Holy Prophet. As such you are dear to us. Stretch your hand so that we may offer our allegiance to you".

Hadrat Umar made Hadrat Abu Bakr stand, and then touched his hand reverently in token of allegiance. Abu Ubaida was the next to pay allegiance. Thereafter all the Ansars assembled there offered their allegiance to Hadrat Abu Bakr turn by turn. Only Sa'd bin Ubadah did not offer allegiance. Thus Hadrat Abu Bakr was elected as the successor to the Holy Prophet on the very day of the death of Holy Prophet, the 8th of June 832 C.E.

Inaugural Address of Hadrat Abu Bakr

Assembly of the people. On the day following the meeting at *Saqeefa Bani Sa'ida*, all the Muslims of Madina assembled in the Prophet's mosque for *Zuhr* prayer, and for offering allegiance to Hadrat Abu Bakr as the Caliph. The Holy Prophet had come from God, and to God he had returned. What could not be cured had to be endured, and for sheer survival the Muslim community had to perforce express faith in some leader who could lead them, and follow in the footsteps of the Holy Prophet. All were agreed that such leader could be no one other than Hadrat Abu Bakr, the bosom companion of the Holy Prophet, the "second of the two" according to the Holy Qur'an, and the man whom the Holy Prophet had himself appointed as the Imam to lead the prayers.

Introductory address of Hadrat Umar. Hadrat Umar addressed the faithful gathered in the mosque in the following terms:

> "I expected that the Holy Prophet would outlive us all, but it was the will of God that after having fulfilled his mission he should return to God. Verily, the Prophet came from God, and to God he has returned. He has left with us the Holy Qur'an from which we can always receive guidance. And we have in our midst, Abu Bakr, Companion of the Prophet, and the "Second of the two in the Cave", who is undoubtedly the worthiest among us to conduct our affairs. To stregthen his hands, and to maintain the integrity of the Muslim community, it is necessary that we should repose our confidence in

him and offer him our allegiance. Now come and offer *bait* (allegiance) to him."

Ceremony of bai at. Having made this appeal, Hadrat Umar requested Hadrat Abu Bakr to take his seat on the pulpit. Hadrat Abu Bakr took his seat on the pulpit, a step below that which used to be occupied by the Holy Prophet. This gesture was expressive of the fact that the leadership of the Holy Prophet was to continue, and the new leader was not to be the successor of the Prophet, he was to be his deputy only. Hadrat Abu Bakr stretched his hand, and the Muslims assembled in the mosque filed past the pulpit touching the stretched hand of Hadrat Abu Bakr reverently as a mark of allegiance. It was a solemn ceremony, each Muslim acknowledged the leadership of Hadrat Abu Bakr.

Inaugural address. When all the Muslims, gathered in the mosque, had offered their allegiance to Hadrat Abu Bakr, Hadrat Abu Bakr rose to address them. After praising Allah and offering his tribute to the Holy Prophet of Islam, Hadrat Abu Bakr addressed the congregation in the following terms:

> "O people, I swear by Allah that I never coveted the caliphate either by day or by night, nor had I any inclination towards it. I never prayed to God openly or in secrecy to confer the office on me. I merely accepted this office lest some mischief might arise at this critical juncture in the history of the Muslims and thereby adversely affect the interests of Islam. In fact a big task has been assigned to me which is beyond my power to fulfil except with the help of the Almighty Allah and your whole hearted cooperation. I wished to see the strongest of men in my place this day. Now, it is beyond doubt that I have been elected your Amir, although I am not better than you. Help me, if I am in the right; set me right if I am in the wrong. Truth is a trust; falsehood is a treason. The weak among you will be strong with me till, God willing, his rights have been vindicated; and the strong among you shall be weak with me till, if the Lord wills, I have taken what is due from him. Obey me as long as

I obey Allah and His Prophet; when I disobey Him and His Prophet, then obey me not. And now rise for prayers; may God have mercy on you."

Hadrat Abu Bakr and the Caliphate

The caliphate issue. Immediately on the death of the Holy Prophet, the caliphate issue came to pose a great threat to the solidarity of the Muslim community. The Ansars insisted that in view of their services of Islam, the office should go to them. The Holy Prophet was a Quraish, and according to the Arab custom, Quraish insisted that the office should go to them. The Ansars by way of compromise proposed that they might have two leaders, one from the Ansars and one from the Quraish. The proposal militated against the solidarity of the Muslim community, and was not agreed to by the Quraish. The issue did not concern the Quraish and the Ansars alone; it pertained to the entire Muslim community. If the Caliph was chosen from the Quraish, the tribe to which the Holy Prophet belonged, the other tribes could accept him, but if the Caliph was chosen from among the Ansars, the other tribes were likely to demand that they should also have their own Caliphs. This would have led to the disintegration of the Muslim community. The Quraish wanted the Caliph to be chosen from among them, not because they coveted power, but because they wanted to maintain the integrity and unity of the Muslim community.

Election of Hadrat Abu Bakr as the Caliph. It was with considerable difficulty and after a good deal of discussion and even exchange of hot words that Hadrat Abu Bakr ultimately succeeded in persuading the Ansars to let the Quraish have the office of the Caliph. Hadrat Abu Bakr did not covet the office for himself. He wanted that any one out of Hadrat Umar or Abu Ubaida should be elected. Hadrat Umar and Abu Ubaida insisted that Hadrat Abu Bakr should have the office. Hadrat Abu Bakr realised that if he hesitated, the Ansars might change their mind. Hadrat Abu Bakr accordingly let the people offer him allegiance. The entire process of election was spontaneous. There was nothing preplanned about it. The things moved in the course they did as ordained by destiny.

Hadrat Abu Bakr's concept of the Caliphate. In the inaugural address which Hadrat Abu Bakr delivered at the time of the assumption of power, he declared his concept of the caliphate in unequivocal terms. He held:

(1) Help me, if I am in the right; set me right, if I am in the wrong;

(2) The weak among you shall be strong with me till God willing his rights have been vindicated, and the strong among you shall be weak with me till, if the Lord wills, I have taken what is due from him.

(3) Obey me as long as I obey Allah and His Prophet; when I disobey Him and His Prophet, obey me not.

Sectarian differences. Unfortunately, the caliphate issue led to sectarian differences. Accounts that have come down to us in this respect are conflicting as well as confusing, and it is difficult for a student of history to assess the correct position. According to one account, Hadrat Ali offered allegiance to Hadrat Abu Bakr along with other Muslims. According to another account, Hadrat Ali did not offer allegiance, and opposed the caliphate of Hadrat Abu Bakr. In this he was supported by the Hashemites. It is alleged that Hadrat Umar threatened to suppress this opposition with force. According to another account, Hadrat Ali offered allegiance to Hadrat Abu Bakr six months later, after the death of Hadrat Fatima. Whatever the case, so much at least is undeniable that Hadrat Abu Bakr's allegiance was duly taken by Hadrat Ali some time during the caliphate of Hadrat Abu Bakr. Hadrat Ali was actively associated with the administration during the caliphate of Hadrat Abu Bakr. When Hadrat Abu Bakr died, Hadrat Ali in his oration dilated at length on the superb qualities of Hadrat Abu Bakr, and expressed full faith in his leadership. Hadrat Ali married the widow of Hadrat Abu Bakr, Asma, and looked after Hadrat Abu Bakr's son Muhammad as his own son. This shows that the differences, if any at all, between Hadrat Abu Bakr and Hadrat Ali were duly reconciled during the lifetime of the Caliph Hadrat Abu Bakr.

Nature of the issue. After Hadrat Ali had taken the oath of allegiance to Hadrat Abu Bakr the controversy about the caliphate issue should have come to an end, and it should not have been made a religious issue. The Holy Prophet was a spiritual as well as a temporal leader. After his death, revelations ceased, and the new leaders of the Muslim community were to be temporal leaders only. The election of such leaders could be nothing but a political issue, and it was not correct to make it a religious issue. On the occasion of the farewell pilgrimage, Allah declared that He had completed the religion for the Muslims. If the caliphate were to be a religious issue, Allah or the Holy Prophet would have given instructions on the point. The very fact that the Holy Qur'an as well as the Sunnah are silent in the matter of caliphate shows that the matter is explicitly political and not religious in character.

Right of Hadrat Ali. Some sections hold that in becoming the Caliph, Hadrat Abu Bakr usurped the rights of Hadrat Ali, and he was therefore a usurper. On the face of the fact that Hadrat Ali did offer allegiance to Hadrat Abu Bakr, though after some time, this argument loses its force. Hadrat Abu Bakr's avowed policy was to follow in the footsteps of the Holy Prophet and to do things as the Holy Prophet would have done if he were alive. Hadrat Abu Bakr was very meticulous in carrying out all the commands of the Holy Prophet, in letter as well as in spirit. When all persons around Hadrat Abu Bakr Holy Prophet him not to despatch Usamah's expedition to Syria as Madina itself was threatened with danger, Hadrat Abu Bakr overruled the objection on the ground that the order of the Holy Prophet had to be carried into effect. When he was asked to appoint someone else as the Commander instead of Usamah, he held that he could not reverse an appointment made by the Holy Prophet. It is well-known that Hadrat Abu Bakr did not covet the office for himself. This is established by the fact that at the time of his death, he refunded all remuneration that he had drawn from the public treasury as Caliph. Under the circumstances, if there had been any indication that the Holy Prophet wanted Hadrat Ali to be the Caliph, Hadrat Abu Bakr would have been the last man to stand in the way of Hadrat Ali.

Choice of the leader. It is well known that the Holy Prophet left no instructions about his successor. Islam is from God, and in whatever way the history of Islam has shaped itself is the unfolding of the Will of God. We cannot, therefore, say that if the Holy Prophet did not nominate a successor, it was an omission or an accident. We must hold that such omission to nominate a successor was deliberate, and in accordance with the Will of God. The intention obviously was that the matter being political in nature, the community should in the matter stand on its legs, and choose the leader for itself.

Claim of Hadrat Ali. Hadrat Ali's claim was not based on seniority or merit; it was based on inheritance. The Holy Prophet declared in unequivocal terms that in the case of prophets, there was nothing to be inherited. The Holy Prophet did beget some sons but they did not survive. It appears that there was a set purpose behind that. The Holy Prophet was the last of the prophets, and it was accordingly the Will of God that with his death, there was the end of the prophethood, and there was nothing to be inherited. The caliphate could not be claimed on the basis of inheritance; it was a political office, and the community was free to choose, whomsoever they liked. If for some reason, Hadrat Ali was not chosen, this could not be made a ground for religious grievance.

Judgment on the caliphate of Hadrat Abu Bakr. In passing any judgment on the caliphate of Hadrat Abu Bakr, two points deserve particular consideration. The first point is that we have definite indications that the Holy Prophet wanted Hadrat Abu Bakr to succeed him. The second point is that the caliphate of Hadrat Abu Bakr must be judged on the basis of its results. With regard to the first point, the Holy Prophet appointed Hadrat Abu Bakr as the Imam, and that vested Hadrat Abu Bakr with the mantle of the leadership of the Muslim community. The Holy Prophet declared that he was under obligation to no one other than Hadrat Abu Bakr. The Holy Prophet also declared that all doors opening in the mosque should be closed except the door of the quarter of Hadrat Abu Bakr.

As regards the second point it has to be borne in mind that when Hadrat Abu Bakr was elected as the Caliph, Islam was confined to Makkah, Madina, and Taif only, and in the rest of Arabia the tribes had risen against Islam. When barely two years later, Hadrat Abu Bakr died, the whole of Arabia was in the fold of Islam and even Iraq and Syria had come under the domination of Islam. The irresistible conclusion is that such a man could not be a usurper.

The verdict of history is that Hadrat Abu Bakr successfully and faithfully carried out the mission of the Holy Prophet, and his policy aimed at securing the integrity and unity of the Muslim community, paid rich dividends. Nothing succeeds like success, and in view of the outstanding success of the caliphate of Hadrat Abu Bakr, it should not be made the subject of any sectarian prejudices.

NOTES

This Chapter gives an account of the election of Hadrat Abu Bakr as the Caliph.

The first section gives an account of the appointment of Hadrat Abu Bakr as the Imam to lead the prayers during the lifetime of the Holy Prophet. In early Islam, the Imamate signified the leadership of the Muslim community. Ordinarily the Holy Prophet acted as the Imam himself. When the Holy Prophet appointed Hadrat Abu Bakr as the Imam it was a positive proof of the fact that the Holy Prophet wanted Hadrat Abu Bakr as the leader of the Muslim community after him. Hadrat Ayesha wanted that Hadrat Abu Bakr should not be appointed as the Imam as he was too tender hearted. The Holy Prophet overruled her. Once when Hadrat Abu Bakr was absent and the prayer was led by Hadrat Umar, the Holy Prophet said, "No, Abu Bakr should lead the prayers". It is reported that the Holy Prophet said that it was not he who had appointed Hadrat Abu Bakr as the Imam, it was God Who had done so. It shows that it was ordained that after the Holy Prophet, Hadrat Abu Bakr should be the leader of the Muslims. During the course of the illness when there was some relief, the Holy Prophet addressed the faithful in the mosque. In his last address, the Holy Prophet singled out Hadrat Abu Bakr for his tribute. The Holy Prophet said that all doors leading to the mosque should be closed except the door of the quarter of Hadrat Abu Bakr. Muir holds in his book *Life of Muhammad* that this was indicative of the fact that the Holy Prophet wanted Hadrat Abu Bakr to look after the Muslims after him.

The second section gives an account of the death of the Holy Prophet. The death of the Holy Prophet led to a great psychological crisis. The Muslims could not believe that their Prophet would die. Even men like Hadrat Umar said, "Who says the Prophet is dead ?" It was Hadrat Abu Bakr who resolved the crisis by declaring, "He who worshipped Muhammad, let him know that Muhammad being a mortal is dead. He who worships the God of Muhammad, let him know that He lives and lives for ever". Hadrat Abu Bakr set an equation between God and the Prophet in the right perspective.

Other religions had fallen into the error of deifying their prophets. Hadrat Abu Bakr saved the Muslims from falling into such an error.

In the third section I have given account of the dialogue between the Ansars and the Muhajirs, and the ultimate agreement of the Ansars to let the Quraish have the office of the caliphate. In writing this section I have derived help from:

(1) *Hadrat Abu Bakr* by Syed Moinul Haq;
(2) *Abu Bakr* by Muhammad Hussain Haykal;
(3) *Abu Bakr, the Caliph* by A. A. Aziz.

In the fourth section I have given the inaugural address that Hadrat Abu Bakr delivered at the time of his assumption of office. This address is contained in the histories of Tabari, Ibn Khaldun and Ibn Hisham. This address of Hadrat Abu Bakr is classical in character and commands significance not only from the historical point of view, but from the political point of view as well. In this address, Hadrat Abu Bakr laid down the basic concepts of statecraft. By asserting that he would support the weak against the strong in the matter of the redress of grievances, he laid down the principle of equality before law. In laying down that he was to be obeyed as long as he obeyed Allah and His Prophet, he laid down the principle that the head of an Islamic state can never be a despot. In his book *Early Caliphate,* M. Muhammad Ali has observed that the inaugural address of Hadrat Abu Bakr is conspicuous for its wisdom, and might well serve as a beacon light for the Muslim world.

In the fifth section I have tried to project Hadrat Abu Bakr's concept of the caliphate, and review the significance of his caliphate. In writing this section I have obtained help from:

(1) *Abu Bakr* by Muhammad Hussain Haykal.
(2) *The Caliphate* by Sir Thomas W. Arnold.
(3) *The Caliphate, its Rise, Decline and Fall* by Sir William Muir.
(4) *Annals of the Early Caliphate* by Sir William Muir.
(5) *Encyclopaedia of Islam.*

8

ENCOUNTER WITH THE TRIBES

Expedition to Syria

Usamah's expedition to Syria. On assuming the caliphate the first issue that Hadrat Abu Bakr was called upon to decide was whether the expedition to Syria which the Holy Prophet had directed to be sent under the command of Usamah should proceed to its destination, or should it be abandoned because of the change in circumstances following the death of the Holy Prophet.

The background. The background of the expedition was that in 629 C.E. the Holy Prophet had sent an expedition against the Syrians under Zaid bin Harith. In the confrontation that had taken place at Mutah, Zaid had been martyred. The command was then taken over by Jafar bin Abu Talib. He too met martyrdom. Abdullah bin Rawahah who next took the command was also martyred. At that critical juncture, Khalid bin Walid took the command. By his superb strategy he succeeded in retrieving the position and bringing back the Muslim forces safely to Madina. For this act of heroism, Khalid bin Walid received from the Holy Prophet the title of *Saifullah*—the Sword of Allah. In 630 C.E. the Holy Prophet himself led an expedition to Tabuk. The Byzantines avoided a confrontation with the Muslim army which returned to Madina without any action. In 632 C.E., on return from the 'farewell pilgrimage', the Holy Prophet ordered a detachment to be sent against the Syrians under the command of Usamah the son of Zaid bin Harith. Some persons objected to the command of Usamah on the ground that he was a mere youth of nineteen. Usamah was very dear to the Holy Prophet. He was the son of Zaid who was an adopted son of the Holy Prophet. The Holy Prophet accordingly loved Usamah as a grandson. When the Holy Prophet entered Makkah after the peace of Hudaibiya, Usamah had the honour of sitting on the camel behind the Holy Prophet. Usamah was very brave, and on the occasion of the battle of Uhud he volunteered to fight when he was only a child. The Holy Prophet wanted the Muslims not to object to the command of Usamah for he was worthy of the command.

When the Holy Prophet fell ill, the detachment of Usamah was encamped at Jorf a few miles from Madina on the road to Syria. On account of the serious illness of the Holy Prophet, Usamah delayed his departure. When the Holy Prophet died, Usamah returned to Madina and sought further orders.

Advisability of undertaking the expedition. Hadrat Abu Bakr was advised that, as at that critical stage in the history of Islam, most of the tribes had apostatised from Islam and Madina itself was surrounded by hostile tribes, it was not advisable to send the army outside the country. Hadrat Abu Bakr said that it was the wish of the Holy Prophet that the army should be sent to Syria and this wish of the Master should be fulfilled at all costs. When some of the companions reiterated the danger to which Madina was exposed, Hadrat Abu Bakr declared in unequivocal terms:

> "Who am I to withhold the army that the Holy Prophet had ordained to proceed? Come what may: let Madina stand or fall, the Caliphate live or perish, the command of the Holy Prophet shall be carried out".

The view of Hadrat Abu Bakr was not based on any obstinacy or foolhardiness. It was based on ideal loyalty to the Holy Prophet envisaging the carrying out of his wish, coupled with the faith that whatever the Holy Prophet had ordered was in the best interests of the community. Against the firmness of the stand of Hadrat Abu Bakr, the companions of Hadrat Abu Bakr could offer no argument.

Command of Usamah. It was contended before Hadrat Abu Bakr with considerable vehemence that in case the expedition was necessarily to be despatched, there should be a change in the command, and some veteran and seasoned General should be appointed as the Commander instead of Usamah. Hadrat Umar was commissioned by the companions to put up this demand before the Caliph. Hadrat Abu Bakr listened attentively to what Hadrat Umar had to say, and then said:

> "Umar, Usamah was appointed by the Holy Prophet, and you want me to veto the appointment made by the Holy Prophet. Does it lie in your mouth to take such a recommendation ? How can I as the Caliph of the Holy Prophet cancel an order made by the Holy Prophet after due consideration. Go, and tell those who have commissioned you to make this recommendation that this is sheer sacrilege, and as long as Abu Bakr lives he cannot be party to such a sacrilegeous act".

This reply considerably embarrassed Hadrat Umar. He felt sorry for making the recommendation which evoked bitter comments from the Caliph. He returned to Jorf and told all concerned as to what had transpired between him and the Caliph. He was very bitter with those who had chosen him as their spokesman for making a recommendation to the Caliph to make a change in the command.

Departure of the army. Hadrat Abu Bakr directed the army to depart on its mission. Hadrat Abu Bakr went to Jorf to bid farewell to the army and addressed them in the following terms:

> "See that you avoid treachery. Depart not in any wise from the right. Do not mutilate anyone. You should not kill children, women or old men. Do not injure the date palm; do not burn it. Do not cut down any tree wherein there is food for men and beasts. Do not slay the flocks of herds of camels save for needful sustenance. You may eat of the meat that the men of the land may bring to you in their vessels, making mention thereon of the name of Allah. Do not molest the monks in the churches, and leave them to themselves. Now march forward in the name of God. Fulfil the mission entrusted to you. May Allah protect you from sword and pestilence !"

Hadrat Abu Bakr walked for some distance along with the army to see it depart. Usamah who was riding on horseback prayed that he should be permitted to dismount, or the Caliph should also ride on a horse. Hadrat Abu Bakr said:

> "No, neither should you dismount, nor would I mount a horse. You ride in the service of God, and I shall account to God for these steps that I take in your company".

The Campaign. The army of Usamah left Jorf towards the close of June 632 C.E. After a ten days march, the Muslim army penetrated into the region of Wadi-al-Qara, and fell on Banu al-Qidzah and other border tribes. Usamah rode on his father's horse "Sabah". He sought the person who had killed his father at the battle of Mutah, and having recognised him put him to the sword. The Byzantine forces avoided confrontation with the Muslim force, and the border tribes left to themselves were no match for the Muslim forces. They were thoroughly discomfited, and hastened to offer allegiance to the authorities at Madina. The expedition proved to be a great success. It secured the safety of the frontier with the Byzantines and averted the threat of any attack from the Byzantines. The success that attended the Muslim arms made the unruly tribes realise that Islam was not dead with the death of the Holy Prophet, and that the Muslims were strong enough to meet all emergencies. Usamah's army returned to Madina, in August 632 C.E. laden with considerable booty. On return to Madina, the army of Usamah was given a tumultuous welcome.

Encounter with the tribes

Tribes around Madina. Madina was surrounded by a ring of tribes, whose attitude to Islam was luke warm. These tribes included Bani Asad; Bani Tha'lba; Bani Ghatafan; Banu Marrah; Banu Abbas; Banu Dhanayan and others. In the battle of the Trench, these tribes had sided with the Quraish of Makkah and had fought against the Muslims. After the conquest of Makkah, when other tribes in Arabia sent delegations to Madina and accepted Islam, the tribes around

Madina also followed suit and offered allegiance to Islam. Their allegiance was based more on diplomacy and expediency than on real faith and conviction of the heart. Islam sat lightly on them. They regarded Islam as a matter of personal allegiance to the Holy Prophet which abated with the death of the Holy Prophet.

Deputation of the tribes. When Usamah's army left Madina for the Syrian front, the tribes around Madina sent a deputation to wait on Hadrat Abu Bakr. Their view was that with the passing away of the Holy Prophet their agreement vis a vis Islam had abated, and it was necessary that the authorities at Madina should make a fresh agreement with them. They said that they would remain on friendly terms with the authorities at Madina provided they were relieved of the obligation to pay Zakat. Hadrat Abu Bakr treated the deputation with due courtesy, and said that he would give his reply after consulting his advisers.

Counsel of the advisers. Hadrat Abu Bakr consulted his advisers. Almost all the eminent companions around Hadrat Abu Bakr advised that as the Muslims were hemed in by danger from all sides, it was expedient that the demand of the tribes should be accepted so that there was no defection from Islam. Even Hadrat Umar known for his strong attitudes favoured the acceptance of the demand of the tribes, in view of the impending danger.

Judgment of Hadrat Abu Bakr. The question became a matter of great concern for Hadrat Abu Bakr. He was conscious of the gravity of the situation, and was aware of the danger to which the Muslim community was exposed. *Prima facie* the advice of Hadrat Umar and others to accept the demand of the tribes appeared to be sound under the circumstances. Hadrat Abu Bakr however could not overlook the other side of the picture. Hadrat Abu Bakr felt that the very basis on which the demand had been raised was open to attack. It was incorrect to hold that Islam was a matter of agreement between the Holy Prophet and the tribes, and that after his passing away this agreement had abated and was open to revision. Islam was an agreement with God, and as

God existed, the passing away of the Holy Prophet after the fulfilment of his mission did not in any way affect their allegiance to Islam. Islam meant total faith, and such faith could not be made subject to any conditions.

Zakat. As regards the demand for Zakat, Hadrat Abu Bakr felt that if he conceded the demand, that might ease the situation temporarily, but that could in turn lead to other demands, and after having accepted one demand it would be difficult to refuse other demands. Islam stood for a central polity, and if any concession was once given in consideration of tribal loyalties, that would be subversive of the solidarity of Islam. Hadrat Abu Bakr felt that as the successor of the Holy Prophet it was his duty to safeguard Islam, and as such he could not follow a policy of appeasement likely to compromise Islam in any way.

Another consideration that weighed with Hadrat Abu Bakr was that Zakat was not a levy subject to political considerations; it was an imperative injuntion ordained by Islam, and was equated with prayers. Hadrat Abu Bakr recalled that when the people of Taif had waited on the Holy Prophet and had sought to be relieved of the obligation to offer prayers, the Holy Prophet had refused to accept the demand on the ground that he was not competent to amend the mandate of God. On this analogy, Hadrat Abu Bakr felt convinced that he was not competent to grant a concession violative of the fundamental principle of Islam. The matter of fact position was that where God and the Holy Prophet left any matter to the discretion of the community, the community could take such action as might be necessary on the basis of expediency, but where the command of Allah or the Holy Prophet was definite and conclusive, it was absolute and mandatory, and it could not be compromised or modified because of any considerations of necessity or expediency. After considering all aspects of the case, Hadrat Abu Bakr arrived at the conclusion that he had no jurisdiction to grant an exemption from Zakat, and that as the representative of the Holy Prophet it devolved on him to enforce the command of Allah in letter as well as in spirit, and not to sit in judgment over such order, and seek to modify it for one reason or the other. Hadrat Abu

Bakr's judgment, therefore, was that under the circumstances he had no option but to refuse the demand of the tribes. This conviction fired him with the determination to stand firm, and to refuse to compromise Islam.

Hadrat Abu Bakr took Hadrat Umar and other companions into confidence. Hadrat Umar tried to insist on his previous advice of giving the concession, but as Hadrat Abu Bakr unfolded his arguments step by step, all the companions came round to the view that truth was what Hadrat Abu Bakr said.

Reply to the tribes. When on the following day, Hadrat Abu Bakr met the delegation of the tribes, he explained to them the philosophy underlying Zakat. He brought home to them the point that he had no jurisdiction to grant any concession in respect of a matter which was a mandate of Allah. He explained to them that if they professed Islam, they had to observe all the injunctions of Islam in toto. There was no half way house in Islam, and it was not permissible for them to pick and choose Islam according to their whims and caprices. Islam had either to be rejected or accepted, and there was no room in Islam for any compromise on fundamentals. Hadrat Abu Bakr argued that Zakat being a fundamental injunction of Islam had to be paid with good grace, and any refusal to pay Zakat implied apostasy.

Addressing the delegates, Hadrat Abu Bakr declared in unequivocal terms:

> "Under the circumstances, if with reference to Zakat you withhold even as much as a string to tie a camel, as the Caliph of the Holy Prophet, it will be my duty to fight for it, whatever the consequences. I will be prepared to face all risks, but I cannot be a party to the compromising of Islam on any fundamental issue."

Battle of Zul Qissa

Challenge of the tribes. When Hadrat Abu Bakr rejected the demand of the tribes to exempt them from the payment of the Zakat, they had no argument to meet the argument of Hadrat Abu Bakr, but in a state of desperateness they took such refusal as a challenge. Islam sat lightly on them, and tribal feelings were most dominant in them. They accordingly decided that if Islam involved the payment of Zakat to Madina, they would prefer to forego Islam, rather than yield to the dictates of the authorities in Madina. During their stay in Madina the delegates of the tribes saw for themselves that with the departure of the main Muslim army under Usamah for Syria, there was hardly any fighting force with the Muslims in Madina and as such the city was vulnerable. When the delegates returned to their tribes and gave an account of what Hadrat Abu Bakr had said feelings ran high among the tribesmen. They decided to attack Madina when the main Muslim army was away, and teach the authorities of Madina a lesson. The tribes concentrated their forces at Zul Hissa and Zul Qissa to the north east of Madina on the way to Nejd, and decided to launch the attack against Madina.

Preparations of Hadrat Abu Bakr. When the delegates of the tribes left Madina in a sullen mood, Hadrat Abu Bakr discerned that they meant mischief, and that an attack by the tribes was imminent. Hadrat Abu Bakr lost no time in making arrangements for the defence of Madina. Strong pickets under Khalid, Zubair, Talha, Abdur Rahman b. Auf, Abdullah b. Masud and Hadrat Ali were posted at strategic approaches to the city. These pickets were required to remain at their posts, and to make immediate report to the Caliph about the movements of the tribes. All the adult male Muslims were asked to collect in the Prophet's mosque. Here Hadrat Abu Bakr apprised them of the impending danger of an attack from the tribes, and asked them to do their duty to Islam. Hadrat Abu Bakr brought home to them the point that if they staked their everything in the way of God, God would come to their help as He had helped them during the life time of the Holy Prophet. A roster of all Muslim male adults in the city was prepared, and their turns for keeping the vigil during the nights were fixed.

The attack of the tribes. One dark night during the month of July 632 C.E. there was brisk movement in the camp of the tribes at Zul Hissa. The Muslim scouts brought the intelligence that the tribes planned to attack Madina that night. Hadrat Abu Bakr collected all the Muslim male adults in the mosque. After the night prayers these men were required to spread out in group to keep vigil in the various quarters of the city. At the head of a contingent Hadrat Abu Bakr took position at a strategic point in the direction of Zul Hissa from where the attack was expected. The tribes launched the attack at midnight. They had hoped that they would take the city by surprise, and that as there was no fighting force in Madina, they would meet no resistance, and it would be an easy walk-over for them. As the tribal force advanced in the darkness of the night fully assured of their victory, the contingent of Hadrat Abu Bakr leapt on the advancing horde, and took them by surprise. Many tribesmen fell victims to the swords of the Muslims; the rest fled in utter confusion.

The counter attack of the Muslims. The Muslims gave chase to the enemy and advanced to Zul Hissa. Here the retreating tribesmen were joined by their reserves. In the battle at Zul Hissa the Muslims were outnumbered but they fought with grim determination. As a stratagem the tribesmen threw inflated water skins in the path of the Muslim army. That frightened the camels on which the Muslims were riding, and the camels did not rest till they reached Madina. The tribes felt jubilant at what they regarded as the repulse of the Muslims. The tribes thinking that all was over with the Muslims retired to their camps at Zul Hissa and Zul Qissa.

The battle of Zul Qissa. Back in Madina, Hadrat Abu Bakr rallied the Muslim forces, and mustering the available reserves decided to fall on the enemy. In the late hours of the night, the Muslim forces rushed out of the city, and led a violent attack against the enemy at Zul Hissa. The tribal forces were taken unawares and they retreated to Zul Qissa. The Muslims pursued them to Zul Qissa. There was an action at Zul Qissa but the tribal force could not withstand the fury of the attack of the Muslims. Many tribesmen were cut to pieces. Those who survived fled in confusion. Before the day dawned the Muslims had won a victory and they were the masters of Zul Qissa. Hadrat Abu Bakr decided to canton his forces at Zul Qissa, and make it a base for further campaigns against the apostate tribes. Hadrat Abu Bakr left a detachment at Zul Qissa under the command of Nauman bin Muqran and himself returned to Madina with considerable booty captured at the battle of Zul Qissa.

Consequences of the battle of Zul Qissa. The victory of Zul Qissa was the first significant event of the caliphate of Hadrat Abu Bakr. When Hadrat Abu Bakr returned to Madina from Zul Qissa he was acclaimed as a hero, a worthy successor of the Holy Prophet. In the midst of most adverse circumstances he remained firm and never lost faith. By his superb leadership he had averted the threat to the city of Madina. By refusing to compromise on principles in spite of heavy odds, he established that he was made of stuff that characterise heroes. In its significance, the battle of Zul Qissa has been compared by some historians with the battle of Badr. The battle of Badr was the first battle after the Hijrat; the battle of Zul Qissa was the first battle after the death of the Holy Prophet. In the battle of Badr the Muslims were outnumbered by the Quraish, and still they won a victory because of the superb leadership of the Holy Prophet. In the battle of Zul Qissa the Muslims were outnumbered by the tribal forces but they won a victory because of the superb leadership of Hadrat Abu Bakr. If the Muslims had lost the battle of Badr, Islam was apt to be extinguished. If the battle of Zul Qissa had been lost, there was the danger of Islam losing its hold. Just as the battle of Badr set the stage for the advancement of the Muslims, thus did the battle of Zul Qissa set the pace for the overthrow of forces hostile to Islam.

Another important consequence of the battle of Zul Qissa was that it crystallised the issues. Heretofore there were tribes which favoured Islam, but still wavered in their allegiance to Madina. Again there were tribes which preferred to sit on the fence and watch developments. After the battle of Zul Qissa such suspense came to an end. Many tribes sent their delegations to Madina, offered allegiance to the authorities in Madina and paid Zakat. The tribes that did not favour Islam openly apostatised. Henceforward the issue was not between Muslims and Muslims; the issue was between the Muslims and the apostates. The battle of Zul Qissa indeed set the stage for the apostasy campaigns.

Battle of Abraq

Concentration of the tribes at Abraq. After their defeat at Zul Qissa the tribes retreated to Abraq. Heretofore the tribes maintained some semblance of allegiance to Islam, and had not made common cause with the tribes who had apostatised from Islam. After their defeat at Zul Qissa these tribes repudiated Islam, and joined the ranks of the apostates. At Abraq there was consequently a great concentration of the apostate tribes, and they were fully poised for attacking the Muslims. These apostate tribes turned viciously in the first instance upon such of their members who still owed allegiance to Islam. Being outnumbered such Muslims were slaughtered mercilessly. Some were put to the sword, some were burnt alive, some were thrown from the cliffs, and some were subjected to tortures of other kinds. When Hadrat Abu Bakr came to know of these atrocities perpetrated against the Muslims he vowed vengeance, but in view of the large strength of the apostate tribes he had to perforce delay action till the return of Usamah's army.

Battle of Abraq. On the return of Usamah's army from Syria, Hadrat Abu Bakr decided to lead an expedition against the apostate tribes concentrated at Abraq. Hadrat Abu Bakr was advised that instead of leading the expedition to Abraq personally he should entrust the command to some one else. His companions said:

> "O Caliph of the Holy Prophet, do not endanger yourself by leading the army in person. If God forbid any harm comes to you that will work to the advantage of the apostates. Appoint some one else to command the Muslim forces, for even if such a commander is martyred he could be replaced."

Hadrat Abu Bakr thanked his advisers for their solicitude about him, but he did not accept their proposal. He said:

"If the Holy Prophet himself led campaigns, it is but meet that as his representative I should also go forth in battle to fight in the name of Allah".

The Muslim army under Hadrat Abu Bakr marched from Madina to Zul Qissa, and from there advanced to the district of Abraq. When the Muslims reached Abraq, they found the hostile tribes already formed in battle array in the plain outside their settlement of Rabza. It was a hot August day, and after prayers, Hadrat Abu Bakr launched the attack. The attack was withheld by the enemy. Then the enemy charged. The enemy contingents led by Haris, Auf, and Huteeyah penetrated into the ranks of the Muslims. The Muslim army fell back and the enemy contingents rushed forward impetuously. Then the Muslims counter charged, and the advance contingents of the enemy were cut to pieces. The enemy leaders Haris and Auf were killed, while Huteeyah who was also a well known poet was captured alive.

With the fall of the leaders the enemy forces were demoralised. Soon the field came to be covered with the dead bodies of the enemy in large numbers. Ultimately the courage of the tribes gave away under the increased pressure of the Muslims, and they found safety in flight. The Muslims thereby won a significant victory.

Consequences of the battle of Abraq. The victory for the Muslims in the battle of Abraq was an important event of the caliphate of Hadrat Abu Bakr. The campaign had a very salutary effect. It showed that the Muslims were strong enough for the offensive. It also brought home to the Muslims and the non-Muslims alike that Hadrat Abu Bakr was not a mere ruler; he was a military General as well. The region of Abraq commanded a strategic position which was vital for the safety of Madina. Hadrat Abu Bakr annexed the district of Abraq to Madina. The vanquished tribes were expelled from the district, and their lands were confiscated and turned into a pasture ground for the state animals. It was the first state pasture in the history of Islam.

NOTES

In this Chapter I have given an account of the Muslims' encounter with the tribes.

The first section deals with Usamah's expedition to Syria. The purpose of this expedition was to protect the Syrian border. The companions around Hadrat Abu Bakr were of the view that in view of the changed circumstances after the death of the Holy Prophet this expedition should be abandoned. Hadrat Abu Bakr remained firm in sending the expedition. This policy led to better results, and we cannot help but admire the firmness and foresight of Hadrat Abu Bakr.

In the second section I have given an account of a delegation of the tribes visiting Madina and insisting that they should not be required to pay Zakat. In this matter again the companions of Hadrat Abu Bakr advised that the tribes be exempted from the payment of Zakat. Hadrat Abu Bakr remained firm and insisted that Zakat should be paid failing which he would fight. This steadfastness of Hadrat Abu Bakr proved to be a great service in the cause of Islam.

In the third section I have given an account of the tribes' attaçk of Madina, their reverse, and the battle of Zul Qissa, in which the tribes were defeated. Just as the battle of Badr set the pace for the advance of the Muslims under the Holy Prophet, thus did the battle of Zul Qissa set the pace for the unification of Arabia under Islam under Hadrat Abu Bakr.

The fourth section gives an account of the battle of Abraq, and the defeat of the tribes. With this battle the threat of the tribes to Madina was over. It established that Islam was to prevail and could not be trifled with.

In writing this Chapter I have derived help from the following books:

(1) *Muhammad at Madina* by Montgomery Watt.
(2) *Abu Bakr* by Muhammad Hussain Haykal.
(3) *Hadrat Abu Bakr* by Syed Moin-ul-Haq.
(4) *Abu Bakr, the Caliph* by A. A. Aziz.

9
APOSTASY CAMPAIGN AGAINST TALEAHA

Plan of Campaign against the Apostates

Plan against the apostates. After the battle of Abraq, Hadrat Abu Bakr felt that a stage had been reached when campaigns against the apostates should be planned and organised on a large scale. Towards the close of August 632 C.E. all the Muslim forces were mustered at Zul Qissa.

At Zul Qissa, Hadrat Abu Bakr formed the Muslim forces into eleven corps each under its own commander. Each commander was given a flag and assigned an objective. The commanders were further authorised to recruit other soldiers on the way in their march to their objectives.

The eleven corps. The first corps was placed under the command of Khalid bin Waleed. It was required to take action against Taleaha of the Banu Asad concentrated at Buzakha. Thereafter they were to proceed against the Bani Tamims at Butaha.

The second corps under 'Ikrama b. Abu Jahl was required to take action against the false prophet Musailmah of the Banu Hanifa tribe at Yamama, but it was required not to engage the enemy till it received further reinforcement.

The third corps under Amr bin Al-Aas was required to take action against the tribes of Quzaa'a, Wadee'a and Harith in the areas of Gaza, and Daumatul Jandal near the borders of Syria.

The fourth corps under Shurahbil bin Hasana was required to follow lkrama and await further instructions.

The fifth corps under Khalid bin Saeed was required to operate on the Syrian border in the Hamqatan region.

The sixth corps under Tureifa bin Hajiz was required to take action against the apostate tribes of Hawazin and Bani Sulaim in the region east of Makkah and Madina.

The seventh corps under 'Ala bin Hadrami was commissioned to operate against the tribes in Bahrain.

The eighth corps under Arafja bin Harsama was required to take action against the tibes in the coastal area of lower Yemen.

The ninth corps under Huzaifa bin Mihsan was required to take action against the apostates in Oman.

The tenth corps under Muhajir bin Abi Umayya was required to operate in Upper Yemen and Hadramaut.

The eleventh corps under Suweid bin Muqran was required to operate in the coastal areas north of Yemen.

Message to the tribes. Before the various corps left Zul Qissa for their objectives, Hadrat Abu Bakr sent envoys to all apostate tribes calling upon them to return to Islam. The message read:

> "I have learnt with regret that under the misguidance of the Devil you have apostatised from Islam, the true faith of God. I am sending to you a Muslim force consisting of the Muhajreen and the Ansar. I have instructed them not to launch the attack against you, without offering you Islam in the first instance. He who repents, re-enters the fold of Islam, desists from hostile activities against Islam, and does good deeds will be forgiven and granted amnesty. He who refuses to accept Islam, and persists in hostilities will be given no quarter. Force will be used against him, and it will not be possible for him to avert that Allah has ordained for him. Such persons

will be put to sword, slaughtered, or burnt to death. Their women and children will be taken captive. Nothing short of allegiance to Islam will be accepted. If after considering this warning, any person seeks his refuge in Islam, such faith will stand him in good stead. But he who persists ia his apostasy will never be able to humble God. I have instructed my envoys that they should read this measage of mine in public gatherings. Calling the Azan will be regarded as an indication of the acceptance of Islam. If there is no Azan this will be taken to mean that the tribe persists in its apostasy."

Instructions to the Commanders. As the various corps left for their abjectives, Hadrat Abu Bakr instructed the commanders to fear God. They were to exert themselves to the utmost in the way of Allah, and to allow no sloth to retard their efforts. They were commanded that if any tribe responded with the Azan it was not to be molested or attacked. Those who did not make such response were to be dealt with by fire and sword. All apostates guilty of murdering Muslims were to be killed. These who were guilty of burning Muslims alive were to be likewise burnt alive. Hadrat Abu Bakr insisted that the only options for the apostate tribes were unconditional surrender or war until total destruction. The commanders were enjoined not to dishonour the word once pledged. They were also forbidden to depart from the targets assigned to them, without further instructions.

Campaign against Taleaha

Taleaha. Taleaha belonged to the Banu Asad tribe. The tribe held the region to the north of Madina. Taleaha had laid claim to prophethood and divine revelation during the lifetime of the Holy Prophet. He ridiculed the Muslim way of prayer, and asked his followers to pray standing. He declared "God does not want us to invert our faces or bend our backs in ugly postures". The Holy Prophet directed punitive action against the imposter. In his anxiety to have the benediction of killing a false prophet, a Muslim stole into the camp of Taleaha with a view to murdering him. The attempt was miscarried, and that made the followers of Taleaha proclaim that no sword could harm their prophet.

Before the Muslim army commissioned by the Holy Prophet could advance against Taleaha, the Holy Prophet was dead. Taleaha declared that the death of the Holy Prophet was a sign corroborative of his prophethood. Many other tribes acknowledged Taleaha as the prophet, and the argument that weighed with them was that while Muhammad (peace be on him) was dead, Taleaha was alive, and a living prophet was to be preferred to the Prophet who was dead. The Banu Fazara joined him under their leader 'Uyaynah. The tribes of Abs, Ghatafan, Banu Bakr and Dhayiban who had been defeated by the Muslims in the battle of Abraq also made common cause with Taleaha. Parts of the Bani Taiy and Banu Jadilah also joined the ranks of Taleaha. That made Taleaha sufficiently strong and powerful, and he came to lead a confederacy of numerous tribes who held North East Arabia.

Movements of the parties. At the time of the battle of Zul Qissa, Taleaha was at Sumera. After the battle of Zul Qissa, Taleaha moved from tribe to tribe who offered their allegiance to him. Ultimately he came to Buzakha and here he mustered a strong force drawn from various tribes anxious to measure swords with the Muslims.

Hadrat Abu Bakr commissioned Khalid bin Walid to undertake operations against Taleaha. In view of the strength of the army at the disposal of Taleaha an effort was made to enlist the flower of the Muslim warriors under the colours of Khalid. Moving northwards the contingent of Khalid penetrated into the mountain region of Aja and Salma, held by Banu Taiy. Here Khalid entered into negotiations with Addi, the chief of Bani Taiy. After the battle of Zul Qissa, Bani Taiy chief had visited Madina, paid Zakat and offered allegiance to Islam. In spite of that although Addi himself remained faithful to Islam, the bulk of his tribe supported Taleaha, and despatched a contingent to Buzakha to fight against the Muslims. Khalid bin Walid carried a special message of Hadrat Abu Bakr for Addi, in which he was asked to use his influence with his people to wean them from the support of Taleaha, and help the cause of Islam. After some difficulty, Addi succeeded in his efforts and his tribe offered allegiance to Islam. The Bani Taiy contingent was withdrawn from Buzakha, and it joined the ranks of the Muslim army. The contingent was commanded by Addi. Through the efforts of Addi, the allied tribe Banu Jadilah also detached itself from Taleaha and joined the fold of Islam. The addition of the contingents of Bani Taiy and Banu Jadilah considerably strengthened the Muslims.

Thus reinforced the Muslim army marched to Buzakha. On the way, the Muslim army was sorely distressed to find that two of the Muslim scouts Akkasha bin Mohsin, and Sapit b. Akram had been slain by the men of Taleaha, and left to be trampled on the road. Khalid bin Walid arranged for the burial of these martyrs. Khalid vowed that he would take vengeance for the death of these scouts.

Battle of Buzakha. When the Muslim army reached Buzakha, they were confronted by the forces of the apostate tribes. In spite of some defections, the forces of the confederate tribes were considerable in strength, and outnumbered the Muslim force. Khalid called upon Taleaha to submit to Islam, but he ridiculed the offer. Thereupon the two armies clashed. The Muslim forces were commanded by Khalid, while the forces of Taleaha were commanded by 'Uyaynah, the chief of Bani Fazara. The two armies were well matched, and the outcome of the battle seemed uncertain.

Taleaha retired to a place of safety, and pretended to await heavenly inspiration. Khalid increased his pressure and 'Uyaynah hard pressed waited on Taleaha to enquire whether he had received any message from the heavens about the outcome of the battle. Taleaha replied that the request made by him was under consideration in the heaven, and a reply was expected any moment. 'Uyaynah led a charge against the Muslim forces, but was beaten back with heavy losses. He again waited on Taleaha, and wanted to know whether any reply had come from the heavens. Taleaha said that God had spoken to him in the following terms:

"Your hopes and that of Khalid shall remain at variance,

and between you matters are so ordained that an event will take place which you will never forget."

At this ambiguous message carrying no sense, 'Uyaynah realised that Taleaha was an imposter, and his cause was doomed to failure. He told Taleaha "Woe to you ! I go." 'Uyaynah asked the men of his tribe to break camp and retreat to save themselves. With the withdrawal of 'Uyaynah and his men the tide of the battle was turned in favour of the Muslims. Khalid intensified the attack, and the battlefield came to be strewn with the dead bodies of the men of Taleaha. Finding resistance useless, Taleaha escaped with his wife to Syria. With the withdrawal of Taleaha the battle was over. The Muslims had won a significant victory. Most of the tribes surrendered and accepted Islam. Those who still remained opposed to Islam retreated and sought refuge further inland.

Sequel to the battle of Buzakha. Khalid made Buzakha his headquarters and re-organised the administration. He appointed his agents for the various districts. General amnesty was granted to those who re-entered the fold of Islam and expressed regret for their past behaviour. Those who had perpetrated atrocities on the Muslims were apprehended and subjected to likewise atrocities. The vacillating tribes in the region who had been sitting on the fence, and had preferred to watch the course of events submitted to the authority of Madina, paid Zakat and were re-admitted to the fold of Islam. The chiefs of the tribes who surrendered were sent to Madina for presentation before Hadrat Abu Bakr. Considerable booty captured from the battlefield was also sent to Madina. Hadrat Abu Bakr treated such chiefs with due courtesy and kindness. Khalid submitted a detailed report to Hadrat Abu Bakr about the operations at Buzakha. Hadrat Abu Bakr approved of the action taken, and appreciated the services of Khalid and his men in strong terms.

Taleaha on escape from Buzakha sought refuge in Syria. When Syria was occupied by the Muslims, Taleaha accepted Islam again and his career as a false prophet came to an end. Later he joined the Muslim army and took conspicuous part in the battles of Qadsiya and Nehavand, during the caliphate of Hadrat Umar.

Campaign against Bani Fazara

'Uyaynah. In the battle of Buzakha, the Bani Fazara had sided with Taleaha. 'Uyaynah a chief of Bani Fazara commanded the forces of Taleaha. At the last moment, Uyaynah came to be disilluioned with Taleaha, and he withdrew from the battlefield along with his men of Bani Fazara.

As soon as the battle of Buzakha was over, Khalid sent out columns in pursuit of the renegades. One column caught up some apostates at Rumman, some thirty miles from Buzakha. They submitted without a fight. They repented and were readmitted to the fold of Islam.

Khalid himself led another fast column in pursuit of 'Uyaynah. Khalid overtook him at Ghamra some sixty miles from Buzakha. Khalid asked 'Uyaynah to surrender, but he remained defiant, and chose to fight. In the sharp clash which followed many of the followers of 'Uyaynah were killed, and he himself was taken captive.

'Uyaynah was sent to Madina in chains. As the procession passed through the streets of Madina, the children gathered round and said "O enemy of Allah; you disbelieved after having believed". He said "No. I had never believed".

'Uyaynah had a chequered career. In the battle of the Ditch, he had sided with the Quraish of Makkah, and had fought against the Muslims. Later he and his men had withdrawn from the siege of Madina. At the time of the conquest of Makkah, he was on the side of the Muslims. Accounts are not clear as to whether 'Uyaynah had at any stage accepted Islam, Islam sat lightly on him, and when the wave of apostasy spread over the land, he saw adventure in siding with Taleaha.

At Madina, 'Uyaynah realised that his defiance of Islam had cost him a good deal. He accordingly repented and accepted Islam. Hadrat Abu Bakr took a lenient view of his past conduct and granted him amnesty. After some time, 'Uyaynah returned to his tribe, and lived in peace as a Muslim.

Umm Zummal. After the battle of Buzakha, some of the followers of Taleaha took refuge with Umm Zummal, a fire brand woman leader of the Bani Fazara. She was a cousin of 'Uyaynah who had commanded the forces of Taleaha. Her name was Salma, who but for her dash and courage she was commonly known as Umm Zummal. Her father was Malik bin Huzaifa, a chief of the Bani Fazara. Her mother Umm Qarfa was a brave and courageous woman of Spartan character. During the lifetime of the Holy Prophet, Umm Qarfa and her followers ambushed and killed some Muslims in the Al-Qara valley. In the counter action, Umm Qarfa along with Salma, and a number of followers were taken captive by the Muslims and led to Madina. At Madina, Umm Qarfa was put to death, and Salma became a maid servant of Hadrat Ayesha. After some time, Hadrat Ayesha freed Salma, and she returned to her tribe. Salma harboured malice against the Muslims and she burnt with the desire to avenge the death of her mother. When the wave of apostasy spread over Arabia she joined the movement and became one of its leaders.

Battle of Zafar. When after the defeat of Taleaha, many of his followers sought refuge with Umm Zummal, she decided to avail of the opportunity, and lead a coalition against the Muslims. She moved from tribe to tribe and excited them to hostility against the Muslims. She mustered a considerable force which assembled at her headquarter Zafar at the western edge of the Salma range, a rugged mountain named after her. When Khalid came to know of the hostile intentions of Umm Zummal, he led a Muslim force from Buzakha to Zafar. Immediately on arrival at Zafar, Khalid took the initative and launched the attack. Umm Zummal and her forces offered stiff resistance, it was by all accounts a hard battle. Mounted on a camel, Umm Zummal personally led the charge, and her undaunted courage was a source of great inspiration for her followers. Failure of his first effort to dislodge the apostates made Khalid reassess the situation. He saw that the centre of the apostates was led by Umm Zummal who rode on a magnificent camel which belonged to her mother. She exhorted her followers to fight bravely. She was surrounded by a ring of warriors who fought desperately, fired with a determination to win or die. For long the result of the confrontation remained uncertain. Khalid realised that the moral strength of the apostate force lay in the leadership of Umm Zummal, and unless she was eliminated somehow the chances of the Muslim victory were not very bright. Khalid directed his archers to aim at the camel on which Umm Zummal was riding. Every bow was bent and every spear of the Muslim was directed towards the camel. The camel was pierced with countless wounds, and it fell. Then Khalid with a picked group of warriors made a determined thrust towards the centre, and as the litter carrying Salma alias Umm Zummal fell to the ground she was killed immediately. The Muslims made free use of their swords and spears. Umm Zummal lay dead on the battlefield, and around her lay the dead bodies of her bodyguards who had fought to the last in her defence. With the death of Umm Zummal all resistance of the apostates collapsed and the battle of Zafar was won by the Muslims. That was in October 632 C.E. The apostate tribles offered submission and were re-admitted to the fold of Islam. Considerable booty fell into the hands of the Muslims which was sent to Madina.

Campaign against Bani Sulaim

The Bani Sulaim. The Bani Sulaim occupied the region north of Madina. Their settlements extended upto the Khyber. Their main concentration was at Naqra.

The tribe was converted to Islam in the time of the Holy Prophet. They participated on the side of the Muslims in the conquest of Makkah. They also fought along with the other Muslims in the battles of Hunain and Taif. A contingent of the Bani Sulaim fought under the command of Khalid and they were very much attached to him.

After the death of the Holy Prophet, the tribe apostatised. They made common cause with Taleaha, and fought against the Muslims in the battle of Buzakha.

The Bani Sulaim were led by a rash chieftain Anu bin Abdul Uzza commonly known as Abu Shajra. He was a poet, and he composed the following doggeral satirising Islam:

"My spear shall play havoc
With the regiments of Khalid,
And I trust thereafter
To crush Abu Bakr and Umar"

After the battle of Buzakha, the Bani Sulaim escaped to Naqra. Khalid pursued them to Naqra and launch the attack. The Bani Sulaim offered stiff resistance, but they could not bear the blows of Khalid for long. In the confrontations which followed many men of the tribe were killed. The aim of Khalid was to capture Abu Shajra alive. By a stratagem he succeeded in this object. With the capture of Abu Shajra all resistance on the part of Bani Sulaim collapsed.

Abu Shajra. Abu Shajra was put in chains and sent to Madina. When presented before Hadrat Abu Bakr, Abu Shajra repented, asked for pardon and chose to be reconverted to Islam. Hadrat Abu Bakr took a lenient way and granted him amnesty. During the caliphate of Hadrat Umar, Abu Shajra came to Madina again. Seeing him Hadrat Umar said, "May God curse you. Were you the man who wrote that doggeral ?" Abu Shujra said, "I wrote that doggeral in my ignorance; my submission to Islam has cancelled all that".

Al-Faja'a. When Khalid undertook operations against Taleaha, another chief of Bani Sulaim, Ayas bin Abd Yaleel commonly known as Al-Faja'a came to Hadrat Abu Bakr at Madina. He declared that he was a Muslim, and was keen to assist the Muslims of Madina in their fight against the apostates. He wanted to be supplied with arms so that he and his people might fight against the infidels. Hadrat Abu Bakr took him at his words, and he was supplied with arms to equip his people to fight against the apostates. Al-Faja'a rode away from Madina with the blessings of Hadrat Abu Bakr, but instead of fighting against the apostates, he formed a gang of bandits who waylaid unwary travellers and put them to death. The gangsters operated in the neighbourhood of Madina and

Makkah, and the Muslims and non-Muslims suffered alike at their hands. When the activities of Al-Faja'a were brought to the notice of Hadrat Abu Bakr, he deputed a column to get the man alive. The column succeeded in its mission and the brigand was brought to Madina in chains. Hadrat Abu Bakr felt very bitter at the treachery of of Al-Faja'a. The Caliph ordered a large pile of wood in front of the Prophet's mosque. When the pile was set on fire and flames rose high, Al-Faja'a still in chains was thrown into the fire and roasted to death. Later on his death bed, Hadrat Abu Bakr expressed certain regrets, Hadrat Abu Bakr regretfully said, "I wish I had Al-Faja'a killed outright and not burnt alive".

This regret was because of a tradition of the Holy Prophet according to which if a person professed to be a Muslim he was not to be punished to death by fire.

NOTES

This Chapter deals with the apostasy campaign against Taleaha of the Banu Asad, and the confederate tribes of Banu Fazara and Bani Sulaim.

The first section tells of the plan of campaigns against the apostates. That shows the skilful planning, strategy, and generalship of Hadrat Abu Bakr. Abu Bakr planned the campaigns in a big way, and looked after the minutest details. He issued a message for the tribes. He also gave detailed instructions to his commanders as to what they were required to do or not to do.

The second section deals with the campaign against Taleaha. In writing this section I have derived help from:

(1) *The Sword of Islam* by A. I. Ikram.
(2) *Abu Bakr, the Caliph* by A. A. Aziz.
(3) *Abu Bakr by* Muhammad Hussain Haykal.
(4) *Hadrat Abu Bakr* by Syed Moin-ul-Haq.
(5) *Ar Riddah and the Muslim Conquest of Arabia* by Elias Shoufani.

Taleaha was defeated not only on the physical plane; he was defeated at the spiritual plane as well. He accepted Islam, and that shows the falsity of his claim to prophethood. That also establishes the truth of Islam.

The third section deals with campaign against Bani Fazara. Here we meet two important characters 'Uyaynah and Umm Zummal 'Uyayna is an adventurer and he ultimately accepts Islam Umm Zummal is a woman of Spartan character. She dies fighting. In writing this section I have derived help from the books mentioned with reference to the second section.

The fourth section gives an account of the campaign against Bani Sulaim. Here we come across two characters Abu Shajra and Al Faja'ạ. Abu Shajra is a poet who writes pungent verses satirising Islam. Ultimately he accepts Islam and dies as a Muslim. Al Faja'a is an adventurer who betrays the trust of Hadrat Abu Bakr, and this costs him life. He is burnt to death.

Because of the successful completion of these campaigns apostasy in Western Nejd was suppressed and the apostate tribes rejoined the fold of Islam.

10

APOSTASY CAMPAIGN AGAINST MUSAILMA

Sajjah, the False Prophetess

Sajjah. Among the false prophets who rose in Arabia as a result of the apostasy movement, a lady named Sajjah claimed to be a prophetess. She was the daughter of Al-Haris who belonged to the Bani Yarbu section of the Bani Tamim. On her mother's side she belonged to the Banu Taghlib tribe who inhabited Iraq. Sajjah and her father lived with Banu Taghlib in Iraq, the tribe of her mother. Sajjah and her tribe were Christians.

Sajjah was beautiful and endowed with an attractive personality. She dabbled in clairvoyance, and professed to predict future. She was a poetess, and mostly talked in verse. She had qualities of leadership, and was popular with her people. When she came to know that after the death of the Holy Prophet, Taleaha and Musailma had declared themselves as prophets, she also declared herself as a prophetess. Soon she succeeded in mustering a good following from among the Banu Taghlib, the clan of her mother.

Malik bin Nuwera. In her attempt to gather some followers from her father's clan as well, Sajjah contacted Malik bin Nuwera the chief of the Bani Yarbu section of the Bani Tamim the clan of her father. At the invitation of Malik bin Nuwera Sajjah came to Bataha. the headquarters of the clan and entered into a pact with him. Malik was a very handsome man, and Sajjah was physically attracted to him.

Malik felt that with the help of Sajjah and her people he could overpower such of the sections of the tribe who were opposed to him. The terms of the pact between Sajjah and Malik are not known. Presumably Malik acknowledged Sajjah as a prophetess, and she undertook to help him in asserting his authority over the section of the Bani Yarbu who were opposed to him. The combined forces of Malik and Sajjah received some initial success. They, however, received a set back at a confrontation that took place at Nibhaj. Peace was won on the condition that Sajjah left the region at once. Sajjah accordingly decided to proceed to Yamama, the stronghold of the false prophet Musailma.

Musailma. Musailma a cunning man did not go to war against Sajjah. Instead he invited Sajjah to visit Yamama as his honoured guest. Sajjah accepted the invitation and proceeded to Yamama in Central Arabia. Musailma held a royal reception in her honour. Musailma was a handsome man of attractive personality. Sajjah was beautiful and passionate. Both were mutually attracted. Musailma flattered the vanity of Sajjah. He argued that as the Muslims were their common enemy, it would be to their mutual interest to join forces, and overpower the Muslims by united action. The idea appealed to Sajjah, and she said that she was prepared to make common cause with him. Musailma recited the verses that he claimed to have been revealed to him. Sajjah also recited her verses. Musailma applauded the verses and said, "Sajjah, you are verily a prophetess". Sajjah complimented him by saying, "I have no doubt that you are indeed a prophet". Then Musailma took another step forward and suggested that in order to strengthen their alliance it was but meet that they should be physically united as well and become husband and wife. Sajjah fell in line with his way of thinking, and agreed to become his wife. Musailma said that in view of their mutual concurrence, it was necessary that such holy alliance should take place at once without losing any time. Under the spell of the magnetic personality of Musailma, Sajjah agreed that the marriage should take place at once. Musailma took Sajjah to his camp where she remained with him for three days and three nights as his wife.

As a wedding gift, Musailma declared that for their common followers the prayers in the morning and in the evening were no longer obligatory and that henceforward the number of prayers per day was to be reduced from five to three. He also agreed to pay Sajjah a share out of the revenues of Yamama.

The end of the adventure. What happened next is not exactly known, for Sajjah instead of remaining with Musailma at Yamama as his wedded wife decided to return to her people in Iraq. The followers of Sajjah felt frustrated at this turn of events, and they did not like their prophetess becoming mistress of Musailma. Presumably Sajjah also realised that in marrying Musailma she had lost the battle. From some accounts it appears that Sajjah was already married, and she surrendered to Musailma under some hypnotice influence. When this spell was over, and she realised the depth to which she had degraded herself she found safety in returning to Iraq. That presumably explains her strange conduct, for if she had been lawfully wedded to Musailma she would have stayed with him in Yamama. When she returned to her people in Iraq that was the end of the adventure of prophethood. She lived in obscurity for the rest of her life. When the Muslims conquered Iraq she became a Muslim along with the other members of her tribe. During the caliphate of Muawiyiah she resided at Kufa, where she died at a sufficiently advanced age.

Campaign against Bani Tamim

The Bani Tamim. Having reduced the Bani Asad and Bani Fazara, Khalid bin Walid decided to march against the Bani Tamim who lived on a plateau to the east. The Bani Tamim had accepted Islam during the lifetime of the Holy Prophet. After the death of the Holy Prophet when the waves of apostasy spread over Arabia, the Bani Tamim were also affected. The tribe came to be divided into two sections. One section remained faithful to Islam, while the other section repudiated their allegiance to Islam. There was however some confusion as to who among the tribe favoured Islam and who were against it. When Khalid gave order to march to Bataha the headquarters of the Bani Tamim, the Ansars in the army refused to march to Bataha. Their stand was that the Caliph had not sanctioned any operation against the Bani Tamim. Khalid said that being the Commander of the forces operating in the region, he was in the best position to know which operations should or should not be undertaken in the interests of the mission for re-establishing the supremacy of Islam. He, however, declared that if the Ansars were unwilling to follow him, it was open to them to withdraw. When the main army of Khalid marched forward the Ansars stayed behind. After some time on second thought, the Ansars also decided to accompany Khalid. They accordingly rejoined the main Muslim army at the next stage of their march.

Murder of Malik bin Nuweira. The orders of Hadrat Abu Bakr were that if any tribe professed faith in Islam, no action should be taken against it. If a tribe did not profess faith in Islam, it was to be invited to repent and be reconverted to Islam. Operations were to be undertaken against a tribe only in the event of its refusal. It was laid down that if on reaching the settlement of a tribe, the Muslim army heard the tribe give Azan it was to be understood that the people of the tribe professed Islam. In the absence of such response it was to be presumed that the people had apostatised. Before the Muslim army reached Bataha, a delegation of Bani Tamim waited on Khalid. They brought with them the amount of the Zakat payable to the Muslims. Khalid took the amount, but continued his advance to Bataha. When the Muslim army reached Bataha, there were no forces of the Bani Tamim to oppose the Muslims. The position was confused. Malik bin Nuweira the chief of the Bani Tamim neither came forward to offer his submission, nor did he come forward to oppose the Muslims. On the other hand he went into hiding. That made him the subjuct of suspicion. Khalid directed his soldiers to forage in the neighbourhood. As a result of such operations, Malik and his wife Laila were taken captive and brought before Khalid. Malik's wife Laila was known far and near for her breath taking beauty. Her long glossy hair flowed upto her knees. She had gorgeous legs, and she carried herself with peculiar grace and charm. What exactly transpired when

Malik and his wife presented before Khalid is not known. According to one account after his talk with Malik, Khalid was satisfied that Malik had repudiated Islam. According to another account, Malik is reported to have said that his wife was his undoing, and that after Khalid had seen her, his death was certain. The prisoners retired for the night. At the dead of night, Malik and his male companions were killed. Here again the accounts differ. According to one account, Khalid had merely ordered that the night being cold, the prisoners should be kept warm, and this order was misunderstood to be an order for murder. The other account is that Khalid in fact ordered the murder of Malik as he had apostatised.

After the Bataha Episode. After the death of Malik, the entire tribe of Bani Tamim surrendered and professed faith in Islam. Khalid immediately married Laila the beautiful widow of Malik b. Nuweira. The campaign against the Bani Tamim was a master stroke from the political point of view. It brought the entire tribe to the fold of Islam. From the military point of view the significance of the action at Bataha was that the rear of Sajjah the false prophetess was cut off and she could no longer count on the support of Bani Tamim. The episode, however, led to considerable scandal. In some quarters it was held that Malik was indeed a Muslim, and that he had been murdered merely because Khalid coveted his beautiful wife. Some of the Ansars in the army of Khalid led by Abu Qatadah refused to fight under the command of Khalid. Abu Qatadah along with Mutamim the brother of Malik set out for Madina to lodge a complaint against Khalid before the Caliph. Mutamim was a distinguished poet, and he composed an elegy mourning the death of his brother, and condemning Khalid as his murderer. These verses became popular in Madina and those who listened to them grieved at the murder of Malik.

Trial of Khalid. Khalid was summoned to Madina and put to explanation. There were two charges against Khalid, firstly, the murdering of a Muslim; and secondly marrying his wife. Khalid's expalantion was that if according to the Holy Prophet he was the "Sword of God" such sword could not fall on the neck of a Muslim. Hadrat Umar was of the view that Khalid was to be blamed, and he should be suitably punished. Hadrat Abu Bakr felt that a military commander, Khalid was indispensable. His view was that even if it was held that Khalid was guilty of a lapse, such lapse could be passed over in the broader interests of Islam. Musailma in the Yamama valley was posing a great threat to the Muslims. Two Muslim Generals sent against Musailma had suffered defeat. The position was critical, and at that stage a General of the calibre of Khalid alone could vindicate the honour of Islam. Hadrat Abu Bakr decided to overlook the lapse of Khalid, and directed him to undertake operations against Musailma. As there were doubts whether Malik was or was not a Muslim, Hadrat Abu Bakr decided that blood money should be paid out of the Baitul Mal to the heirs of Malik for his murder.

Hadrat Umar did not feel happy at this decision of Hadrat Abu Bakr. When Hadrat Umar remonstrated, Hadrat Abu Bakr observed:

> "Umar, I cannot sheathe the sword, which God has intended to be wielded against the non-Muslims."

Campaign Against Musailma

Musailma. Of all the imposters and false prophets who rose in Arabia after the death of the Holy Prophet, the most notorious and dangerous was Musailma who belonged to the Banu Hanifa tribe of Central Arabia. Musailma visited Madina during the lifetime of the Holy Prophet, and enjoyed the privilege of his company for some time. On return from Madina, Musailma, however, laid claim to a divine mission and founded a new creed. He relieved his followers from the obligations of fasting, and Zakat. He reduced the number of daily prayers. He legalised adultery and drinking. He forbade his followers to cohabit with their wives, once they had become mothers. In imitation of the Holy Qur'an he recited rythmical sentences and bits of doggeral which he had himself composed, but gave out as having been revealed by God. He was endowed with a superb physique, and an attractive personality. He was a good speaker, and could sway the masses. He exploited these qualities and succeeded in winning over a considerable following. When asked by the Holy Prophet to abandon his pretensions, Musailma sent an impudent letter demanding the division of the Arabian peninsula into two halves, one part to be earmarked for the Muslims, and the other to be the exclusive reserve for Musailma and his followers. The Holy Prophet addressed him as Musailma, the Liar, and said that all land belonged to God, and He gave its control to such person as He willed. The Holy Prophet deputed Nahr-ar-Rajjal a Muslim convert from the tribe of Banu Hanifa to go back to his people and propagate Islam. On return to his tribe, Nahr-ar-Rajjal fell a victim to the blandishments of Musalima. He declared falsely that he was witness to the fact that the Holy Prophet had acknowledged Musailma as co-sharer in the divine mission. That established the credentials of Musailma, and the number of his followers increased considerably.

Campaigns against Musailma. With the death of the Holy Prophet, Musailma gained in strength further. The general argument which prevailed with the people was that Muhammad (peace be on him) was dead while Musailma was alive, a living prophet was to be preferred to a dead prophet. Many tribes who were hostile to Islam joined his ranks. Hadrat Abu Bakr originally entrusted the operations against Musailma to 'Ikramah son of Abu Jahl. Shurahbil bin Hasnah was to advance with another column to the assistance of 'Ikramah. Hadrat Abu Bakr issued strict orders that action against Musailma was to be taken only when the two columns joined together. 'Ikramah was the first to reach the Yamama valley where Musailma was lodged. Without waiting for Shurahbil, 'Ikramah launched an attack against Musailma. The Muslims were beaten back with considerable losses. When the news of the defeat reached Madina, Hadrat Abu Bakr felt much distressed. He asked 'Ikramah not to return to Madina, but to proceed to fight in South Arabia.

Some time later, Shurahbil arrived in the yamama valley with his column. He also opened an attack against Musailma without waiting for help. He was also beaten with considerable loss. Two successive defeats created an embarrassing situation for the Muslims. That raised the morale of the followers of Musailma who proudly declared that Musailma was indeed a prophet and divine help was on their side.

Commission of Khalid bin Walid. It was at this critical juncture that Hadrat Abu Bakr commissioned Khalid bin Walid to undertake operations against Musailma. Elaborate arrangements were made to reinforce the army of Khalid. Seasoned soldiers were included in the force under his command. Bar'a bin Malik and Thabit bin Qais led the contingents of the Ansar, while Abu Khadhifa bin Utba and Zaid bin Khattab led the contingent of the Muhajreen. Against his declared policy, Hadrat Abu Bakr permitted the veterans of Badr to join the forces of Khalid. Among others, those who joined the force included: Abdur Rahman son of Hadrat Abu Bakr; Abdullah son of Hadrat Umar; Abu Dujana the renowned warrior of Uhud; and Mauwiyiah who later founded the Umayyad rule.

From Madina the Muslim army proceeded to Butaha. Here contingents from the Muslim tribes joined the force. From there the Muslim army marched south to Yamama valley under the command of Khalid bin Walid. In the way the Muslim army came across some men of Banu Hanifa led by Maja'a bin Murrah. All of them except Maja'a were put to death under the orders of Khalid. Maja'a was kept in custody to serve as a hostage. He was put in chains, and entrusted to the custody of Laila, the new wife of Khalid who accompanied him to the battlefield.

The battle of Aqraba. The advance of the Muslim army was intercepted by Musailma at the plain of Aqraba. Here the two opposing armies arranged their ranks for the battle. The battle that followed was hotly contested. The forces of Musailma numbered over forty thousand, while the strength of the Muslim army did not exceed fifteen thousand. Besides being outnumbered the Muslim forces suffered from certain disabilties. There were differences between the tribes, the Ansar and the Muhajreen. A dust storm blew across the valley against the faces of the Muslims. Taking advantage of this the forces of Musailma increased their pressure, and the Muslims had to fall back. Some men of the Banu Hanifa even reached the tent of Khalid where Maja'a was in chains guarded by Laila. These men wanted to kill Laila, and rescue Maja'a. Maja'a called upon them to desist from raising their hands against a woman. He wanted them to go and kill some men. These men left the camp, and said that they would return after some time to rescue Maja'a. In the confusion that followed the party could not come back, and in the meantime the Muslims were able to take precautionary measures.

When the battle for the first day ended there was jubilation in the camp of Musailma. Though Khalid had been forced to withdraw he refused to admit defeat. He regrouped his army in tribal commands and exhorted the various tribes to show their valour on the battlefield. From within the Makkah and Madinite horsemen he created a reserve force of a thousand cavalrymen and kept them under his personal command.

When the battle began on the next day, the forces of Musailma elated by the pride of victory on the first day made the bid to push forward. Bara'a was the commander of one of the Muslim wings. He was a brother of Anas, the personal attendant of the Holy Prophet. There was a strange peculiarity of Bara'a. Whenever he would go to fight his whole body would shake necessitating others to hold him. After some time his body would stop shaking, and he would feel electrified. He would then rush forward against the enemy and fight like a lion. At the battle of Aqraba he had his fit of shivering, and thereafter he plunged into the thick of the battle crying "O Muslims where do you go ? Here am I, Bara'a bin Malik; come to me." Bara'a and his men made a determined charge. Abdur Rahman the son of Hadrat Abu Bakr shot an arrow from his bow which killed Muhkam bin Tufail who commanded the forces of Musailma. At this stage the two armies faced each other in a headlong combat. As the forces of Musailma were larger in number such state of affairs was advantageous to them. While the front ranks of the two armies grappled with each other in hand to hand fight, Khalid collected his cavalry reserves and carrying out a wide outflanking movement dashed for the mounds where the camp of Musailma was located. The boldness of the move of Khalid took Banu Hanifa completely by surprise. The body guard of Musailma fought valiantly, but they could not hold ground for long. As Khalid increased his pressure, Musailma lost his nerves, and retreated to a neighbouring fortified garden.

Battle of the Garden. With the withdrawal of Musailma his army lost the will to fight, and they too found safety in seeking refuge in the garden. The garden was surrounded by a huge wall, and the fugitives closed the gate thus shutting access to the pursuing Muslims. Bara'a bin Malik asked his companions to lift him to the top of the garden wall and from there he jumped into the garden. Some other Muslims did likewise. Thus, hazarding their lives, this group of Muslims rushed to the gate and opened it. With the opening of the gate, the Muslim army rushed into the garden, and let lose a reign of slaughter on the Banu Hanifa. The Banu Hanifa fought desperately for sheer survival, but theirs was a losing battle. All advantages now lay with the Muslims. The men of Banu Hanifa were cut to pieces in large numbers, and the garden was virtually drenched with blood. So bloody was the battle of the garden, that in the Arab annals it came to be known as the "Battle of the Garden of Death".

In the Muslim ranks there were some women as well. One of them was Umm 'Ammarah. She had fought in the battle of Uhud, and when wave after wave of the enemy rushed to attack the Holy Prophet she shielded him in which task she received no less than a dozen wounds. After the death of the Holy Prophet her son Habib while returning from Uman fell into the hands of Musailma, the Liar. Habib was required to disown the Holy Prophet of Islam, and offer allegiance to the false prophet Musailma. Habib refused, and for his faith in Islam he was put to death. Umm 'Ammarah thereupon vowed vengeance against Musailma. When Hadrat Abu Bakr ordered operations against Musailma, Umm 'Ammarah accompanied the Muslim force fired with the urge to take revenge. In the "Garden of Death" penetrating through the ranks of the enemy she reached close to Musailma. At that time Wahshi an Abyssinian fighting in the Muslim ranks threw in a javelin at Musailma. At the battle of Uhud Wahshi had fought on the side of the Quraish against the Muslims, and he had killed

Hamza an uncle of the Holy Prophet with his javelin. Later he became a Muslim and he fought in the various battles during the caliphate of Hadrat Abu Bakr. When Wahshi threw his javelin, Abdullah another son of Umm 'Ammarah who was with her in the battle rushed forward and fell on Musailma with his sword. Musailma fell dead, and his severed head was hoisted for all to see. Thereupon the Banu Hanifa formally surrendered. With such surrender the valley of Yamama which had so long defied Islam lay prostrate at the feet of the Muslims.

Treaty of Yamama

Consequences of the Yamama. The battle of Yamama was the bloodiest battle so far fought by the Muslims. It was a decisive battle which established the supremacy of Islam in Central Arabia. It proved to be a great trial of strength, and though the Muslims won the victory, this was achieved at a heavy cost. The casualties of Banu Hanifa were staggering. As many as 7,000 followers of Musailma died in the battle of Aqraba, and equal number fell in the Garden of Death. Twelve hundred Muslims met their martyrdom in this action, and although the number was very much less than the number of the dead of Banu Hanifa, the loss was nevertheless colossal. Almost every family in Makkah and Madina sufferred the loss of some dear one. Most of the Muslims who had memorised the Holy Qur'an died in this battle, and their loss was most acute. Among the martyrs were Abu Hudhaifa, Zaid bin Khattab, Abu Dujana, Yazid bin Aus, Yazid bin Thabit; Abu Hababa bin Ghazia: Zarara bin Qais; Saib bin Awwam; Salma bin Masud, and many other distinguished persons from among the Ansars and the Muhajreen.

Release of Maja'a. All the important leaders of the Banu Hanifa were killed, and there was no leader to negotiate terms of surrender. Maja'a who had won the confidence of Khalid by saving the wife of Khalid, Laila, undertook to make negotiations with the Banu Hanifa. Maja'a was released on parole, and he went to negotiate terms with the Banu Hanifa. He returned to say that the major portion of the army was still in the fort of Yamama, and that they were poised for another action. Khalid decided that he would himself go to the city to assess the situation Maja'a sent a secret message to the Banu Hanifa that all women, old men and children should mount the battlements and display their arms. When Khalid went to the city he saw that the battlements were crowded. That set Khalid thinking. After the disastrous war of Aqraba, the Muslim forces though victorious, were too exhausted to risk another action. Khalid was under the circumstances keen to avoid another war. Maja'a played upon the feelings of Khalid and said that if lenient terms were offered he might be able to arrive at some settlement with the Banu Hanifa. Khalid allowed him to go to his people again. Maja'a returned to say that if the Muslims were to be content with taking only one fourth of the property of the Banu Hanifa, peace could be negotiated. Khalid agreed and the peace treaty was signed whereunder the Banu Hanifa were to surrender one fourth of their property.

Khalid s marriage with Bint Maja'a. After the treaty, Maja'a was allowed freedom and he returned to his people. The gates of the city were thereafter thrown open. When Khalid rode into the city, the Banu Hanifa army was no where to be seen. "Where are your warriors" asked Khalid of Maja'a and Maja'a pointing to the women and children said, "These women and children were the warriors. I had them dressed as warriors, and made them parade on the battlements." Khalid turned furiously to Maja'a and said, "This means that you deceived me". Maja'a merely shrugged his shoulders and said, "You may kill me, if you like, but I had to resort to this ruse to save my people". Khalid felt very bitter, but as he had given his promise to the people of Banu Hanifa, he was not in favour of withdrawing from the terms of the treaty. Khalid had heard of the beauty of the daughter of Maja'a, and he asked Maja'a to marry his daughter to him in case he wanted to escape his wrath. Maja'a said, "I am at your disposal, but you know what happened when you married Laila. The Caliph did not approve of that marriage, and he will not approve of your marrige with my daughter".

Khalid retorted, "You need not bother about the approval of the Caliph. I wed.your daughter to-night. You may go and make your arrangements accordingly". That night Khalid married the beautiful daughter of Maja'a. Laila merely sulked in her tent.

Hadrat Abu Bakr's reactions. As the Muslims had suffered heavily at the hands of Banu Hanifa, Hadrat Abu Bakr sent instructions to Khalid that no mercy should be shown to the Banu Hanifa and all the male adults should be killed. Before these instructions reached Khalid, he had given these people general amnesty and they had accepted Islam. Under the circumstances the instructions of Hadrat Abu Bakr could not be complied with. Khalid sent a delegation of the people of Abu Hanifa along with the booty to Madina. The delegates expressed regrets and said that they had been deceived by Musailma. They assured Hadrat Abu Bakr that they were sincere in their profession of Islam. Hadrat Abu Bakr treated them with due courtesy and let things rest at that. He was, however, very bitter at Khalid's marriage with Bint Maja'a. He addressed the following letter to Khalid:

> "O son of the mother of Khalid. What has gone wrong with you? You are out to wed women when the land around your camp is still drenched with blood of over a thousand martyrs".

Apart from this mild censure, Hadrat Abu Bakr chose to take no further action against the Victor of Aqraba.

NOTES

In this Chapter an account is given of campaigns against Bani Tamim and the false prophet Musailma of Banu Hanifa. An account is given of the false prophetess Sajjah.

The false prophetess Sajjah emerges from Iraq makes common cause with Malik b. Nuweira of Bani Tamim, joins Musailma, becomes his wife and then returns to Iraq. In later life she accepts Islam. Sajjah is a mysterious character. We do not have much particulars about her life. It appears she was an adventuress, and possessed some attributes of leader-ship.

In the campaign against Bani Tamim, there is not much of fighting and the Muslim victory is a walk over. This campaign carries interest because of the murder of the Banu Tamim's chief Malik b. Nuweira, and Khalid b. Walid marrying his beautiful wife Laila. Khalid was accused of murdering a Muslim. Hadrat Umar advocated strong action against Khalid, but Hadrat Abu Bakr took a leninent view, saying that he could not sheathe the sword God wanted to be wielded against the non-Muslims.

In Central Arabia the most serious confrontation of the Muslims was against Musailma, the false prophet. The battle was the bloodiest of all the wars so far waged in Arabia. The Muslims won a victory. Musailma and thousands of his followers died in the battle. The Muslims suffered the loss of many companions. The romantic side of the campaign is that here again Khalid married the daughter of a Banu Hanifa chief. This shows that though Khalid was a great General, women were his weakness. Verily every great man has his eccentricities. With the death of Musailma and the surrender of Banu Hanifa, the apostasy campaigns in Central Arabia ended successfully, and this part of Arabia came to be unified under Islam.

In writing this chapter I have derived help from the following books:

(1) *Abu Bakr* by Muhammad Hussain Haykal.
(2) *Abu Bakr, the Caliph* by A. A. Aziz.
(3) *Hadrat Abu Bakr* by Syed Moin-ul-Haq.
(4) *Ar Riddah and the Muslim Conquest of Arabia* by Elias Shoufani.
(5) *The Sword of Islam* by A. I. lkram.

11

APOSTASY CAMPAIGNS IN EAST AND SOUTH ARABIA

Campaign in Bahrain

Bahrain. After the fall of Musailma and the overthrow of the Banu Hanifa, Hadrat Abu Bakr decided that a campaign should be undertaken against the people of Bahrain who had supported Musailma in the fight against the Muslims. Bahrain comprised the coastal strip to the west of the Persian Gulf. During the life time of the Holy Prophet. Mundhir bin Sawa was the ruler of Bahrain. The Holy Prophet sent a mission to Bahrain, and invited Mundhir to Islam. Mundhir accepted the call and was converted to Islam. Mundhir continued to be the ruler of Bahrain under the suzerainty of Madina. Under the influence of Mundhir most of the people of Bahrain accepted Islam. He deputed Jarud bin Mualia a scholar of Bahrain to study Islam at Madina. Jarud returned to his people after some time, and made dedicated efforts to promote Islam with his people. The Holy Prophet appointed Al-'Ala bin Al-Hadrami as the Resident at the court of Bahrain.

After the death of the Holy Prophet. Mundhir died soon after the death of the Holy Prophet. His death led to anarchy and chaos, and like the people of the other regions in Arabia, most of the people of Bahrain also apostatised. Jarud remained steadfast in his faith in Islam. His tribe, however, wavered in their allegiance to Islam. The argument of his tribe Abdul Qais was that if Muhammad (peace be on him) had been a Prophet, he would not have died. Jarud asked, "There were prophets before Muhammad (peace be on him); where have they gone?" They said that they had died. Thereupon Jarud said, "As other prophets before him died, so Muhammad (peace be on him) has also died. If the deaths of the other prophets could not affect their prophethood, how can the death of Muhammad (peace be on him) affect his prophethood? I testify that there is no god but Allah and that Muhammad (peace be on him) whether dead or alive is His messenger". The argument of Jarud carried weight with his tribe, and they continued their allegiance to Islam. The other people of Bahrain repudiated their allegiance to Islam, and revolted under the leadership of Al-Hotam b. Dubayah. The rebels captured power and installed al- Gharur a Lakhmid prince as their ruler. Al-Gharur was a descendant of the Arab kings of Hirah, and was a bitter enemy of Islam. He was crowned as the king of Bahrain and he took the pledge to fight against Islam. He brought pressure on Jarud and his people to denounce Islam. But they remained steadfast in their faith. Thereupon the Bahrain forces led an attack against the Muslims. The Muslims of the Banu Abdul Qais shut themselves in the fort of Jarasi, and the non-Muslims pressed the siege with considerable vehemence.

Action in Bahrain. Al-Hadrami returned to Madina to seek help and Hadrat Abu Bakr sent a force under the command of Al-Hadrami to the relief of the besieged Muslims. In the meantime the battle of Yamama was over, and the Banu Hanifa had been won over to Islam. Many men of Banu Hanifa joined the ranks of Al-Hadrami, as his forces passed through the Yamama valley on their way to Bahrain. In the meantime the non-Muslims of Bahrain received considerable help from the Persians, and they were fully prepared for a confrontation with the Muslims. Al-Hadrami called upon the Bahrain authorities to offer submission. They ridiculed the offer and declared that the issue would be decided by the sword. The Bahrain forces were sufficiently strong, and that made Al-Hadrami halt. He sent words to the besieged Muslims at Jarasi to persevere for he was coming to their relief. He had a ditch dug round his camp, and the Muslims waited for a suitable opportunity to overpower the enemy. This state of stalemate lasted for a month, and that made the Bahrain forces feel that the Muslims were no match for them. One night the Muslims heard a lot of noise from the non-Muslim camp. It was reported to Al-Hadrami that the non-Muslims were celebrating their national festival, were dead drunk and were giving themselves to fun and frolic. Al-Hadrami decided to avail of this opportunity. He ordered his troops to take up arms, cross the ditch and pounce upon the enemy. The surprise attack unnerved the Bahrain forces. They ran helter skelter in all directions and were cut to pieces by the pursuing Muslim forces. Hotam the Commander of the Bahrain forces was killed, while Prince Gharur was captured alive. Over 10,000 non-Muslims died in the action. The Bahrain forces laid down arms and surrendered. Jarud and his Muslim forces came and joined the victorious Muslim army. The people of Bahrain were admitted to the fold of Islam. Those who refused to accept Islam escaped to the island of Darim in the Persian Gulf.

The battle of Darim. Al-Hadrami re-organised the administration and appointed his agents in various parts of Bahrain. After settling the affairs in Bahrain proper, Al-Hadrami decided to take action against the persons who had taken refuge in the island of Darim. There is a report that on the approach of the Muslim army the water in the channel dried, and they crossed it as if it were a shallow beach. This was interpreted as a sign from the Heaven that God favoured the Muslims. Brought to bay the fugitives on the island capitulated and were admitted to the fold of Islam.

Consequences of the battle of Bahrain. The victory of the Muslims in Bahrain was significant in more than one way. Bahrain was at considerable distance from Madina, and the victory at Bahrain showed that the Muslim military arm was sufficiently long and powerful, and could reach far. The assistance that the Persians gave to the people of Bahrain was originally a cause of great concern to the Muslims, but in the long run this worked to the advantage of the Muslims. The Muslims had originally intended to confine their operations to Arabia proper, but the alliance of the people of Bahrain with the Persians provided the Muslims an opportunity for settling accounts with the Persians. The Banu Hanifa who had been at one time the greatest opponents of Islam now became the ardent supporters of the faith. Muthanna a chief of the Banu Hanifa organised a flying column, and undertook to protect the barriers against the Persians. The battle of Bahrain thus proved a prelude to the war with Persia. But for the interference of the Persians in the affairs of Bahrain, the Muslims might not have advanced in Persia, and history would have taken a different course.

Campaigns in Uman and Mahrab

Jayfar bin Al Julanda. During the lifetime of the Holy Prophet, Uman bordering on the Persian Gulf was under Persian influence. It was ruled by Jayfar bin Al-Julanda who owed allegiance to Persia. When the Holy Prophet sent letters inviting the various rulers to Islam, a letter was addressed to Jayfar as well. As the Persian power was on the decline, Jayfar stood in need of some outside support to bolster up his rule. He responded favourably to the invitation of the Holy Prophet. He said that he was inclined to accept Islam, but the difficulty was that his people were not likely to agree to the payment of Zakat to Madina. The Holy Prophet assured him that if he and his people became Muslims, the amount realised from Zakat could be distributed among the poor and the destitute in Uman itself. Thereupon Jayfar became a Muslim, and under his influence most of his people were also converted to Islam. The Holy Prophet appointed Amr bin Al-Aas as the Muslim Resident in Uman.

Laquit bin Malik. After the death of the Holy Prophet, like other parts of Arabia Uman also fell a prey to chaos and anarchy. A false prophet Laquit bin Malik came into prominence. He belonged to the Azdi tribe, which was very numerous. The Azdi felt elated at having a prophet of their own. They apostatised from Islam, and accepted the new creed. Laquit exempted his followers from the disciplines of fasting, prayers, and Zakat. He sanctioned adultery as well as the use of wine. He claimed that he was the recipient of divine revelations. Jayfar remained faithful to Islam, but he lost his hold on the people of Uman most of whom accepted the new creed. Laquit gained in strength, overthrew Jayfar and captured political power. Jayfar and the few people who remained true to Islam had to seek refuge in the hill. Laquit declared himself as the king of Uman. He assumed the title of "Zul Taj"—the crowned head. He established his capital at Daba.

Muslim campaign against Uman and Mahrah. With the change in the affairs of Uman, the Muslim Resident Amr b. Al-Aas left Uman for Madina. Back in Madina, Amr gave a detailed report of the developments in Uman to the Caliph. Hadrat Abu Bakr despatched a force under Hudhaifah b. Muhsan to undertake operations in Uman. The wave of apostasy overwhelmed the neighbouring state of Mahrah as well. The Caliph sent another force under the command of 'Urfajah to operate in Mahrah. Both the forces under Hudhaifah and 'Urfajah were required to collaborate. The operations were required to be commenced from Uman. The instructions of Hadrat Abu Bakr were that if there was a battle in Uman, Hudaifah was to lead the combined forces, and if the operations were undertaken in Mahrah, 'Urfajah was to hold the command. When 'Ikramah met a reverse at Yamama, he was required not to return to Madina, but to proceed with his men to Uman and Mahrah. All the three forces of Hudhaifah, 'Urfajah and 'Ikramah were directed to act in concert.

Battle of Daba. 'Ikramah and his force reached Uman first. He was soon joined by the force of Hudhaifah. Word was then sent to Jayfar and his followers to descend from the hills and join the Muslim forces. After descending from the hills, the forces of Jayfar joined the relief forces from Madina at Sa'a. The combined forces thereafter marched to Daba. The battle between the forces of Laquit and the Muslims took place in the plain outside Daba. Laquit had a large force at his command and the Muslims were outnumbered. It was a hotly contested battle, and to start with, the forces of Laquit appeared to dominate the field. At the nick of time when the Muslim ranks were likely to disintegrate under the pressure of the forces of Laquit, the Muslims received unexpected reinforcement in the shape of contingents from Bahrain and the tribe of Abdul Qais. That turned the tide of the battle. The

Muslims charged with great vehemence, and the forces of Laquit were unable to stand the charge. They found safety in retreat. As the enemy fled, the Muslims pursued them, and overtaking them cut them to pieces. As many as ten thousand followers of Laquit fell on the battlefield. Laquit himself was killed, and with his death all resistance broke down, and the forces of Uman laid down the arms. As a result of the battle of Daba, Jayfar was restored as the ruler of Uman, and the apostates were re-admitted to the fold of Islam.

The campaign in Mahrah. After order was restored in Uman, and the Muslim rule was re-established, 'Ikramah crossed over with his force to attend to the affairs of Mahrah. Like the people of other parts of Arabia the people of Mahrah also apostatised after the death of the Holy Prophet. The people of Mahrah came to be divided into two sections. One section which was the majority section was led by Shikrit, while the other party which was in minority was led by Al-Musabbah. Taking stock of the affairs in Mahrah, 'Ikramah felt that instead of fighting against the people of Mahrah as a whole, it would be expedient to take advantage of the rift between the two sections. 'Ikramah accordingly opened negotiations with the minority party led by Shikrit. The negotiations succeeded. Shikrit and his men were converted to Islam, and 'Ikramah offered them full support to capture political power and overthrow their rival section. The majority section was asked by 'Ikramah to return to Islam but they ridiculed the offer. The combined forces of Shikrit and 'Ikramah accordingly marched to give battle to the people of Al-Musabbah. In the battle that followed the fighting was severer than the fighting at the battle of Daba. It was a hotly contested battle, and the apostates fought with a spirit of venegeance. The chances of victory were balanced but ultimately the faith and determination of the Muslims carried the day, and the forces of Al-Musabbah found safety in capitulation. Immense booty fell into the hands of the victor Muslims, including two thousand dromedaries and a large supply of arms. The defeated people accepted Islam, and they were granted amnesty. 'Urfajah carried the booty to Madina while 'Ikramah stayed in Mahrah to re-organise the administration. When order was fully restored, 'Ikramah was asked by Hadrat Abu Bakr to proceed to Yemen.

Campaign in Yemen

Khusro Parwez. During the time of the Holy Prophet of Islam, Yemen was under the suzerainty of Persia, and a Persian noble Badhan was the Governor. In 628 C.E. the Holy Prophet sent, despatches to the various contemporary rulers inviting them to embrace Islam. Among others the invitation was sent to Khusro Parwez as well, the 'Kisra' of Iran. When Khusro Parwez got the letter, he was infuriated. He tore the letter to pieces and instructed Badhan to send some agents to Madina to summon the Holy Prophet to his court.

Badhan complied with these orders, and sent some agents to Madina. These agents tried to prevail upon the Holy Prophet that it would be in his interest if he accompanied them to the court of the Kisra. The Holy Prophet suppressed his rage at the insolent message, and asked the agents of Badhan to see him the following day.

When the men from Yemen waited on the Holy Prophet the next day, he said:

> "The Kisra who had the audacity to summon me in his court has been summoned to the court of my Allah, and his abode is in hell. He has been murdered by his son. Go, tell your masters that the prophets of God do not attend the courts of temporal sovereigns. And tell Badhan that his interest in this world as well as in the world hereafter lies in accepting Islam. If he accepts Islam, he can continue to be ruler of Yemen on behalf of the Muslims".

Badhan. When the message of the Holy Prophet was communicated to Badhan in Yemen that set him thinking. These were no ordinary words, and obviously the man who had sent the message could not be an ordinary person. In the meantime news was received from Iran that Khusro Parwez had in fact been murdered and his son had ascended the throne. The new rular of Iran also sent a command to Badhan not to interfere in any way with the affairs of the Arabian Prophet, and that the order of his father summoning the prophet of Islam to the court of Kisra was not to be enforced. At this turn of events, Badhan was much impressed. He became a Muslim, and many people of Yemen accepted Islam likewise. Yemen threw off its allegiance to Persia. Badhan continued to be the ruler of Yemen on behalf of the Muslims. The Holy Prophet appointed a Resident at the court of Yemen.

Aswad 'Ansi. A year later, Badhan died and was succeeded by his son Shahr. At this stage a false prophet rose in Yemen. He was one Aswad 'Ansi, an ugly man who kept his face veiled to hide his ugliness and was nicknamed, "The Veiled Prophet". By dubious methods, Aswad 'Ansi succeeded in winning a considerable number of followers. Within a short time, he became powerful enough to challenge Shahr who remained faithful to Islam. In the confrontation that followed, Shahr was defeated and killed, and power was captured by Aswad 'Ansi. Aswad 'Ansi now crowned himself as the king of Yemen, and repudiated allegiance to Madina. He forcefully married the beautiful widow of Shahr, Azad by name. Feroz a Minister under Shahr became a Minister under Aswad 'Ansi although he remained a Muslim. Qais bin Abu Yaghus the commander-in-chief of the forces of Shahr became the commander-in-chief of the forces of Aswad 'Ansi. Aswad 'Ansi was a man of suspicious nature. He felt that in order to strengthen his position he must overthrow Feroz and Qais. Feroz and Qais soon fell out with Aswad 'Ansi. Azad bitterly hated Aswad 'Ansi. In conspiracy spearheaded by Qais, Feroz and Azad, Aswad 'Ansi was assassinated. Feroz who still professed Islam became the ruler of Yemen. He however, could not pull on with Qais for long. Feroz was of Persian descent while Qais belonged to the Arab tribe, of Bani Hamir. Qais made common with some other Arab tribes, and thought of capturing power. Feroze was no match for the combined strength of the Arab tribes. Lacking strength, Feroz fled to the hills. Thereupon Qais captured political power and became the ruler of Yemen.

Campaign in Yemen. On being ousted from power,

Feroz who remained true to Islam sought help from Hadrat Abu Bakr. Qais apostatised from Islam, and won the cooperation of all those who had previously supported Aswad 'Ansi. Some tribes in Yemen, however, remained firm in their faith in Islam, and they rallied round Feroz. With the aid of these tribes, Feroz sallied down from the hills and advanced against Sana'a the capital of Yemen. There was a confrontation in the plain outside Sana'a. In this confrontation, the forces of Qais were defeated, and he found safety in flight. Feroz once again became the ruler of Yemen. The restoration of Feroz did not bring peace to Yemen. Qais though defeated continued to be a source of trouble. He approached the Arab tribes and tried to win them to his cause in opposition to Feroz. Qais succeeded in winning Umr bin Maadi Kurb to his side. Umr was a poet and a firebrand fighter and his alliance with Qais made the position of Feroz difficult.

Feroz appealed to Hadrat Abu Bakr for help. Hadrat Abu Bakr ordered a two pronged advance on Yemen. Muhajir b. Umayya was directed to march from Makkah to Yemen. 'Ikramah bin Abu Jahal was directed to march from Mahrah to Yemen. 'Ikramah entered Yemen and camped at Abyan. Muhajir with his force advanced from Makkah and Taif. At the border of Yemen the advance of the force to Muhajir was intercepted by a tribe allied with Qais. The Muslims charged with great fury, and in the battle that ensued practically the whole of the tribe was exterminated. This victory of the Muslims unnerved the apostates. Instead of making common cause to give another battle to the Muslims, Qais and Umr fell out with each other. One day Umr surprised Qais and after taking him captive presented him before Muhajir. Umr had hoped that thereby he would win the favour of Muhajir. Muhajir, however, arrested Umr as well for his past misconduct. With the elimination of the two leaders, the apostate tribes had no will to fight. They laid down arms, and those who accepted Islam were granted amnesty, the rest were killed. That brought peace to Yemen. Qais and Umr were both sent in chains to Madina and there they were presented before Hadrat Abu Bakr. At Madina, both Qais and Umr repented and were re-admitted to the fold of Islam.

Campaign in Hadramaut

The revolt of the Kinda. Early in 633 C.E. the Kinda in Hadramaut broke into revolt. The people of the Kinda tribe did not apostatise, but something went wrong with the way they were handled. The Muslim Governor of Hadramaut was Ziyad bin Lubeid, and his headquarter was at Zafar. On of the Kinda chiefs offered a camel as Zakat. Later he found that the animal which he had offered in Zakat belonged to his brother. He approached the Governor with the request that the animal which he had offered in Zakat should be returned to him, and he would offer another camel in its stead. Ziyad the Governor rejected the request, and that led to trouble. The chieftain thereupon sent some persons to steal the camel in question. Ziyad had the camel lifters arrested. A riotous assembly of the Kinda people demanded the return of the arrested persons. Ziyad refused, and on such refusal the situation exploded.

Large sections of the Kinda revolted. In protest they apostatised from Islam and refused to pay any taxes. In defiance of the Muslim authority they took up arms. Ziyad sent a column against the rebels. There was a confrontation at Riyad not far from Zafar. Here the apostates were defeated and many were captured. As the captives were being taken to Zafar, they passed through a settlement which belonged to Ash'as bin Qais, a Kinda chief. Ash'as was a typical Arab chief, a man of considerable charm and wit, and of a colourful personality. The captives appealed to Ash'as for his help. They cried "O Ash'as, we are of your clan and we invoke your help". Ash'as by that time had not apostatised, but his tribal loyalty proved stronger than his faith. With his men, Ash'as intercepted the Muslim column, and liberated the captives. When Ziyad took notice of this breach of faith on the part of Ash'as, Asha's revolted and apostatised. The rebel Kinda flocked to the standard of Ash'as, and prepared for battle.

Campaign in Hadramaut. Ziyad wrote to the Caliph Hadrat Abu Bakr for reinforcement. Hadrat Abu Bakr directed Muhajir to march from Yemen to Hadramaut to the relief of the administration in Hadramaut. Muhajir marched with his force to Hadramaut. There was a battle in late January 633

C.E. in which Ash'as was defeated. Though the defeat was not decisive. Ash'as withdrew his army from the battlefield and shut himself in the fort of Nujeir. Here he was joined by other dissident tribes. The Muslims besieged the fort of Nujeir. To strengthen the Muslims, 'Ikramah also marched with a column from Yemen to Hadramaut. The Muslims thereafter pressed the siege, and some time in February 633 C.E., Ash'as opened negotiations with Muhajir and 'Ikramah. Ash'as agreed to surrender if the lives of ten persons and their families were spared. The Muslims accepted the proposal and Ash'as was asked to write the names of the persons for whom he wanted amnesty. Ash'as went to his people, and prepared the document containing the names of the persons who were to be granted amnesty. It was his intention to write the names of other ten persons, and thereafter write his own name as the tenth. He did not notice that one man Jahdam stood over his head reading the names. As Ash'as was going to write his own name as the tenth person, Jahdam drew his dagger saying "Write my name, or I will kill you". Overawed, Ash'as wrote the name of Jahdam as the tenth person, and the list of ten persons having been completed was handed over to Muhajir who had it sealed. In pursuance of the pact, Ash'as laid down arms, and opened the gates of the fort. The Muslim forces thereafter entered the fort. Ash'as had not taken the garrison with him into his confidence. The garrison, therefore, opposed the Muslims. The apostates suffered from terrible slaughter, and the few who were left laid down their arms. All the men were taken captive. The Kindas now realised that Ash'as had betrayed them. As the captive men and women of the Kindas were led past Ash'as they looked at him reproachfully and said "You traitor".

Ash'as bin Qais. When after the fall of the fort of Nujeir the sealed document with Muhajir was opened it was found that the name of Ash'as was not included in the list of ten persons who were to be granted amnesty. Muhajir felt delighted at this and said "O enemy of Allah, your name is not included in the list, and thus prepare yourself for death". 'Ikramah came to the rescue of Ash'as, and at his instance, it was decided that Ash'as should be sent to Madina, where Hadrat Abu Bakr would decide his fate. Ash'as was accordingly put in chains, and taken to Madina along with other captives.

At Madina, Ash'as was presented before Hadrat Abu Bakr. The Caliph reproached him for apostatising from Islam. He also criticised his conduct in betraying his own people. Ash'as bore these reproaches without being ruffled in any way, and then pressing into service all the wit, eloquence, and charm of which he was master, made the Caliph believe that instead of having sinned, he had been sinned against. He tried to create the impression that he had been forced to take the stand that he had taken because the Muslim administration at Zafar had mishandled the affairs and acted tactlessly. He assured the Caliph that he was always a Muslim, and that even when forced to take up arms against the Muslim administration he had remained at heart a Muslim.

Hadrat Abu Bakr felt that Ash'as was a man of great parts and that the prepare course for the administration should have been to win his collaboration rather than drive him to the hostile camp. Hadrat Abu Bakr granted him amnesty. Ash'as won the favour of the Caliph to such an extent that he was married to Umm Farwa a sister of Hadrat Abu Bakr. It is related that in honour of the celebration of his marriage, Ash'as went to the camel market at Madina, and inflicted cuts with his sword on the hamstrings of every animal that came his way. In a few moments dozens of camels were thus disabled. When the owners protested he paid them the price that they demanded. A large crowd gathered, and he asked them to have the animals slaughtered and feast upon the meat to celebrate his marriage to the sister of the caliph. He said that if he had been in his home town he would have celebrated the marriage on a grander scale. Ash'as settled at Madina. In later years of his life he fought with distinction in Syria, Iraq, and Persia. Under Hadrat Usman he was made the Governor of Azarbaijan.

Treachery was, however, in the very blood of Ash'as. One of his daughters married Imam Hassan, and she poisoned her husband at the instance of Amir Muawiyiah. On his death bed Hadrat Abu Bakr gave expression to some of the regrets of his life. One of his regrets was that he should not have pardoned Ash'as, but should have beheaded him.

NOTES

In this Chapter I have given account of the apostasy campaigns in Bahrain, Uman, Mahrah Yemen, Kinda, and Hadramaut. Two false prophets arise in this region, namely Laquit b. Malik in Uman, and Aswad 'Ansi in Yemen. Aswad 'Ansi was killed by his own people before the beginning of the apostasy campaigns. Laquit fell fighting.

The circumstances of this region were somewhat different from those of Central Arabia, the Muslims had to fight against the tribes as a whole. In the coastal region, the "Abna", the nobles of Persian origin remained firm in their faith in Islam; it was only the Arab tribes that revolted. The battles in this region were won more by diplomacy than by resort to the sword. This shows that Hadrat Abu Bakr was not only a skilful General and tactician; he was a great diplomat as well.

In Central Arabia the campaigns were led by Khalid. In the coastal regions the campaigns were led by other commanders.

This shows that while Khalid was unique as a General, the Muslims had many other Generals as well who won victories for Islam.

In writing this Chapter I have obtained help from the following books:

(1) *Abu Bakr* by Muhammad Hussain Haykal.
(2) *Hadrat Abu Bakr* by Syed Moin-ul-Haq.
(3) *Hadrat Abu Bakr the Caliph* by A. A. Aziz.
(4) *Ar Riddah and the Muslim Conquest of Arabia* by Elias Shoufani.

12

CAMPAIGNS IN EASTERN IRAQ

Muthanna's Reconnaissance Campaign in Iraq

Muthanna. Muthanna was a chief of the tribe of Bani Bakr who inhabited the north eastern part of Arabia. In the apostasy campaign in Bahrain, Muthanna and his band fought on the side of the Muslims. Records are silent as to when Muthanna became a Muslim. Presumably he became a Muslim during the lifetime of the Holy Prophet. When the wave of apostasy engulfed the Arabian peninsula, Muthanna remained firm in his faith in Islam.

Conflict with Persia. In the apostasy campaign in Bahrain, the Persians had aided the apostates. After the successful termination of the apostasy campaigns, the stage was set for taking action against the Persians across the borders, from whom trouble could be expected any time for the Muslim state. There was considerable disarray in the affairs of Persia, and the Arab tribes in Persian territory were dissatisfied with the Persian rule. Muthanna felt that his position could be exploited to the advantage of the Muslims, and the Arab tribes could be liberated from the Persian yoke.

Reconnaissance campaigns of Muthanna. With a band of his followers Muthanna began his raids in Iraq. In the first instance he stuck to the periphery of the desert, so that in the case of danger, he could withdraw to the safety of the desert. Most of his raids were conducted in the region of Uballa in the lower valleys of the Tigris and the Euphrates. From these raids, Muthanna was able to collect much booty.

The Persian were unable to take any action against Muthanna because his ghost like riders struck rapidly and then disappeared in to the desert.

Muthanna's visit to Hadrat Abu Bakr. These reconnaissance campaigns which took the form of desultry raids brought home to Muthanna that Iraq was vulnerable, and that if active operations were undertaken there were prospects for success. Early in February 633 C.E., Muthanna went to Madina and saw Hadrat Abu Bakr. He pointed out to the Caliph that the people who inhabited the border areas in Iraq were Arabs who legitimately belonged to Arabia, and that if the Muslims undertook campaigns to liberate such tribes from the irksome yoke of the Persians, that would be a step forward in history towards building a greater Arabia.

Decision of Hadrat Abu Bakr. Hadrat Abu Bakr listened patiently to all that Muthanna had to say. Hadrat Abu Bakr was aware of the prophesies of the Holy Prophet that erelong Islam would spread to Iraq and Syria. Now that the apostasy campaigns had ended in victory for Islam, and the entire Arabia stood unified, Hadrat Abu Bakr felt that if campaigns were undertaken beyond the borders of Arabia that would provide an outlet for the energies of the Muslims. Such campaigns, if successful, were also likely to bring considerable money. It would extend the sphere of the influence of Islam, and it would also lead to more people coming within the fold of Islam. Hadrat Abu Bakr felt convinced that if Islam was to fulfil its destiny, it must necessarily expand. Hadrat Abu Bakr held a council of war, and after due deliberation it was decided that in the name of God a campaign should be launched against Iraq. Muthanna was given the necessary aid and he was required to operate with his column on the Iraq front. He was assured that the main Muslim army under Khalid bin Walid would soon launch the attack against Iraq.

Battle of Kazima

March to Iraq. In March 633 C.E. when Khalid bin Walid was quartered with his army at Yamama, he received orders from Hadrat Abu Bakr that he should march to Iraq and start operations in the region of Uballa where the two rivers, the Tlgris and the Euphrates met. Four other columns each under the command of Muthanna, Mazar, Harmala, and Salma were also directed to proceed to Iraq to reinforce the main Muslim army under the command of Khalid bin Walid.

Hormuz. Uballa was the main port of lraq and was the headquarter of the district then known as "Dasht Meisan". Uballa being a junction of many land routes was the gateway of Iraq and commanded great strategical importance. The Governor of the district was Hormuz, a veteran General and a skilful administrator. In the Persian administrative hierarchy he held 'one lakh dirham' rank, and was entitled to wear a gem studded cap worth one lakh dirhams. He was an imperialist, very haughty and arrogant. He held the Arabs in contempt. His harshness and high handedness became the subject of a saying among the local Arabs "More hateful than Hormuz".

Khalid's letter to Hormuz. As soon as Khalid received orders to march to Iraq, he addressed a letter to Hormuz calling upon him to accept Islam. The letter read:

> "Submit to Islam and be safe. In the alternative you may agree to the payment of 'Jizya', and you and your people will be under our protection. Otherwise you will have only yourself to blame for the consequences for I bring a people who desire death as ardently as you desire life."

Preparations of Hormuz. Hormuz mustered his forces and set out from Uballa to meet the Muslim forces. On the direct route from Uballa to Yamama the first stage was Kazima, and Hormuz decided to give a battle to the Muslims at that place. His idea was that the Muslim forces should be kept away from Uballa. On arrival at Kazima, Hormuz deployed his army with a centre and two wings, the right and the left. His men were linked together with chains, and in this state of affairs the Persians awaited the arrival of the Muslim forces.

Tactics of Khalid. Khalid gave a slip to the Persians, and instead of following the direct route to Uballa via Kazima, he followed the indirect route via Hufeir. Hufeir was much closer to Uballa than Kazima, and when Hormuz came to know that Khalid had already reached Hufeir, he was very much upset. He immediately ordered his forces to march to Hufeir. It was a weary two days march for the Persian forces, but when they reached Hufeir they found that the Muslim forces had left for Kazima. The Persians had no option but to march back to Kazima.

By the time the Persian forces reached Kazima, they were thoroughly exhausted. Khalid allowed them no time to rest. As the Muslim forces were already deployed for battle, the Persians were forced to go into action. The Persian forces were linked in chains, and it was the use of these chains which gave the battle of Kazima, the name of the "Battle of Chains".

Duel between Khalid and Hormuz. The battle started with a duel between the army commanders. Hormuz the Commander of the Persian forces stepped forward and invited Khalid the Commander of the Muslim forces to a duel. Hormuz instructed some of his men to remain close to him, so that when he gave a signal they should fall on Khalid and kill him. Hormuz and Khalid began to fight with swords and shields. Both the Generals were expert swordsmen, and the fight with swords proved to be a drawn battle. Thereupon Hormuz suggested that they should drop the swords and wrestle. When the wrestling match was in full force. Hormuz gave the signal to his men to step forward and kill Khalid. Khalid realised the gravity of the situation. He was without sword and shield, and was obviously at the mercy of the Persian soldiers. Khalid, however, did not lose nerve. He held Hormuz fast in his grip, for as long as he held Hormuz in his grasp the other Persian soldiers could not harm him. In the Muslim ranks, a warrior Qa'qa'a bin Amr saw through the Persian game and decided to take immediate action. He spurred his horse and rushed to the spot where Khalid and Hormuz were wrestling. Before the Persians could realise, Qa'qa'a had killed all the Persians who had treacherously conspired to kill Khalid. Having been freed from the threat of the Persian soldiers, Khalid tightened his grip on Hormuz. Within a few moments, Hormuz lay motionless on the ground. Khalid picked up his sword, and drove it into the body of Hormuz.

Battle of the Chains. After having killed Hormuz, Khalid ordered an immediate attack on the Persian forces. The death of Hormuz had demoralised the Persians, but nevertheless, they fought hard. The Muslims assailed vehemently, but all attacks were withstood by the chain-linked Persian infantry. The Muslims redoubled their attacks, and the Persians were forced to fall back. The Persians found their chains to be a death trap, and as they retreated held together in chains they were slaughtered in thousands. Before night set in, the Muslims had won the battle.

Consequences of the battle of Kazima. In the battle of Kazima which was the first confrontation between the Muslims and the Persians, the Persians so proud of their power met a humiliating defeat. Thousands of Persians were killed, and thousands of them were taken captive. The war booty which fell into the hands of the Muslims comprised wagons, armour, stores, costly garments, horses and a good amount of money. Four-fifth of the booty was distributed among the Muslim soldiers and one-fifth was sent to the Caliph at Madina. So large was the booty that the share of each cavalry man came to a thousand dirhams. The booty included the one lakh dirham cap of Hormuz studded with diamonds and pearls. The Caliph offered this cap as a present to Khalid. The battle of the Chains at Kazima unchained for the Muslims the gate of Iraq. The so-called uncivilised Arabs had defeated the Persians so proud of their civilisation extending over a thousand years.

Battle of Mazar

Occupation of Uballa. After winning the battle of Kazima, Khalid rested his men for a few days and then advanced further inland in Iraq. Khalid sent a contingent under Ma'qal bin Muqarrin to occupy Uballa. There were no Persian forces at Uballa, and the town was occupied without any resistance.

Hisn ul Mar'at. Muthanna with his column rode ahead of the main Muslim army. The task of this column was to reconnoitre and kill the strugglers left behind the retreating Persians.

North of Zubeir stood a fort known as "Hisn ul Mar'at" —the fort of the lady. It was held by a Persian princess Qamarzad who was related to the Persian emperor. Muthanna left a contingent under his brother Mu'anna to lay siege to the fort of the lady and himself proceeded with his column further north Muthanna assaulted the fort and finding the resistance futile Qamarzad surrendered. She was offered to accept Islam or to pay 'Jizya'. She accepted the first alternative and became a Muslim. Thereupon Mu'anna proposed marriage, and she married him.

The Persian force. In the meantime another Persian army assembled at al-Madain. It was placed under the command of a top ranking Persian General, Qarin bin Quryana. Like Hormuz, Qarin was also a 'one lakh dirham' man. The original mission of Qarin was to march with his army to Uballa to reinforce Hormuz.

From al-Madain, the Persian army marched along the left bank of the Tigris. They crossed the Tigris at Mazar, and here they came to know of the defeat of the Persians at Kazima. Qarin camped at Mazar, and soon the remnants of the army of Hormuz who had escaped from Kazima joined the camp. They included the Generals Qubad and Anushjan who had commanded the wings of the army of Hormuz at Kazima.

Qarin was shocked that the imperial army of Persia under such a General as Hormuz should have been defeated by the uncouth Arabs. He resolved that he would avenge the defeat of Kazima and drive the Arabs to the desert.

Khalid's march to Mazar. The advance guard of Muthanna who scoured the countryside came to know of the Persian concentration at Mazar. Muthanna informed Khalid of such concentration. Qarin came to know that some Muslim forces were lurking in the neighbourhood, and his plan was to fall on this Muslim force and destroy it, before it could get help from the main Muslim army. Khalid realized the danger which beset the column of Muthanna. Khalid was keen that he should destroy the Persian force under Qarin while the impact of the defeat at Kazima was still fresh in the Persian mind. By forced marches, Khalid reached Mazar in the third week of April 633 C.E. before Qarin could take any action against the column of Muthanna.

Battle of Mazar. Qarin concluded that one of the causes of the defeat of the Persians at Kazima had been that the Muslims had been able to carry flanking manoeuvres which had made the Persians lose their nerve. In order to avoid such a situation at Mazar, Qarin deployed his forces with the main river in the rear so that there may be no possibility of outflanking them.

As Khalid surveyed the situation, he felt that at Mazar, he would have to fight a frontal set piece battle. This was the usual Persian style, and in this respect the advantage lay with the Persians. Khalid, however, hoped that with the blessings of God, he would be able to defeat the Persians at their own game.

Khalid deployed the army with a centre and wings. He commanded the centre himself, while the wings were commanded by Asim bin Amr and Adi bin Hatim. The Persian army was similarly deployed with Qarin commanding the centre, and Qabad and Anushjan commanding the wings.

The battle began with a call for a duel. Qarin stepped forward from the Persian side and gave the challenge. Before Khalid could step forward in response to the challenge, another Muslim commander, Ma'qal bin Al-Ashi rode out of the Muslim front to grapple with Qarin. Khalid let Ma'qal have the chance. Ma'qal was an expert swordsman, and he killed Qarin.

As Qarin fell, Qabad and Anushjan stepped forward and gave the challenge for duel. Asim and Adi the commanders of the wings of the Muslim forces accepted the challenge. In the personal combats which followed, Asim killed Anushjan and Adi killed Qabad.

After the fall of the three Persian Generals. Khalid gave the Muslim forces the order for a general attack. In spite of the demoralisation that followed in the deaths of their three topmost Generals, the Persian forces fought with great tenacity. Khalid intensified the pressure, and the Persian ranks began to give way. With the increased violence of the Muslim attacks, the Persian army broke up and made for the river.

The retreat of the Persian army soon became a rout. The lightly armed Muslim soldiers soon overtook the heavily equipped Persians and slaughtered them mercilessly. According to the Muslim historian Tabari, 30,000 soldiers were killed in the battle of Mazar. The Muslims won the second victory against the Persians as well.

Consequences of the battle of Mazar. In the battle of Mazar, heavy spoils were won by the Muslims. These exceeded the booty gained at Kazima. Four-fifths of the spoils were distributed mong the soldiers and one-fifth share was sent to Madina.

After the victory of Mazar the local inhabitants offered submission and agreed to pay 'Jizya' to the Muslims. Khalid established his headquarters at Hufeir, and a team of Muslim officials was appointed to attend to the administration of the country and collect taxes.

Battle of Walaja

Preparation of the Persians. After the defeat of the Persians at Mazar, the Persian emperor Ardsheer ordered the assembling of two more Persian armies to fight against the Muslims. One army was placed under the command of Andarzaghar, a military Governor of considerable standing. He had grown up among the Arabs, and was familiar with the Arab way of war. He commanded considerable popularity among the Arab tribes allied with the Persians. In addition to the regular Persian army, Andarzaghar was commissioned to raise contingents from the Arab auxiliaries. The other force was placed under the direct command of Bahman, the Commander-in-Chief of the Persian forces.

Andarzaghar was required to move with his army to grapple with the Muslims. The other force under Bahman was to follow after some time. Andarzaghar set off from al-Madain and moved along the east bank of the Tigris. He crossed the

Tigris at Kaskar, the site where the city of Wasit was founded later. From there he moved southwest to the Euphrates, and after crossing it established his camp at Walaja.

At Walaja, Andarzaghar was joined by the Arab auxiliaries as well as the remnants of the army of Qarin who had escaped from the battlefield of Mazar. The strength of the army of Andarzarghar was very considerable, and if it were reinforced by the army of Bahman, the Persian army was likely to assume formidable dimensions. Khalid's strategy, therefore, was that he should tackle the army of Andarzaghar before the main army under Bahman could join it.

Battle of Walaja. By forced marches, Khalid reached Walaja. As Andarzaghar surveyed the field, the Muslim army did not consist of more than 10,000 persons and the Muslim cavalry was no where to be seen. The strength of the Persian army was thrice the strength of the Muslim army, and Andarzaghar thought that in no time he would be able to make mince meat of the Muslim force, and thus avenge the defeats of Kazima and Mazar.

The battle at Walaja began as usual with a duel. Out of the Persian ranks stepped forward their champion 'Hazar Mard', the giant of a man supposed to have the strength of a thousand warriors. Khalid stepped forward from the Muslim front to grapple with the giant. Khalid appeared to be no match for the giant, but surprisingly enough after a few minutes of duelling Khalid struck a heavy blow at his adversary who reeled under the weight of his own heavy body. Khalid repeated the strokes until the giant was dead.

After the death of 'Hazar Mard', the Muslim army advanced for a general attack. The two armies met with a clash of steel, and the battle raged with unabated fury. The Muslims struck at the heavily armed Persians, but the Persians stood their ground, and repulsed all attacks. Then Andarzaghar ordered a counter attack. The Muslims were able to hold the attack for some time, but as the Persians intensified their pressure, the Muslims began to lose ground and fell back. Andarzaghar exhorted his men to step up their pressure for victory was very much in sight.

At that critical juncture, Khalid gave a signal. The next moment over the crest of the ridge which stretched behind the Persian army appeared columns of mounted Muslim warriors. Raising shouts of 'Allah-o-Akbar', the Muslim cavalry charged at a gallop, and the plain of Walaja shook under the thundring hooves of the Arab horse.

The Persians who were pressing forward were now caught in a trap. When they turned their face to meet the charge of the Muslim cavalry, the main Muslim army delivered a furious charge. The ring of steel became tighter round the Persians and in whatever direction they turned they were struck down by sword and dagger.

The battlefield of Walaja became a slaughter house for the Persians. The very helplessness of the Persians excited the Muslims to greater violence. The bulk of the Persian army was annihilated. Andarzaghar fled from the battlefield and penetrated deep into the desert where he lost his way and died of thirst. The battle of Walaja ended in a victory for the Muslims. That was the third consecutive victory of the Muslims over the Persians.

Consequences of the battle of Walaja. The victory of Walaja established the superiority of the Muslim fighting forces. Once again a large booty fell into the hands of the Muslims. Four-fifth of the spoils were distributed among the Muslim warriors on the spot, and the remaining one-fifth were sent to Madina. As the news of the Muslim victory reached Madina, Hadrat Abu Bakr offered special prayers of thanksgiving to Allah.

Battle of Ulleis

Christian Arabs. After their defeats in the battles of Kazima, Mazar and Walaja, the Persians felt that there should be a change in their strategy. They decided to set the Christian Arabs against the Muslim Arabs. In pursuance of this policy, after the battle of Walaja, the Christian Arabs mustered at

Ulleis, ten miles from Walaja in another bid to drive the Muslims from Iraq. The Persian Commander-in-Chief decided to send another Persian force to Ulleis to reinforce the Christian Arabs. This force was commanded by Jaban.

Khalid's march to Ulleis. The strategy of Khalid was to pounce upon the Christian Arabs before the arrival of the army of Jaban. Khalid, therefore, rushed to Ulleis to meet the Christian Arabs. When Khalid reached Ulleis with his force, he found that the Persian army under Jaban had already arrived there. Khalid, thereupon decided to surprise the enemy. The Persian soldiers were having their meals when Khalid ordered his force to launch the attack. Hurriedly, Jaban deployed his forces to face the Muslims. The Persian troops were massed in the centre, while the Christan Arabs led by Abdul Aswad and Abjar formed the right and left wings.

The battle of Ulleis. The battle ground lay between the river Euphrates and its tributary Kaseef. The battle front extended to about two miles. The battle began with a personal duel between Abdul Aswad the Christian Arab commander and Khalid. The combat was evenly matched, but Khalid succeeded in killing his adversary. Thereafter the Muslims launched the attack against the Persians. The Persians stood as a rock, and showed no signs of any weakening. The Muslims renewed the charge, and the Persians offered stiff resistance. The Muslim attack did not yield the desired result, and as the Muslim attacks appeared to lose force, a counter attack from the Persians was expected. In view of the limited space, there were no possibilities of a manoeuvre here, and Khalid was afraid that in frontal attack, the Persians in view of their superioirty of strength had the advantage and were likely to carry the day.

Khalid prayed to Allah for victory. He pledged "O God, if you give us victory, I shall see that no enemy warrior is left alive until the river runs red with their blood". It was typical soldier's pledge, and it inspired Khalid and his men to greater violence and fury. That paid dividends, and against the Muslim pressure, the Persian resistance ultimately broke down. By the afternoon a greater part of the Persian and Christian Arab army had been shattered, and the battle was over. The Muslims had secured a brilliant victory against the Persians for the fourth time.

Consequences of the battle of Ulleis. As the Persian army fled from the battlefield, the Muslim cavalry galloped out in pursuit of the fugitives, who had crossed the river Kaseef, and were fleeing in the direction of Hirah. These fugitives were overtaken, disarmed, and driven back to Ulleis. As each group was brought back, it was herded to the river. They were beheaded on the river bank, and their blood ran into the river. This process of slaughter went on for three days and so large were the killings that the river virtually became the river of blood. According to the historian Tabari, 70,000 Persian and Christian Arabs lost their live as a result of the battle of Ulleis.

The Ulleis disaster unnerved the Persian and the Christian Arabs. The local inhabitants of the region of Ulleis entered into a pact with the Muslims whereunder they agreed to pay 'Jizya' in lieu of Muslim protection. They also undertook to act as spies and guides for the Muslims.

Of all the battles fought by Khalid the battle of Ulleis was the toughest. At the battle of Mauta, which Khalid had fought during the lifetime of the Holy Prophet he had to face a grave situation, but the situation at Ulleis was graver still. Khalid is on record to have said:

> "At Mauta I broke nine swords in my hand. But I have never met an enemy like the Persians, and among the Persians I have never met an enemy like the Persian army at Ulleis."

Conquest of Hirah

Amgheeshiya. When Khalid bin Walid was asked to undertake operations in Iraq, he was given by Hadrat Abu Bakr, the target of Hirah. After the battle of Ulleis, the road to Hirah lay open. Khalid and his army immediately took the road to Hirah. After a day's march from Ulleis, the Muslim army reached Amgheeshiya. It was a large city rivalling Hirah in importance and splendour. The city was deserted, and there was no one to oppose the Muslims. The flower of the manhood of Amgheesiya had fallen at Ulleis, and the population of the city had found safety in flight. The Muslims occupied the deserted city. The wealth of Amgheeshiya in spite of the fact that residents had taken away their precious belongings with them, dazzled the Muslims.The booty amassed from the deserted city exceeded the spoils of war that the Muslims had won at the battles of Kazima, Mazar, Walaja, and Ulleis put together. When the state share of the booty from Amgheershiya reached Madina, Hadrat Abu Bakr addressing the faithful assembled in the Prophet's mosque said, "O Muslims, rejoice that your lion has empowered the Persian lion. Verily, women can no longer bear sons like Khalid."

Advance to Hirah. After the occupation of Amgheeshiya, Khalid decided to advance to Hirah. Hirah was under the nominal rule of an Arab chief Layth bin Qubeisa. The actual administration of the city was, however, the responsibility of the Persian Governor Azarbeh. When Azarbeh came to know of the advance of the Muslim force, he organised the defences of the city. He sent forward a cavalry group commanded by his son to hold the advance of the Muslims. This cavalry group was commissioned to dam the Euphrates in order to hold the advance of the Muslim army.

In the advance to Hirah, while the main Muslim army marched by riding on camels and horses, the heavy military loads were carried by boats on the river. The Muslim forces had traversed a short distance only, when due to the damming of the river, the water level fell, and the boats carrying the military loads came to be grounded. Seeing this situation, Khalid dashed off at great speed on the road to Hirah at the head of a cavalry detachment. At Badqala, some twelve miles from Hirah, the son of Azarbeh and his column were surprised, and cut down to a man. Khalid thereafter opened the dam, and as the water level in the river rose, the Muslim army resumed their advance by land as well as the river.

Occupation of Hirah. Khalid was expecting that he

would have to fight for Hirah. Therefore, instead of approaching Hirah from the front, Khalid made a detour and approached Hirah from the rear. When the Muslims reached the gates of the city, there was no Persian army to oppose them. When Azarbeh came to know of the death of his son, he was smitten with grief. In the meantime Ardsheer the emperor of Persia died and Persia came to be rocked by succession disputes. That unnerved Azrabeh. He abandoned Hirah, and fled with the Persian forces to Madain. Under the circumstances, the Muslims occupied the city of Hirah without any resistance.

The Christian Arabs. The Christian Arabs, however, locked themselves in four citadels, and refused to surrender. These citadels were the white palace commanded by Iyaz bin Qubeis; the Al- Adassiyeen palace commanded by 'Adi bin 'Adi; the Bani Mazin palace commanded by Ibn Akal; and Ibn Buqela palace commanded by Abdul Maseeh. The Muslims pressed the siege of the four citadels, and it was not long before the Christian Arabs were forced to ask for terms. The Christian Arabs surrendered, and agreed to pay an annual tribute to the Muslims.

Dialogue between Khalid and Abdul Maseeh. On the occasion of the surrender of the Christian Arabs, the dialogue that took place between Khalid and Abdul Maseeh, one of the Christian Arab chief has been preserved in history. Abdul Maseeh reported to be two hundred years old, was known as the sage of Hirah. This dialogue is one of the most unusual dialogues recorded in history.

Khalid: "How many years have you come upon."

Abdul Maseeh. "Two hundred."

Khalid: "What is the most wonderful thing that you have seen?"

Abdul Maseeh: "The most wonderful thing I have seen is a village between Hirah and Damascus to which a woman travels from Hirah with nothing more than a loaf of bread."

Khalid: "Have you gained nothing from your great age. You even do not know from where you come?"

Abdul Maseeh: "Truly, I know from where I come."

Khalid: "Where do you come from."

Abdul Maseeh: " From the spin of my father".

Khalid: "Where are you going?"

Abdul Maseeh: "To my front".

Khalid: "What is your front?"

Abdul Maseeh: "The end."

Khalid: "Where do you stand?"

Abdul Maseeh: "On the earth."

Khalid: "In what are you?"

Abdul Maseeh: "In my clothes."

Khalid: "Do you understand me ?"

Abdul Maseeh: "Yes."

Khalid: "The earth destroys its fools, but intelligent destroy the earth. I suppose your people know you better than I do."

Abdul Maseeh: "It is the ant, and not the camel that knows what is in the hole."

Khalid: "Tell me something that you remember."

Abdul Maseeh: "I remember the time when the ships of China sailed behind these citadels."

Khalid: "I call upon you to accept Islam or pay Jizya."

Abdul Maseeh: "We have no wish to fight you. We will pay you the Jizya, but we shall stick to our faith."

After the signing of the pact, when the old sage was to depart, Khalid noticed a pouch. Khalid asked, "What is in the pouch?"

Abdul Maseeh; "It is the poison."

Khalid: "But why the poison?"

Abdul Maseeh: "I feared that this meeting might turn out otherwise than it has. I would prefer death to seeing more horrors befall my people."

Princess Kirama. One interesting but rather strange clause in the peace pact pertained to the Christian Arab princess Kirama, the daughter of Abdul Maseeh. At one time Kirama was known for her extraordinary breath taking beauty. A story goes that one day when the Holy Prophet of Islam was sitting in the mosque at Madina surrounded by his followers he prophesied that erelong Hirah would fall to the Muslims. Among the Muslims who listened to this prophesy was a simple unlettered Muslim warrior Shuweil, by name.

Addressing the Holy Prophet, Shuweil said, "O Prophet of God, if the Muslims conquer Hirah, may I have Kirama ?" The Holy Prophet laughed and said, "Yes, you shall have her."

Now, when Hirah fell, Shuweil was in the Muslim army. He waited on Khalid and told him of the promise that the Holy Prophet had made with him regarding the princess Kirama. The statement of Shuweil was corroborated by some other Muslims. Thereupon Khalid had a clause inserted in the peace pact to effect that the princess Kirama was to be awarded to Shuweil.

Abdul Maseeh protested, but as Khalid insisted on the stipulation, Abdul Maseeh wanted some time so that he might consult Kirama. When Kirama was consulted, she said to her father, "You may agree to the condition. I will myself find a way out of the difficulty. The fool Shuweil would have heard of my beauty when I was young, and has forgotten that youth is not eternal".

When in pursuance of the agreement, the princess Kirama came to Shuweil the rough soldier was shocked that the princess was an old hag of eighty years. At one time Kirama enjoyed the reputation of being the most beautiful woman of Arabia, but age had withered her, and she was now nothing but wrinkles and old bones.

Shuweil did not know what to make of the old woman, Seeing his predicament the princess suggested to him "Of what use can an old woman be to you? You may let me go, and have some money instead". The suggestion appealed to Shuweil and he wanted to be paid a sum of three thousand dirhams. The priness paid the amount and secured her release. It was a good riddance for both.

Mass victory prayer. After signing the pact, Khalid led a mass victory prayer at Hirah. When the news of the conquest of Hirah reached Madina, along with the amount of the tribute realised from the people of Hirah, Hadrat Abu Bakr led a thanksgiving prayer at Madina. Central Iraq was now under the complete occupation of the Muslims.

NOTES

In this Chapter I have given an account of the campaigns in eastern Iraq. In this connection the main campaigns are:-

(1) Muthanna's reconnaissance campaign;
(2) battle of Kazima;
(3) battle of Mazar;
(4) battle of Walaja;
(5) battle of Ulleis;
(6) battle of Amgheeshiya and
(7) occupation of Hirah.

These campaigns began in March 633 C.E. and Hirah was occupied before the close of the year. One wonders at these victories of the Muslims one after the other within the short space of six or seven months, in spite of the larger resources at the disposal of the Persians. One cannot help but feel that God helped the Muslims in some mysterious way.

Against this background of blood and sword we come across some episodes of romance and general interest. The story of Kirama the princess of Hirah is of great interest. Khalid bin Walid's dialogue with Abdul Maseeh the sage of Hirah is very interesting. Mu'anna's marriage with a Persian Princess is also very interesting.

Khalid bin Walid is the hero of these battles. Hadrat Abu Bakr paid him the highest tribute when he said that mothers had yet to give birth to a son like Hadrat Khalid b. Walid. He also referred to him as a lion of the Muslims.

In writing this chapter I have derived the greatest help from Lt. General A. I. lkram's book *The Sword of Allah* which is a comprehensive biography of Khalid bin Walid, and which describes the battles fought by Khalid bin Walid in considerable detail. I have also derived help from:

(1) *Abu Bakr* by Muhammad Hussain Haykal;
(2) *Abu Bakr the Caliph* by A. A. Aziz; and
(3) *Hadrat Abu Bakr* by Syed Moin-ul-Haq.

13

CAMPAIGNS IN WESTERN IRAQ

Battle of Anbar

After Hirah, what? With the conquest of Hirah, Khalid had achieved the objective which Hadrat Abu Bakr had set for him. Having succeeded in his objective, a man like Khalid could not be expected to rest on oars. The question before Khalid was: after Hirah, what next? After taking stock of the situation around him, Khalid decided to advance further afieid.

Anbar. Khalid chose Anbar as his next objective. It was an important town and commercial centre to which caravans came from Syria and Persia. It was towards the end of June 633 C.E. that Khalid marched with his army from Hirah to Anbar. The Muslim force marched along the west bank of the Euphrates, and crossed the river somewhere below Anbar.

Anbar was the headquarter town of the district of Sabat. The Governor of the district was Sheerzad, and he decided to defend the town with the help of his Persian garrison and the Arab auxiliaries. The town was protected by walls, and a large deep moat.

The battle. The town of Anbar was situated at a height, and the Muslim army had to camp at the low plain below the town. As the Persians saw the height that intervened between them and the Muslim army, they felt that their position was invulnerable. The Persians stood on the top of the walls of the citadel carelessly in groups looking at the Muslim army as if they were watching a tournament.

Khalid collected the best of his archers, and commanded them to shoot at the eyes of the Persians. The Muslim archers shot several rounds and as a result thousands of Persians lost their eyes. Because of this action the battle of Anbar came to be called 'the battle of the eyes'.

The fall of Anbar. As a result of the efforts of the Muslim archers, a panic was created in the ranks of the Persians, and Sheerzad sent an offer to negotiate terms. Khalid rejected the offer and demanded that the surrender should be unconditional. Under the circumstances, Sheerzad decided to continue resistance.

The moat stood between the Persians and the Muslims, and the problem before Khalid was to cross the moat. Khalid selected a point where the moat was the narrowest. Here he placed his archers in position to shoot at the enemy ruthlessly. Under the cover of these archers Khalid pushed his army. The old and weak camels of the army were slaughtered and dumped into the moat. As the pile of carcasses rose it formed a bridge over which the Muslim army crossed the moat and assaulted the fort.

Finding his position insecure, Sheerzad made another offer to surrender provided the Persian army was allowed to withdraw in safety. Khalid agreed to the offer provided the Persians did not carry any arms or other property with them.

Withdrawal of Sheerzad. Sheerzad accepted the terms given by Khalid. The Persian soldiers and their families evacuated the fort at Anbar, and left for Al-Madain. Thereafter the Muslims occupied the town of Anbar. The Christian Arabs, the auxiliaries of the Persians had no option but to lay down arms after the withdrawal of the Persian forces. They agreed to pay *Jizya*. Khalid stayed at Anbar for a few days, and received the submission of the clans living in the neighbourhood.

When Sheerzad reached Al-Madain, he was severely rebuked by the Persian military authorities at his failure to defend Anbar. He attributed his failure to the betrayal of the Christian Arabs. He said, "I was among a people whose roots were among the Arabs, and their resistance to the invading Muslim Arabs was half hearted."

Battle of 'Ein-at-Tamr

'Ein-at-Tamr. Khalid left a garrison at Anbar under the command of Zabarqan bin Badr, and himself marched further afield with the main Muslim army. In early August 633 C.E. the Muslim army recrossed the Euphrates, and marched southward. This time his objective was 'Ein-at-Tamr. 'Ein-at-Tamr was a large fortified town surrounded by date palms. 'Ein-at-Tamr in fact meant "Spring of dates". It was a place of strategical importance, and was garrisoned by Persian forces and the Arab auxiliaries.

Christian Arabs. The Persian forces at 'Ein-at-Tamr were commanded by Mehran bin Bahram Jabeen who was a skilful military commander. The Christian Arabs belonged to the tribe of Namr, and were led by their chief Aqqa bin Abi Aqqa. Aqqa was a man of formidable dimensions and enjoyed great reputation for his prowess. He was a devout Christian and was very hostile to Islam.

Aqqa was proud of his bodily strength and Arab lineage. In a war council with Mehran, Aqqa volunteered to fight against the Muslims with his men. He argued "Diamond cuts diamond, and we Christian Arabs know best as to how to fight against the Muslim Arabs. Let us fight against the Muslims in the first instance". Mehran accepted the offer and said, "You are right; you are the best men to fight against the Muslims. Go ahead, and give the Muslims a tough fight. We will remain close to you, and will come to your assistance, when you need reinforcement."

Battle of 'Ein-at-Tamr. The Persian forces remained at 'Ein-at-Tamr, but the Christian Arab auxiliaries under the command of Aqqa marched on the road to Anbar to intercept the advance of the Muslim force under Khalid. The two forces met at a distance of some ten miles from 'Ein-at-Tamr. As soon as the two forces came in sight, they went in for action immediately. Khalid deployed the Muslim forces in the usual way, the centre and the wings. Khalid had heard .of the boastings and vaunts of Aqqa, and the plan of Khalid was to take Aqqa captive alive Aqqa led the centre of his force, and with his heavy body he looked very defiant. When the battle began, the wings of the Muslim army charged with considerable vehemence, but the centre under the direct command of Khalid charged in a luke warm way. That gave Aqqa the impression that the centre of the Muslim army was showing signs of exhaustion. He decided to avail of this advantage. He launched an attack at the central wing of the Muslim force with considerable vehemence. Before this attack, the Muslim centre withdrew. That made the central wing of Aqqa's force rush forward. By such impetuous advance, the central wing of Aqqa's force was cut off from the other wings of the army of the Christian Arabs. At this stage the Muslim force turned a somersault, and launched a furious charge enveloping the forces of Aqqa. In the hand to hand fighting that followed, the men surrounding Aqqa were cut to pieces, and Aqqa was captured alive according to plan.

Occupation of 'Ein-at-Tamr. With the capture of Aqqa, the Christian Arabs lost nerve, and fled to 'Ein-at-Tamr, hoping to be reinforced by the Persian forces. When the Arab fugitives reached 'Ein-at-Tamr, they found that the Persian forces under Mehran had already evacuated the town, and left for Al-Madain. Finding themselves abandoned and betrayed the Christan Arabs rushed into the fort, closed the gates and prepared for a siege.

The Muslims soon arrived at 'Ein-at-Tamr, and laid siege to the fort. Aqqa and other prisoners in the Muslim camp were paraded outside the fort, and that had an unnerving effect on the defenders. The Christian Arabs soon asked for terms, but Khalid said that there would be no terms and that the surrender must be unconditional. After a few days the resistance of the Christian Arabs broke down, and they surrendered unconditionally. Aqqa and the leaders of the Christian Arabs were beheaded. The people agreed to pay *Jizya.* A huge booty was collected, and distributed according to the usual formula.

Monastery at 'Ein-at-Tamr. At Ein-at-Tamr was a monastery where boys were trained for priesthood. These boys were converted to Islam. Among these boys was one Naseir whose son Musa later became the Governor of Africa, and the Conqueror of Spain.

Battle of Daumatul Jandal

Daumatul Jandal. Daumatul Jandal, the present day Al-Jauf was in the time of Hadrat Abu Bakr, a place of great strategic importance. It lay at the border of Iraq and Syria, and was the meeting place of the routes from Central Arabia, Iraq and Syria. In the strategy for the defences of Arabia, Daumatul Jandal was a key point, and even the Holy Prophet was conscious of the importance of Daumatul Jandal.

Akeider. When in 630 C.E., the Holy Prophet undertook a campaign to Tabuk, Khalid was directed to lead a campaign to Daumatul Jandal. Khalid succeeded in his mission, and Akeider the Christan Arab ruler of Daumatul Jandal was taken captive. Akeider paid a heavy ransom, and on agreeing to pay an annual tribute, he was restored to his principality.

'Ayad bin Ghanam. After the death of the Holy Prophet, Akeider broke the pact with the Muslims, and defaulted in the payment of the tribute. Hadrat Abu Bakr sent a column under 'Ayad bin Ghanam to capture Daumatul Jandal. 'Ayad laid a siege to Daumatul Jandal, but failed to capture it. The siege lasted for over a year, but still the resistance of the defenders was not broken. Many Christian Arabs driven from Iraq as a result of the operations of Khalid found refuge at Daumatul Jandal, and that created further difficulties for 'Ayad.

March of Khalid to Daumatul Jandal. At this critical juncture, 'Ayad wrote to Khalid to come to his help. Hadrat Abu Bakr also asked Khalid to go to the help of 'Ayad. Khalid received the call for help when he was at 'Ein-at-Tamr. Khalid decided to go in for the help of 'Ayad forthwith. Leaving a garrison at 'Ein-at-Tamr, Khalid marched on with his main force to the relief of Daumatul Jandal. Khalid covered the journey of three hundred miles to Daumatual Jandal in ten days.

The battle of Daumatul Jandal. The Christian Arab forces at Daumatul Jandal were led by two chiefs, namely Akeider and Judi bin Rabee'a. Akeider, who had personal experience of the prowess of Khalid, was unnerved when he came to know that Khalid had arrived for the help of 'Ayad. He advised the Christian Arabs to make peace with Khalid. His advice was, however, not accepted by his people, who decided to fight. Thereupon 'Akeider withdrew from Daumatul Jandal, and set off on the road to Jordan. He was soon overtaken by a detachment of Khalid's cavalry. Accounts differ as to the fate of Ukeider. According to one account, when Ukeider was presented before Khalid, he ordered his execution, as he had broken his oath of allegiance. According to another account, Ukeider was sent to Madina, where he repented and was granted amnesty by Hadrat Abu Bakr.

Thereafter, Khalid pressed the siege of Daumatul Jandal. The Christian Arabs under Judi bin Rabee'a offered resistance, but they could not hold on for long. Daumatul Jandal fell in the last week of August 633 C.E. Over two thousand Christian Arabs were killed in the battle of Daumatul Jandal. Judi bin Rabaee'a was captured alive. The people of Daumatul Jandal were offered amnesty on their agreeing to pay *Jizya*. Immense booty fell to the share of the Muslims. Judi bin Rabee'a had a beautiful daughter who was among the captives. She was a typical beauty. When Khalid saw her, he felt attracted and married.

Reaction of Hadrat Abu Bakr. When the news of the fall of Daumatul Jandal were communicated to Hadrat Abu Bakr at Madina, he felt very happy. He felt proud of the exploits of Khalid, who had succeeded where others had failed. When the Caliph was told that Khalid had married Bint Judi, he merely smiled and said:

> "Great men have their eccentricities, and Khalid a great General has a soft corner in his heart for beautiful women. He is the victor of Daumatul Jandal, and he may very well have Bint Judi as his prize, if that is his pleasure."

Campaigns in Western Iraq

Persian forces. After the victory of Daumatul Jandal, Khalid returned to the Iraq front in September 633 C.E. By this time, the Persians had raised more forces, and they were once again on the war path. One force of the Persians commanded by Ruzbeh was quartered at Huseid, northeast of 'Ein-at-Tamr. Another Persian force under Zarmahr was cantoned at Khanafis northwest of Huseid.

Plan of the campaign of Khalid. Khalid had his headquarters at 'Ein- at-Tamr. From there he sent one column under Qa'qa' to Huseid, and another column under Abu Leila to Khanafis. The instructions of Khalid were that the operations at Huseid and Khanafis should take place simultaneously.

The battle of Huseid. Qa'qa' reached Huseid before Abu Leila could reach Khanafis, and thus the original plan of simultaneous action could not be followed. The battle at Huseid began with a personal duel between Qa'qa' and Ruzbeh. In the duel, Ruzbeh was overpowered and killed. Then Zarmahr, the Commander of the forces at Khanafis, who was also at Huseid, stepped to give the challenge. Qa'qa' accepted the challenge and in the duel that followed, Zarmahr was also killed. Thereafter the Muslims charged. After some resistance, the Persians lost nerve, and withdrew from the battlefield leaving a large number of the dead at the site of the battle.

Confrontation at Khanafis. The survivors of the Persian army from Huseid, fled to Khanafis. When the Persian garrison at Khanafis came to know of the Persian defeat at Huseid, and of the death of their own Commander Zarmahr, they felt that any stand at Khanafis against the superior Muslim forces would be futile. Mabhuzab the new Commander considered discretion to be the better part of valour. He abandoned Khanafis and with his forces moved to Muzayyah further north where more forces were available and defences were stronger. When the Muslim forces under Abu Leila arrived at Khanafis, they found that there were no Persian forces to meet them. The Muslims accordingly occupied Khanafis without firing any shot. Khalid was, however, not happy with the operations for the entire Persian garrison at Khanafis had escaped slaughter at the hands of the Muslims.

March to Muzayyah. When Khalid came to know that the Persian garrison from Khanafis had escaped to Muzayyah, he directed that the Persians should be pursued to Muzayyah. Three Muslim columns started separately for Muzayyah from 'Ein-at-Tamr, Huseid and Khanafis. They had to follow different routes, but they were required to reach a point close to Muzayyah at the same time.

The battle of Muzayyah. The movements of the Muslim forces were carried out according to plan, and the three corps mustered at the appointed place according to schedule. In the Persian camp there was a large concentration of the Persian forces and the Christian Arab auxiliaries at Muzayyah. Muzayyah was at considerable distance from Huseid and Khanafis, and the Persians were under the impression that the Muslim forces would take considerable time to reach Muzayyah.

When the Muslim forces reached unexpectedly at Muzayyah, it was night and the Persians and the Christian Arabs slept peacefully. Roaring masses of Muslim warriors hurled themselves on the Persian camp. So sudden was the Muslim attack that Persian army was unable to take any firm stand. There was confusion and panic in the ranks of the Persian army, and the Persians were slaughtered in thousands. The disaster that met the Persians at Muzayyah was more or less of the same order as they had suffered at Walaja. Helped by the darkness of the night many Persians and their auxiliaries found safety in withdrawing from the battlefield.

When the sun rose the following day, not a single Persian soldier could be seen at Muzayyah. Most of them lay dead at the battlefield, and the rest had found safety in flight. Among the Arabs who had lost their lives at Muzayyah were two persons, Abdullah and Labid who were Muslims and had certificates to that effect from Hadrat Abu Bakr himself. Some of the critics of Khalid held him guilty of killing Muslims. Hadrat Abu Bakr held that such things were likely to occur when Muslims chose to live in the midst of non-Muslims, against whom military operations were undertaken. Hadrat Abu Bakr, however, paid blood money to the heirs of the two persons from the Muslim Baitul Mal.

Battle of Saniyy. The victory of the Muslims at Muzayyah exposed the Christian Arab pockets of Saniyy, Zumeil, and Ruzab to Muslim attack. Saniyy being close to Muzayyah become the first objective of the attack of the Muslim forces. From Muzayyah three Muslim columns marched through separate routes and arrived at Saniyy according to plan on pre-determined time and date. A three pronged attack was launched on the Christian Arab camp at Saniyy. The Christian Arabs were no match for the trained forces of Khalid, and were slaughtered in thousands. The Christian Arab Commander Rabee'a bin Bujeir was slain on the battlefield. Among the captives was the beautiful daughter of Rabee'a. She was sent to Madina, where Hadrat Ali married her.

Battle of Zumeil. From Saniyy the Muslim forces marched to Zameil. Here again a three pronged attack was launched by three columns according to a pre-determined plan. The Christian Arab forces at Zumeil met with disaster and were annihilated. The Muslims won considerable booty both at Saniyy and Zumeil.

Battle of Ruzeb. From Zumeil, the Muslim forces proceeded to Ruzab. Here Hilal the son of the Christian Arab chief Aqqa who had fallen at 'Ein-at-Tamr had collected a large force of the Christian Arabs to give a fight to the Muslims and avenge his father's death. When Hilal came to know of the fate of the Christian Arabs at Saniyy and Zumeil, he lost heart. When the Muslim forces arrived at Ruzab, there was no enemy to oppose them, and they occupied Ruzab without any resistance. Hilal and his forces withdrew before the arrival of the Muslims.

Muslim domination. With the completion of these operations, the entire region to the west of the Euphrates from Uballa to Anbar came under the complete domination of the Muslims, and all pockets of the Persians of the Christian Arabs in this region were completely liquidated.

Battle of Firaz

Firaz. By the end of 633 C.E., the Muslims were the masters of the Euphrates valley. In this valley, Firaz at the outermost edge of the Persian empire still had a Persian garrison. Khalid decided to drive away the Persians from this outpost as well. Khalid marched to Firaz with a Muslim force and arrived there in the first week of December 633 C.E. Firaz was the frontier between the empires of Persia and Byzantium, and the garrisons of the Persians as well as the Byzantines were cantoned there. In the face of the Muslims, the Byzantine garrison decided to come to the aid of the Persian garrison. The united forces of the Persians, the Byzantines, and the Christian Arab auxiliaries were ten times the number of the Muslim force. Impressed by the imposing array of the coalition, the Byzantine General sent a haughty message to Khalid, demanding an unconditional surrender. Khalid replied that he would give reply on the battlefield.

The battle of Firaz. Khalid gave the enemy the option to cross the Euphrates. As soon as the enemy had crossed the Euphrates, Khalid commanded the Muslim force to go into action. The united forces of the Persians and the Byzantines had the river at their back, and the position was similar to that at the battle of Mazar. At Firaz, Khalid adopted the same tactics as he had adopted at Mazar. As the front ranks of both the forces committed themselves in the fighting, Khalid fixed his enemy on either flank with the help of his rear wings. Making a swift lighting movement, the Muslims dashed for the bridge on the river, and succeeded in occupying it. The enemy was thus held in a pincer movement. The Muslims intensified the attack and closed the noose round the neck of the enemy. In the mortal conflict that ensued, the enemy soon lost the ground. The withdrawing forces of the Persians and the Byzantines either jumped into the river in a state of horror or confusion or allowed themselves to be squeezed to death. It was a bloody battle, and over fifty thousand men of the enemy fell on the battle ground. The battle was soon over, and Firaz the last stronghold of the Persians fell to the Muslims. The battle of Firaz added further lustre to the Muslim arms.

Khalid's pilgrimage to Makkah. In the beginning of the battle of Firaz when the odds appeared to be against the Muslims, Khalid undertook an oath that if he was victorious, he would undertake pilgrimage to Makkah, the House of God. After the victory of Firaz, Khalid stayed at Firaz for some days and made the necessary arrangements for the administration of the territory. In January 634 C.E., while a garrison was kept at Firaz, orders were issued to the main Muslim army to return to Al-Hirah. Khalid stayed behind with the rear of the army. As the army moved forward on the road to Al-Hirah. Khalid separated himself from the army, and took an unfrequented route to Makkah with a small escort. Khalid reached Makkah in time to perform the 'Hajj'. After performing the pilgrimage secretly and fulfilling his vow, Khalid and his party rode back to Al-Hirah. Before the last contingent of the main army from Firaz had entered Hirah, Khalid was also there, as if he had been all the time with the rear guard. Although Khalid had taken pains to ensure that he was not recognised at Makkah, news was nevertheless carried to Hadrat Abu Bakr that leaving his charge in Iraq, Khalid had visited Makkah incognito. When Khalid reached Al-Hirah, he got a letter from Hadrat Abu Bakr asking him not to indulge in such adventure again.

Battle of Babylon

Muthanna's command of the Iraq front. After the transfer of Khalid bin Walid to the Syrian front, Muthanna became the commander of the Muslim forces in Iraq. Khalid had taken one half of the troops with him to Syria, and left the other half with Muthanna in Iraq. With the reduction in the strength of the troops in Iraq, Muthanna was not in a position to take the offensive. He accordingly withdrew from the advanced posts, and cantoned the troops at Hirah.

Shahr Iran. For long the affairs in Persia had been in a state of disarray because of succession disputes. With the accession of Shahr Iran, stability was restored to Persia. The new king was ambitious, and on assuming authority, he decided to take action against the Muslims and drive them from the soil of Iraq. Khalid who was a terror for the Persians was no longer in Iraq. The Muslim forces on the Iraq front had been considerably reduced. The Persian Kisra, therefore, felt that it was the ideal time to take action against the Muslims. A large Persian force was mustered, and placed under the command of a veteran General Hormuz.

Letter to Muthanna. Shahr Iran sent an insulting letter to Muthanna demanding immediate withdrawal of the Muslim forces from Iraq. The Kisra observed that the Muslims were so despicable before him that he was not sending the main Persian army against them. He was sending an army of "fowl men and swine herdmen." Muthanna replied that the Muslim forces were not there to withdraw, they were there to fight and they would give a good account of themselves, Commenting on the Kisra's letter Muthanna said that it appeared that he was either a braggart or a liar, and in any case unless he chose to see the light of reason, his army of "fowlmen and swine herdmen", God willing, would be destroyed.

Battle of Babylon. In spite of the heavy odds against him, Muthanna did not lose nerve. He decided to give the battle away from Hirah. He accordingly marched with his troops from Hirah, crossed the Euphrates, and arrived at the site of Babylon where the Persian forces under Hormuz were already camped. When the battle began, the Persians had all the advantages in their favour. The Persians had a fierce war elephant in front of their ranks, and the beast threw the Muslim ranks in confusion and paralysed their action. At this stage, Muthanna directed his archers to aim every arrow at the beast. Soon the beast was pierced with innumerable wounds. It groaned, staggered and fell. With the fall of the beast the offensive of the Persians lagged. Muthanna ordered his men to fall at the Persians. In the hand to hand fight that followed the Persians were routed. Hormuz fell on the battlefield. With his death the Persian resistance was over, and the Persians retreated post haste leaving thousands of their soldiers on the battlefield.

Muthanna's visit to Madina. Muthanna felt that the battle of Babylon was not the end of the matter. The Persians had considerable resources at their disposal, and they were likely to raise a still larger army against the Muslims. Muthanna wrote to Hadrat Abu Bakr for reinforcement. There was some delay in reply from Madina and Muthanna dashed to Madina to apprise the Caliph personally of the situation in Iraq. When Muthanna arrived in Madina, Hadrat Abu Bakr lay on death bed. He, however, saw Muthanna, and listened to his account attentively. Thereafter Hadrat Abu Bakr summoned Hadrat Umar, and directed him to command levy for Muthanna. He said:

> "If I die this day wait not till the evening; if I linger till night wait not till the morning. Let not sorrow for me divert you from the service of Allah".

This direction was the last offcial act of Hadrat Abu Bakr as the Caliph.

NOTES

This Chapter gives an account of the campaigns in western Iraq. These include;

(1) battle of Anbar;
(2) battle of 'Ein-at-Tamr;
(3) battle of Daumatul Jandal;
(4) battle of Huseid;
(5) battle of Khanafis;
(6) battle of Mazayyah;
(7) battle of Saniyy;
(8) battle of Sumeil:
(9) battle of Ruzab;
(10) battle of Firaz; and
(11) battle of Babylon.

It is a matter of wonder how the Muslims won all these battles. The hero of these battles, except the battle of Babylon was Khalid bin Walid. The battle of Babylon was won by Muthanna after Khalid had left for the Syrian front. This shows that apart from Khalid, the Muslims had among them other outstanding Generals as well.

During these campaigns we have the spell of romance as well. After the conqest of Daumatul Jandal, Khalid bin Walid married a daughter of the chief of Daumatul Jandal. We may feel curious at such marriages of Khalid bin Walid, but we may agree with Hadrat Abu Bakr when he said, "Great men have their idiocyncracies, and as the victor of Daumatul Jandal, let Khalid have Binte Judi if he so desires."

In writing this chapter I have derived help from the following books:

(1) *The Sword of Allah* by A. I. Ikram;
(2) *Abu Bakr* by Muhammad Hussain Haykal;
(3) *Abu Bakr the Caliph* by A. A. Aziz; and
(4) *Hadrut Abu Bakr* by Syed Moinul Haq.

14

CAMPAIGNS IN SYRIA

Campaigns in Syria

The garrison at Tayma. When active operations were being undertaken in Iraq, Hadrat Abu Bakr stationed a garrison at Tayma to the east of Tabuk to protect the border against any attack by the Byzantines from Syria. The garrison at Tayma was commanded by Khalid bin Saeed.

Discomfiture of Khalid bin Saeed. The Muslims won spectacular success on the Iraq front. That created in Khalid bin Saeed the urge to score some victory on the Syrian front as well. Early in 634 C.E., Khalid bin Saeed sought the permission of Hadrat Abu Bakr to advance into Syria. Hadrat Abu Bakr permitted Khalid bin Saeed to enter into Syria, but he was directed that the operations should be undertaken as a reconnaissance measure only, and no attempt should be made to get involved in any serious hostilities with the Byzantines.

Khalid bin Saeed advanced into Syria, and the Byzantine forces retreated before him. That gave Khalid bin Saeed the impression that the victory of Syria would be a walk over, and that he could win laurels on the Syrian front as his namesake had won on the Iraq front. Khalid bin Saeed accordingly penetrated deep into Syria in pursuit of the Byzantine forces. When Khalid bin Saeed was cut off from his base, the Byzantines enveloped the Muslim forces and launched a vigorous counter attack. In this encounter, the Muslims suffered a serious defeat. Khalid bin Saeed lost his son in action and that unnerved him. In a state of desperateness he escaped from the battlefield. The command was thereafter assumed by Ikrama bin Abu Jahl, who retrieved the position by evacuating the Muslim forces. Hadrat Abu Bakr felt annoyed at the discomfiture of Khalid bin Saeed, and directed him not to come to Madina. Khalid bin Saeed accordingly retired to the interior of the desert at some distance from Madina.

Jihad on the Syrian front. On return from the pilgrimage in February 634 C.E., Hadrat Abu Bakr issued a call to arms for Jihad on the Syrian front. In response to the call, tribal contingents came over to Madina from all parts of Arabia. By March 634 C.E., a large force assembled at Madina ready to march to Syria. Hadrat Abu Bakr organised all these warriors into four corps, each comprising 7,000 men.

The first corps was placed under the command of 'Amr bin Al- Aas. It was required to advance to Palestine via Eila and the valley of Araba.

The second corps was placed under the command of Yazeed bin Abi Sufyan. It was directed to proceed to Damascus via Tabuk.

The third corps under Shurahbil bin Hasana was required to proceed to Jordan.

The fourth corps under Abu Ubaida bin Al-Jarrah was required to advance to Emessa. All the columns were required to act independently, if the forces were to integrate, Abu Ubaida was to be the Commander-in-Chief.

Hadrat Abu Bakr's address to the Muslim forces. The Muslim forces marched from Madina in the first week of April 634 C.E. The corps led by Yazeed bin Abi Sufyan was the first to leave. Thereafter, other corps left according to programme. Hadrat Abu Bakr addressed the forces at the time of their departure in the following terms:

> "In your march be not hard on yourself or your army. Be not harsh with your men or your officers whom you should consult in all matters. Be just and abjure evil and tyranny, for no people, who are unjust, can prosper or achieve victory over their enemy. When you meet the

> enemy turn not your backs except to manoeuvre for the battle or to re-group, for he, who does so, earns, the wrath of Allah. His abode will be hell, and what a terrible place it is ! And when you have won a victory over your enemies, kill not women or children or the aged. Do not slaughter any beasts except for eating. And break not the pacts that you make with other people. You will come upon persons who live like hermits in monasteries, believing that they have given up all for God. Let them be as they are, and do not harm their monasteries. You will meet other persons who are partisans of Satan and worshippers of the Cross who shave the centre of their heads so that you can see the scalp. Assail them with your swords, until they submit to Islam or pay the *Jizya.* In all transactions fear God, and when in difficulty invoke His aid. Now depart in the name of God. May He protect you."

Yazeed and his corps sped on the road to Tabuk. The corps of Amr bin Al-Aas took the route to Eila. Then followed the corps of Shurahbil, and next came the corps of Abu Ubaida, each a day's march from the other.

Encounter with the Byzantines. At the border, the corps of Yazeed struck against a force of the Christian Arabs sent forward by the Byzantines as a reconnaissance force. The Christian Armies withdrew and Yazeed marched to the valley of Araba. The corps of 'Amr bin Al-Aas reached Eila. Both the corps fought against Byzantine detachments sent to intercept their advance. The Byzantine detachments suffered defeat, and had to retreat after suffering considerable loss. In the meantime the corps of Shurahbil and Abu Ubaida reached the region Basra and Jabiya.

Plan of the Byzantines. The Byzantine emperor, Heraclius now planned action on a large scale. He mustered forces at Ajnadeen numbering over one lakh. The position became critical for the Muslims for the four small corps that had penetrated into Syria were no match for such a large concentration of the Byzantines. Abu Ubaida wrote to Hadrat Abu Bakr asking for reinforcement, and Hadrat Abu Bakr decided to send Khalid bin Walid from Iraq to Syria.

Khalid's March to Syria

Khalid's transfer to Syria. In May 634 C.E. while Khalid bin Walid was at Al-Hirah, he received orders from Hadrat Abu Bakr that he should proceed with all possible haste to Syria to take over the command of the Muslim forces in Syria, and lead the operations there. With the departure of Khalid from Iraq, Al-Muthanna was to be the Commander of the Muslim forces in Iraq. On receiving these orders, Khalid divided the Muslim forces in Iraq in two corps. One corps he left with Al-Muthanna in Iraq, and with the other corps he proceeded to Syria.

Route to Syria. The main point that Khalid had to decide was as to the route by which he should march to Syria. The southern route led via Daumatul Jandal. It was the easiest and the simplest route. It was, however, a long route, and the march was likely to take a considerable time. The other route in the north lay along the Euphrates. It was not the proper route to be followed for it was studded with numerous cantonments garrisoned by the Byzantine soldiers.

Khalid was keen to know of some other shorter route to Syria. One of the soldiers of the army of Khalid, Rafe' bin Umeira declared that there was another route through the land of Samawa. Through this route, the entire journey was to take five days only. The difficulty, however, was the region was a barren and waterless desert, and because of the want of water considerable difficulties had to be faced by the travellers. Rafe' was of the view that the Samawa route was not a proper route for the army, as it involved extreme hardships, absence of water, and the risk of losing the way.

Urged by the spirit of adventure, Khalid, decided that he would follow the Samawa route, whatever the risks. This dangerous decision alarmed them, but he addressed them "Let not your resolve be weakened. Allah will help you, and why should you fear anything when you have the help of Allah?"

March to Syria. In early June 634 C.E., Khalid marched from Al-Hirah with his corps of 9,000 men. From Al-Hirah they proceeded to 'Ein-at-Tamr, Sandauda, Mazayyah and Qaraqir. At Qaraqir, the army filled the water skins and other containers with water which could last for five days. Old camels were made to drink water to their full, so that they could serve as reservoirs of water in case of emergency.

Plunge into the desert. On the following morning, taking the name of Allah, the army plunged into the trackless desert. The journey through the desert proved to be very hard and oppresive. Things became difficult when the water supply expected to last for five days was exhausted in three days. On the fourth day, in the absence of water, things became very difficult for the army. Some of the camels were slaughtered and the water stored in their stomachs was utilised for the watering of horses. By the end of the fourth day, the men of Khalid reached the limits of human endurance. On the fifth day, the army reached the site where according to the guide there should have been a spring of water. The spring of water was, however, no where to be found. That led to a feeling of great disappointment and frustration among the army. On further search and some trial diggings, a spring of water was after all found. That was the end of all trouble and anxiety. Men and animals drank their fill, and praised God for His mercy.

Suwa. The rest of the march through the desert was no longer oppressive. After a day's march, the Muslim army reached Suwa. That was the first settlement in Syria. It was an oasis surrounded by a pasture land where there were large flocks of sheep and herds of cattle. The Muslims captured all the flocks and herds to serve for the army's food during the campaigns to follow.

Arak. The following day, the Muslim army reached Arak, which was a fortified town. The Byzantine garrison found resistance futile. They laid down arms, and the people of the town agreed to pay *Jizya*. The pact of peace was signed and the fort was occupied by the Muslims.

Tadmur. From Arak, the Muslim army advanced to

Tadmur, where was a Christian Arab garrison, who shut themselves in the fort at the arrival of the Muslim army. The Muslims besieged the fort, and finding resistance useless the Christian Arabs asked for terms. They surrendered and agreed to pay *Jizya.*

Qaryatein. From Tadmur, the Muslim army marched to Qaryatein. The Byzantine garrison here decided to resist. In the fight that followed the Byzantine garrison was annihilated to a man. The people of the town sued for terms, and agreed to pay *Jizya.*

Huwareen. From Qaryatein, the Muslims marched to Huwareen, some ten miles away. Here the Muslims had to fight against the local inhabitants reinforced by a contingent of the Ghassans who had come to the relief of the local inhabitants. The Byzantines and the Ghassans were cut to pieces. The survivors laid down arms, and a peace pact was signed whereunder people agreed to pay *Jizya.*

Pass of the eagle. From Huwareen the Muslim army took the road to Damascus. They halted at a pass twenty miles from Damascus. At this pass in the Jabal-us-Sharq range, Khalid fluttered his standard bearing the 'Eagle, and because of such standard, the pass came to be known as "Saniyyat-ul-Uqab", i.e. the pass of the eagle.

Marj Rahit. From the pass, the Muslim army advanced to Marj Rahit. A garrison here offered some resistance, but was soon overpowered. The garrison surrendered and the Muslims amassed considerable booty. From Marj Rahit, the Muslim army under Khalid marched to Busra.

Battle of Busra

Campaign against Busra. Over running the southern frontier posts, Abu Ubaida and Shurahbil occupied the Hauran district lying east of the river Yermuk, with a view to guarding against a surprise attack from Busra, Abu Ubaida despatched a detachment of four thousand warriors under Shurahbil to capture Busra.

Khalid's march to Busra. At Marj Rahit, Khalid came to know that a Muslim detachment was fighting at Busra. By-passing Damascus, Khalid and his army set off for Busra. Khalid sent a message to Abu Ubaida, the Commander-in-Chief of the Muslim forces in Syria that he should meet him at Busra.

Khalid's arrival at Busra. At Busra the Muslim forces were heavily out numbered. Taking advantage of their numerical strength, the Byzantines launched a vigorous attack, and under the intensity of the attack, the Muslim forces began to reel back. The position for the Muslims became critical, and Shurahbil prayed to God for help. Miraculously the army of Khalid arrived at the scene at the nick of time. That turned the tide of the battle. Seeing that the Muslims had received reinforcement, the Byzantine garrison withdrew to the city and shut its gates.

Commencement of the battle. The following day, the two armies faced each other in battle array. The battle was preceded by a call for personal combat between the Commanders of the armies. Khalid stepped forward from the Muslim ranks, and out of the Byzantine ranks their commander Romanus stepped forward. Before duelling, Khalid offered Islam to Romanus and surprisingly enough, Romanus after asking a few questions about Islam, declared the article of faith and became a Muslim. He crossed over to the Muslim camp.

Romanus. From the Muslim camp, Romanus addressed the Byzantines in the following terms:

"O ye, enemies of God and His prophet. You must not forget that I have accepted the true faith of Islam to please God. Now no common ties exist between you and me, either in this world, or in the world hereinafter. I deny him who was crucified, and sever my connections with his followers. I choose Allah for my Lord, and Muhammad (peace be on him) as my prophet, the Ka'aba as my sanctuary, and the Muslims as my brethren. In sooth, I bear witness that there is no God but Allah. He has no partner, and Muhammad (peace be on him) is His prophet, whom He selected to direct mankind to the right way. I am fully convinced that God would exalt the true religion of Islam over the religion of those who join partners with His Divinity."

Muslim occupation of Busra. The conversion of Romanus to Islam unnerved the Byzantine forces, and instead of giving the fight, they withdrew to the city and shut the gates against the Muslims. That night, Romanus led a Muslim detachment to a subterranean passage under the ramparts of the city. This contingent was led by Abdur Rahman the son of Hadrat Abu Bakr. This contingent entered the city through the underground passage and then dashing towards the city gates opened them for the main Muslim army to enter. The Muslim forces attacked right and left raising the cries of "Allah-o-Akbar." The Byzantines were slaughtered in thousands and the survivors laid down arms. The citizens of Busra agreed to pay *Jizya,* and thereupon a peace pact was drawn up.

Consequences of the conquest of Busra. The conquest of Busra in the second week of July 634 C.E. was the first important victory gained by the Muslims in Syria. The Muslims lost 130 men in the battle, while the Byzantines lost several thousand persons. Khalid informed Hadrat Abu Bakr of the victory and despatched the usual one fifth of the spoils of war. The conquest of Busra opened for the Muslims the gate for the conquest of Syria.

Abu Ubaida. At Busra, Abu Ubaida came to meet Khalid. Khalid had replaced him in the over all command of the Muslim forces in Syria, but Abu Ubaida had no grudge on that score. Addressing Khalid, he said, "O father of Sulaiman, I have received with gladness the letter of Hadrat Abu Bakr appointing you as the Commander-in-Chief. There is no resentment in my heart over this, for I know of your skill in matters of war". Addressing Abu Ubaida, Khalid in reply said "By Allah, but for the necessity of obeying the orders of the Caliph I would never have accepted the command over you. You are much higher than me in Islam. I am a companion of the Holy Prophet, while you are one whom the Messenger of Allah called the 'trusted one of the nation'."

Siege of Damascus

Khalid's march to Damascus. From Busra, Khalid marched northward to Damascus. The Muslim forces occupied the outskirts of Damascus. Damascus was heavily guarded, and the Muslim force was too small to press the siege of a city like Damascus. After the defeat of Busra, the Byzantine emperor was much upset. He vowed vengeance and undertook preparations on a large scale to drive away the Muslims from the soil of Syria. Heraclius garrisoned all forts in Syria. He ordered a huge concentration of forces in the south at Ajnadein west of Jerusalem.

Lifting the siege of Damascas. The Muslim scouts brought the intelligence that a Byzantine force over one lakh strong had assembled at Ajnadein. That set Khalid thinking. If he pressed the siege against Damascus the danger was that the Byzantine army from Ajnadein might attack the Muslim army from the rear, and in that case the position for the Muslims would become very critical. Khalid accordingly changed his strategy, and decided to deal with the Ajnadein Byzantine forces in the first instance. In pursuance of this decision, the siege of Damascus was lifted and the Muslim forces were ordered to march to Ajnadein. Upto this time the various Muslim forces in Syria were operating in different sectors. Khalid directed the integration of all the Muslim forces, and required the entire Muslim army to assemble at Ajnadein.

Byzantine attack on the Muslims. When the siege of Damascus was lifted by the Muslims that emboldened the Byzantines. A Byzantine contingent with a force of six thousand horse and ten thousand foot soldiers fell upon the Muslim rearguard as they were retreating from Damascus. So fierce and unexpected was the Byzantine attack that the Muslims had to give way. The Byzantines were able to capture a number of women who were in the Muslim camp.

Khaula. The Muslim women captured by the Byzantines were kept in a separate camp. The Byzantines intended to carry these women to Damascus after they had collected other booty. Among the women prisoners was a beautiful lady, Khaula, the sister of the Muslim commander Zarrar. Peter the commander of the Byzantine contingent was struck by her beauty, and chose her for himself. Khaula was a firebrand lady of extraordinary courage. She exhorted her companions to muster courage, and defy their capture. Her companions asked as to how they were to resist their captors when they were unarmed. Khaula asked them to get hold of the tent poles. They were required to keep close to one another, and to fall upon the Byzantine soldiers who came near them.

Some Byzantine soldiers tried to get hold of the Muslim women. The women struck them with tent poles, and smashed their skulls. Then Peter addressed Khaula from a safe distance "Surrender and I will see that you are not only safe, but that I make you the queen of my heart." Khaula retorted "You Byzantine dog, how can you dare marry a Muslim virgin. I will kill myself in the case of any such exigency." Peter ordered his men to surround the women and disarm them. The women were in a defiant mood, and would not allow any one approach them. Thereupon Peter ordered his soldiers to step forward with drawn swords.

Khalid's vengeance. When Khalid bin Walid who was leading the vanguard came to know of the disaster that had befallen his rearguard, he turned back and rushed to the relief of his men. Khalid struck with vengeance. The Byzantines were not only routed; they were massacred. Out of six thousand Byzantine horsemen only one hundred escaped back to Damascus to tell the story of the disaster that had fallen them. When Peter and his men were stepping forward to overpower the Muslim women, Khalid, Zarrar, and other Muslim warriors arrived at the spot to the aid of the Muslim women. Peter thereupon turned to flee but was intercepted by Zarrar the brother of Khaula. Addressing Zarrar, Peter said, "She is your sister; I make you a present of her." Zarrar said that he accepted the present, and then in return he had to give him the point of his spear. Thereupon Zarrar struck off the head of Peter and impaled it on his lance.

Battle of Ajnadein

March to Ajnadein. From Damascus and other parts of Syria, the Muslim forces marched to Ajnadein, and there camped at some distance from gigantic camp of the Byzantines.

Khalid's address. The total strength of the Muslim army was 40,000, while the strength of the Byzantine army was over one lakh. The odds appeared to be against the Muslims, but Khalid had firm faith in God. He inspected the ranks, and addressed the Muslim warriors thus:

> "O Comrades-in-arms, you are to face the biggest army that the Byzantines could muster. Should you come out of battle victorious all is yours. Fight in good earnest and remain steadfast to the teachings of Islam. See that you do not turn back for God sees you. Close your ranks; keep your heads; and do not lose heart".

Khalid's address to women contingent. Halting before the women's contingent in the Muslim army, Khalid said:

> "Sisters-in-faith, make sure that your actions be acceptable to Allah and His prophet. Your participation in this war will go down in history, and I know that you will acquit yourself honourably. Should the Byzantines attack you, show your mettle and the heroic stuff you are made of. Should you find any Muslim fleeing from the field reproach him until he turns again to face the enemy. It is by these means that you will infuse the menfolk with a spirit that can stand up against the heaviest odds."

Zarrar. Khalid sent Zarrar on a reconnaissance mission. He stripped himself to the waist and rode up to the centre of the Byzantine camp. Here he was seen by the Byzantines, and a body of thirty Byzantine soldiers rode out to catch him. Zarrar killed nineteen of the Byzantine soldiers before the survivors turned and galloped back to their camp. In the Byzantine camp, Zarrar became a legend for daredevilry.

The Byzantine spy. The Byzantines sent a Christian

Arab to the Muslim camp to get information about the strength and quality of the Muslim forces. The spy when went back in the Byzantine camp reported about the Muslims in the following terms:

> "By night they are like monks; by day they are like warriors. If the son of the ruler were to commit theft, they would cut off his hand, and if he were to commit adultery, they would stone him to death."

On getting this report, Qubuqlar the Deputy Commander of the Byzantine forces declared:

> "If what you say is true, it would be better to be in the belly of the earth than to meet such people upon its surface."

Commencement of the battle of Ajnadein. The battle of Ajnadein began on 30th July 634 C.E. The Muslim army was deployed on a front of about five miles. The centre was placed under M'uadh bin Jabal; the right wing was placed under Saeed bin 'Amir; while the left wing was placed under Abdur Rahman the son of the Caliph Hadrat Abu Bakr. Khalid commanded the force as a whole, and he kept a reserve with him who could be commissioned for special jobs. This reserve included among others: 'Amr bin Al-Aas; Zarrar; Rafe' and Abdullah the son of Hadrat Umar.

Peace offer of the Byzantines. The Byzantines took the battle position about half a mile away from the Muslim front line. Before the battle began, a venerable old man dressed in black emerged from the Byzantine ranks and walked up half way towards the Muslim army. Khalid stepped forward to meet him. Addressing Khalid, the Byzantine bishop said:

> "Lo', we have an army numerous as the atoms, and it is not like the armies you have met before. With this army, Caesar has sent his mightiest Generals. My master is nevertheless inclined to be generous with you. Withdraw and we will give each of you a dinar, a robe, and a turban, and for you there will be a hundred dinars, hundred robes, and hundred turbans."

Khalid repudiating the peace offer said:

"We have not come here to accept alms. Your choice is either to accept Islam or pay *Jizya*. The third alternative is sword. We are not afraid of the strength of your army. Our one man may fight against ten of your men."

The first day of the battle. The battle began with personal combats. From the Muslim camp, Zarrar stepped forward, and he gave the battle cry:

"I am the death of the pale ones;
I am the killer of the Byzantines;
I am a scourge sent for you;
I am Zarrar bin Al-Azwar".

All the Byzantine champions who came forward to meet the challenge of Zarrar were killed by him. These included three Byzantine Generals. Thereafter, Khalid ordered a charge, and the entire Muslim front dashed forward hurling itself at the Byzantine army. The battle raged furiously for several hours. By the evening, both sides broke contact, and fell back to their original lines.

Werdan's conspiracy. Werdan, the Commander-in-Chief of Byzantines, was distressed that on the first day of the battle, thousands of Byzantines had been killed, while the casualties on the Muslim side were very few. Werdan was overawed by Khalid, and he felt that as long as Khalid was there to command the Muslim forces, there was little chance for the Byzantines to win a victory. He, accordingly hatched a plot to ambush Khalid.

A Christian Arab was sent to Muslim camp with a message from Werdan that Khalid should meet him for peace parleys. So great was the awe of Khalid that the emissary disclosed the details of the plot Werdan had hatched, and indicated the spot where under the instructions of Werdan, the Byzantines were to lie concealed to fall upon Khalid unawares.

Death of Werdan. The next day as the two armies again took the field, Khalid and Werdan stepped forward to negotiate peace parleys. Werdan desired that the Muslim force should withdraw, and they could have some money. Khalid ridiculed the offer and said that in case the Byzantines did not accept Islam or pay Jizya, the sword alone would decide the issue. Thereupon, Werdan gave the signal, and from behind the hillock emerged ten warriors dressed in Byzantine uniforms. As they came forward, Khalid saw that they were Zarrar and his companions. They had killed the Byzantine soldiers sent by Werdan and had donned their uniforms. Zarrar, at once, fell on Werdan and severed his head with his sword.

The Muslim victory. With the death of Werdan, the Muslims launched the attack. The Muslims struck violently, and the Byzantines struggled desperately to hold the assault. Then Khalid brought in his reserves. That turned the tide of the battle. The Muslims drove deep wedges into the Byzantine army. Some Muslim soldiers advanced and killed Qaubuqlar who commanded the Byzantine forces after the death of Werdan. With the death of Qubuqlar, the Byzantines lost heart and fled from the battlefield. The Muslim cavalry pursued the fugitives and the Byzantines were slaughtered in thousands. The Muslims won a complete victory. The large Byzantine army at Ajnadein was practically annihilated.

Report of the battle. Khalid sent a detailed report of the Muslim victory to Hadrat Abu Bakr along with the state share of the booty. At the battle of Ajnadein over 50,000 Byzantine soldiers died against 450 Muslims only. At Madina the news of the victory was received with great joy. Hadrat Abu Bakr lay ill, and this good news cheered him up.

Siege of Damascus

Yaqusa. After the battle of Ajnadein, the Muslims broke the camp at Ajnadein in the first week of August 634 C.E. and set out for Damascus. The advance of the Muslims was resisted by a Byzantine force at Yaqusa on the bank of the Yermuk. The Byzantine force was defeated with considerable loss, and Muslims pushed on towards their objective Damascus.

Marj-us-Saffar. After three days march from Yaqusa, the Muslim forces arrived at Marj-us-Saffar, twelve miles from Damascus, and here their way was barred by a Byzantine force. The battle began on the 19th August with personal duels. In these duels the Muslim cavaliers won and their Byzantine counterparts lost their lives. When after the personal combats, the battle began, the Byzantines stood firm for a few hours, but as the Muslims increased their pressure, the Byzantine forces withdrew. Two Byzantine Generals, Kulus and Azazeer were captured alive. Many Byzantine soldiers were killed. The survivors withdrew post haste to Damascus.

Gibbon. In his well known work *Decline and Fall of the Romau Empire,* Gibbon has a passage giving a graphic description of the arrival of the Muslim forces at Damascus. He writes:

> "The sad tidings of the fall of Ajnadein were carried to Damascus by the speed of grief and terror, and the inhabitants beheld from the walls of the city the return of the Muslim heroes of Ajnadein. Amr bin Al-'Aas led the van at the head of nine thousand horse; the bands of the Muslims followed each other in formidable review; and the rear was closed by Khalid in person, with the standard of the black eagle. To the activity of Zarrar, he entrusted the commission of patrolling round the city with two thousand horse, of scouring the plain and of intercepting all succour or intelligence. The rest of the Arabian chiefs were fixed in their respective stations before the seven gates of Damascus and the siege was renewed with vigour and confidence."

Byzantine garrison. The Byzantine garrison in Damascus was commanded by Thomas, a son-in-law of the Byzantine emperor Heraclius. At the principal gate of the city, the Byzantines erected a lofty crucific before which prayers were offered that the Son of God would defend his servants and vindicate his truth.

The siege. The siege of Damasus began on the 21st of August, and on the 23rd of August 634 C.E., Hadrat Abu Bakr was dead. Damascus fell in the hands of the Muslims in September 634 C.E. during the caliphate of Hadrat Umar.

NOTES

This Chapter gives an account of the campaigns in Syria.

When in the apostasy campaigns Hadrat Abu Bakr constituted eleven corps each under its own commander and each corp was assigned a destination, one of the corps under 'Amr b. Al-Aas was required to take action against the apostate tribes of Quza'a and Wadee'a in the area of Tabuk and Daumatul Jandal along the borders of Syria. While the sources give an account of the apostasy campaigns in central, south and east Arabia no account is given of the action on the western front. This appears to show that the tribes in the western region were reconverted to Islam without any difficulty and there was no military action. As the Muslim forces later penetrated into Syria under the Byzantines this shows that the border tribes had been generally won over to Islam by this time. It is obvious that the Muslims could not have penetrated in Syria with hostile tribes in the rear.

The first section tells of the plan of the campaign in Syria and Khalid bin Saeed's discomfiture. In order to strengthen the front at Syria, Hadrat Abu Bakr directed Khalid bin Waleed to march to Syria. The second section tells of Khalid's march to Syria. The third section gives an account of the battle of Busra. The fourth section tells of the siege of Damascus and its lifting. The fourth section gives an account of the battle of Ajnadein. The fifth section gives an account of the second siege of Damascus. The account is incomplete as Hadrat Abu Bakr died when the campaign had just begun and the conduct of the campaign thereafter concerns the caliphate of Hadrat Umar.

In writing this Chapter I have derived help from the following books:

(1) *The Sword of Allah* by A. I. Akram.
(2) *Abu Bakr, the Caliph by A. A. Aziz.*
(3) *Abu Bakr, Sidiq-i-Akbar* by Muhammad Hussain Haykal.
(4) *Hadrat Abu Bakr by* Syed Moinul Haq.

15

POLITICAL, SOCIAL, ECONOMIC AND MILITARY ORGANISATION

Political Organisation

Government of Hadrat Abu Bakr. As Caliph, Hadrat Bakr was the Head of the Government of the Islamic State Hadrat Abu Bakr held Government to be a sacred trust, and he ran Government as if he were administering the affairs of a trust. To Hadrat Abu Bakr, the office of the Caliph was not a means of earthly glory; he regarded it as a burden that he had to discharge in the interest of Islam. About the nature of his office, and his responsibilities he declared in unequivocal terms:

> "O ye men, now do I long that some one else may take the burden of the State on his shoulders. If you expect from me that I should come upto the standard set by the Holy Prophet, then you must know that I cannot fulfil your expectations because he was immune from all sins and had the assistance of divine revelations while I am an ordinary man subject to human fallibility."

Character of Polity. Hadrat Abu Bakr took pains to impress upon the people that he was only the first among the equals. For him, all men, rich or poor, high or low were equal. His rule was the rule of the law, but the law that he had to administer was not man made law; it was divine law. There is no priesthood in Islam, and as such the caliphate was not a theocracy. As all power lay with the people, the political order was democratic in character, but the democracy was not like the democracy we know today. In the polity that Hadrat Abu Bakr administered the will of the people was paramount, but it was subject to divine will. As such the polity was neither theocracy nor democracy in the sense in which the West understands these terms. It was democracy under the umbrella of divinity, the vicegerency of the people organised to carry into effect the will of God as embodied in Islam.

Constitutional ruler. Hadrat Abu Bakr was a constitutional ruler as his rule was subject to constitution. But the constitution in this case was not man made; it was divine. As a ruler, Hadrat Abu Bakr had to discharge a three fold responsibility. He was responsible to God, and it was his responsibility to enforce the commandments of God as contained in the Holy Qur'an. He was responsible to the Holy Prophet, and it was his endeavour to follow in the footsteps of the Holy Prophet, and prove himself to be a true representative of the Holy Prophet. In this respect he had to seek guidance from the Sunnah. He was also responsible to the people. It was his endeavour to ensure that all that he did commanded the approval of the people. As Caliph, Hadrat Abu Bakr was the Head of the State as well as the Government. As representative of the Holy Prophet he was also the religious head. He wielded power, but the polity was organised in such a way that power did not lead to corruption; it served as an instrument of service. As Caliph, Hadrat Abu Bakr was more of a father to the people than as the ruler.

Advisory Council. The Caliph was aided by an Advisory Council. It comprised all companions. There was, however, nothing hard and fast about the Advisory Council. Its constitution, its conduct of business were all informal. All decisions were arrived at through the process of concensus. There was no monopoly about the Advisory Council. Even an ordinary Muslim could express his views and render advice. It was open to the Caliph to accept or not to accept the advice offered to him, but whenever Hadrat Abu Bakr did not accept the advice tendered to him, he advanced reason therefor.

Secretariat. The Government of Hadrat Abu Bakr carried correspondence. Hadrat Ali, Hadrat Usman, and Zaid b. Thabit acted as Secretaries. There was, however, no elaborate Secretariat. No remuneration was paid to the Secretaries. There were no palatial buildings to house the Government offices. All Government business was conducted in the main mosque at Madina. There were no elaborate departments for the conduct of Government business. There was however division of functions among the Companions, and each Companion was responsible for specified functions. Hadrat Umar acted as a Minister to the Caliph, and was in charge of judicial administration. Hadrat Abu Ubaida Jarrah was in charge of the financial administration.

Caliphal duties. As Caliph, Hadrat Abu Bakr did not live in any palace. He lived in an ordinary house as a commoner. He was accessible to every person. If any person had any grievance, he could place it before the Caliph without any difficulty or formality. Hadrat Abu Bakr always took prompt steps to redress the grievances of the people. Hadrat Abu Bakr personally led the prayers. He reviewed the problems every week in the Friday Khutba, and took the people in confidence in formulating his policies.

Local administration. For the purpose of local administration the country was divided into provinces each under a Governor. Arabia proper was divided into ten provinces, namely, Madina, Makkah, Taif, San'a, Hadramawt, Khaulan, Zubaid, Jund, Bahrain, and Najran. Iraq was divided into three provinces, namely: Hirah, Dumatul Jandal, and Muzainah. Syria was divided into four provinces: Hims, Damascus, Jordan and Palestine. The Governor was required to lead prayers. He superintended the army, collected taxes, administered justice, maintained law and order, supervised public morals, and provided social services. He was aided by an Amil who collected revenues, and a Qadi who administered justice. Subject to the payment of 'Jizya', the minorities enjoyed cultural autonomy and managed their affairs themselves.

Social Organisation

Social values of Islam. Islam revolutionised social life in Arabia. The Holy Prophet set the pattern for Islamic society, and it was the endeavour of Hadrat Abu Bakr to follow in the footsteps of the Master, and promote the social values of Islam. Hadrat Abu Bakr was the embodiment of all the social values for which Islam stood. Islam stood for piety, and by all accounts, Hadrat Abu Bakr led a pious life. He led the prayers in the mosque. All the Muslims in Madina gathered for prayer in the mosque five times a day. On Fridays there were special congregations. Hadrat Abu Bakr addressed such congregations and delivered eloquent addresses. Hadrat Abu Bakr took steps to ensure that there was no lapse in the matter of the observance of the injunctions of Islam. When his son Abdullah lost in the love of his wife Atika failed to fulfil his religious obligations, Hadrat Abu Bakr asked him to divorce his wife. When some tribes suggested that they would offer prayers, but would not pay Zakat, Hadrat Abu Bakr declared that if they withheld even a moiety of what was payable in Zakat he would fight against them. As a result of this strictness on the part of Hadrat Abu Bakr, the society came to be fully impregnated with the values of Islam.

Egalitarian Society. Hadrat Abu Bakr took pains to build an egalitarian society in which there was no distinction between the high and the low. He said, "None should look down upon any Muslim for in the eyes of Allah even an inferior Muslim is great". It was suggested to him that the spoils of war should be distributed according to the status of the people. He did not accept the suggestion, and insisted on equal distribution regardless of the rank or status of the people. It was the endeavour of Hadrat Abu Bakr that all those who were destitute were provided maintenance at state expense. A story is told of a blind woman who lived in a suburb of Madina who had no one to support her. Hadrat Abu Bakr visited her every day and looked after her needs. Wherever there was any person in distress, Hadrat Abu Bakr was always there to relieve the distress. As a result of this policy of Hadrat Abu Bakr, a society emerged which was free from social distress.

Social justice. Hadrat Abu Bakr was very particular that due justice should be done to all the members of the community without fear or favour according to the injunctions of Islam. At the time of the assumption of office as Caliph he declared:

> "The weak among you shall be strong with me till God willing his rights have been vindicated and the strong among you shall be weak with me till, if the Lord wills, I have taken what is due from him."

Hadrat Abu Bakr strictly followed this policy and administered even handed justice. As a result of this policy, a society came to be established in Madina which was practically litigation free.

Simplicity. Hadrat Abu Bakr took pains to ensure that the people led simple lives free from ostentation. Hadrat Abu Bakr himself set the pattern for simple living. He slept on the floor. His meals were abstemious. He attended to his jobs himself. He lived in an ordinary house. There were no guards to attend to him. According to Gibbon, "The pride of his simplicity insulted the vain magnificence of the kings of the earth". It is related that one of the wives of Hadrat Abu Bakr once wished for a sweet dish. The Caliph said that he had no money for such luxury. She said, "Then permit me to save something daily, and then have a sweet dish when sufficient amount has been collected." He gave the permission, and in a few days she saved some amount. Hadrat Abu Bakr deposited this amount in the public treasury, and got his daily allowance reduced by such amount as had been saved by his wife. When some members of the ruling family of Yemen arrived in Madina they wore rich attire. When they saw that the Caliph wore simple coarse clothes they felt ashamed and discarded their finery. All the companions of Hadrat Abu Bakr followed his example, and vied with one another in simple and unostentatious living. In this way the social life in Madina came to be marked by simple living devoid of all show and ostentation.

Society of action. The pre-Islamic society was tribal in concept and complexion, the new Islamic society was universal in character. There was thus a broadening of social horizons. The society impregnated with Islamic values came to be characterised by social refinement, social decorum, social justice, and social health. That led to social solidarity and social happiness. The people living in such social environments came to feel that they had a destiny to fulfil. That motivated them to play their part in the fulfilment of their destiny. The society thus came to have a creative outlook, and the Arabian desert heretofore known for the ignorance and backwardness of its people became the nursery of heroes. The static society thus came to be transformed into a society of action.

Moral values. The moral values of Islam provided the guidelines for the social life. The people became accustomed to a disciplined life in which there was no place for any frivolity. Care was taken to ensure that in business matters there were no unfair deals. Great emphasis was laid on above board transactions. In Islam there was no place for fraud or deception. Islam called a spade a spade. The society over which Hadrat Abu Bakr presided was accordingly an elevated and purified society conspicuous for its high social and moral values.

Women. In the new society women played a creative role. They rocked the cradles in which heroes were bred. Women wrote poetry. Some women like Hadrat Ayesha were eminent scholars. Women fought in battles, e.g. Umm 'Amara, Khaula, and Jawariya. The age produced beautiful women like 'Atika, Umm Hakim, Laila the wife of Khalid and princess Kirama.

Economic Organisation

Character of the State. In the Islamic State under Hadrat Abu Bakr, the emphasis was on moral values, and the people were not motivated by material considerations. There was no race among the people to get rich overnight. Islamic laws operated to discourage the amassing of wealth. Islam favoured trade, but the faithful were enjoined not to indulge in any unfair practices. In the Muslim society there was no economic exploitation of one class by another. Although there were slaves, they were not exploited, and in the families the slaves were treated like other members of the families.

The economic levies. The economic levies were few. These were limited to Zakat, Ushr, Kharaj, Jizya, and Fay. When the Muslims embarked on their career of conquest "Ghanimah" i.e. the spoils of war became a major source of revenue.

Zakat. Zakat had some characteristics of a tax, but it was basically a religious obligation. It was levied on the basis of capital assets, and the idea was that one who was endowed with assets should pay a part in the way of Allah for distribution to the poor. It was in theory an instrument for the equalisation of wealth. A scale for the levy of Zakat was prescribed. Usually the criterion was that for every forty rupees of capital, one rupee should be paid as Zakat.

Ushr. Ushr was a tax on land produce. It was levied at one-tenth of the produce, and hence the name 'Ushr'—one-tenth.

Kharaj. In the case of land in conquered territories, the land owners had to pay a levy called "Kharaj". The rate of Kharaj was slightly higher than the rate of Ushr in Arab lands.

Jizya. In conquered territories where the people did not become Muslims they had to pay Jizya in lieu of protection to be afforded by the State. It was a poll tax payable at a certain rate per able bodied adult male. The poor, the disabled, and the monks as well as the women and children were exempt from the levy.

Fay. Fay was the income accruing from State land.

Ghanimah. In the days of Hadrat Abu Bakr much wealth came to the state on account of the spoils of war. The movable property won as booty on the battlefield was known as "Ghanimah". Four-fifth of the spoils of war were immediately distributed among the soldiers who had taken part in the battle. The remaining one-fifth went to the State. The State's one-fifth share was further divided into three parts. One part went to the family of the Holy Prophet, one part went to the

Caliph, and one part was spent for welfare purposes.

Annuities. When Hadrat Abu Bakr assumed office as Caliph there was no money in the treasury. After the end of the apostasy campaigns, Zakat came to be paid by all the tribes and that eased the situation. With the conquest of Iraq and Syria untold wealth poured into State treasury. The economic condition of the people improved to such an extent that there was no one to get Zakat. Hadrat Abu Bakr, therefore, distributed annuities to the entire Muslim community, every one receiving an equal share.

Economic prosperity of the people. The economic organisation of the Islamic State under the Holy prophet and thereafter under Hadrat Abu Bakr was unique in the annals of mankind. The State had no salaries bill to foot. All State functionaries at the higher level worked honorarily. Military service was performed on voluntary basis. Nominal taxes were levied on the people, and these were returned to the people as annuities. In most cases what the State paid to the people was more than what it had realised from them as taxes. Under Hadrat Abu Bakr the Muslim community was thus the most prosperous community ever known to history.

Military Organisation Under Hadrat Abu Bakr

Army. In the time of Hadrat Abu Bakr, no standing army or mercenary force was kept by the State. In the case of any emergency, recruiting parties were sent to the various tribes to recruit volunteers. Inspired by religious fervour for 'Jihad' and for patriotic and economic considerations, volunteers willingly enrolled themselves in large numbers whenever there was a call to arms. On this basis for every military expedition, a new militia was raised, and when the expedition was over, the militia was disbanded.

Military service. Military service constituted the noblest of professions in the eyes of the Arabs. "Jihad" was according to the tenets of Islam incumbent on every adult male Muslim, and the entire community was regarded as the army of Islam. No salary was paid to the soldiers. They were allowed a share in the spoils of war. During the caliphate of Hadrat Abu Bakr, so great were the spoils of war, particularly in the campaigns in Iraq and Syria that every soldier amassed so much wealth as sufficed for his lifetime.

The Caliph. As the Caliph, Hadrat Abu Bakr was the Generalissimo or the Supreme Commander. A commander was appointed for each column by the Caliph. The Caliph personally awarded the standard to each commander. The commander was responsible to the Caliph, and the Caliph issued directions from time to time to direct military operations. The commander as the representative of the Caliph presided at daily prayers, and all soldiers in the column were required to attend the congregation.

Composition of the army. The army was composed of cavalry and infantry. The cavalry was armed with shields, swords and long lances. The infantry was armed with shields, and bows. The formation of the infantry was generally in line three deep with lancers in front and the archers in the rear. The cavalry was usually posted on the flanks. The cavalrymen wore chain armour with steel helmets. The infantry men were clad in tight fitting tunics. The armies were always well provisioned. Long marches were made on camels.

March to the battlefield. The army marched to the battlefield chanting verses from the Holy Qur'an. Orators were attached to every column who exhorted the soldiers to do their duty to Islam, and to live upto the standards of the Arab ideals of chivalry. The Muslims marched to the battlefield with the beat of drums. They delivered the attacks with the shouts of "Allah-o-Akbar".

Offer to the enemy. Before attack, the enemy was always offered three alternatives, namely acceptance of Islam, payment of Jizya or decision by sword. Where a people accepted Islam, they were treated as part and parcel of the Muslim community and no conditions were imposed. Where a people wished to stick to their faith, and pay Jizya they were allowed cultural autonomy and were guaranteed full protection. I Where a people chose to fight, the Muslim attacks were always violent, and in many cases the entire force of the enemy was exterminated. Those who were taken captive were either released on ransom or kept as slaves.

On the battlefield. All battles began with personal duels between chosen warriors from both the sides. In such duels the Muslim champions always won. After such duels the battle developed into a general hand to hand fight in which all the troops took part. On the battlefield the army divided itself in five units called "Khamis". These were the centre, the right wing, the left wing, the vanguard and the rear guard. The flanks were covered by the cavalry. The archers were so disposed as to cover both cavalry and infantry. The organisation of the army was based on tribal units. Each tribe had its own distinct contingent with its own leader and banner. Many tribes marched to the battlefield with their families in their train. There were special contingents of women. They were employed as nurses, cooks, store guards and water carriers.

Code of conduct. The soldiers were required to follow strict code of conduct. They were required to observe strict discipline and scrupulously obey the command of their superiors. Persons found guilty of breach of discipline were punished. Where a soldier displayed any cowardice on the battlefield he was subjected to the humiliation of his turban being taken off his head. The soldiers had strict orders not to kill monks, priests, women, children, the slaves, the sick and the aged. They were not to sack any town or village, or destroy or ravage any arable land. There was to be no wanton pillaging, no trees were to be cut, and no crops were to be burnt or destroyed. No corpses of the enemy were to be burnt or mutilated. The dead of the enemy were to be buried with due respect, and where requests were made for particular corpses by the enemy, these were to be freely handed over.

Victories of the Muslims. During the caliphate of Hadrat Abu Bakr all the military campaigns undertaken by the

Muslims ended in their victory. The Muslims fought against forces superior to them in strength and numbers, but victory always lay with the Muslims. The Muslims won reputation for their invincibility. Even the biased western writers have been forced to admit that during the period of the caliphate of Hadrat Abu Bakr, the desert of Arabia became the nursery of heroes. The story of the Muslim conquest of Iraq and Syria, the miraculous exploits of the Muslim heroes, and the manner in which they dealt blows after blows on the armies of Persia and Byzantium read like some fiction from the Arabian Nights. And if truth were to be ever stranger than fiction, that is so in the case of Muslim conquests under Hadrat Abu Bakr.

Causes of Muslim victories. The main causes of the victories of the Muslims during the caliphate of Hadrat Abu Bakr were the high morale of the Muslim soldiers, their religious enthusiasm, their endurance, their mobility, and the superb directions of Hadrat Abu Bakr. To these basic causes may be added the unique generalship of Khalid, heroism of Muslim soldiers and the blessings of Allah and His Prophet.

NOTES

In this Chapter the first section deals with the political organisation under Hadrat Abu Bakr. The second section deals with social organisation. The third section deals with economic organisation. The fourth section deals with military organisation. In writing this Chapter I have derived help from the following books:

(1) *Arab Administration* by S.A.Q. Hussaini: and
(2) *Studies in Muslim Thought and Administration* by H. K. Sherwani.

Hadrat Abu Bakr did not introduce any new organisation. He continued the organisation as introduced by the Holy Prophet. Such organisation was fool proof and perfect in every way. Such organisation stood the Muslim in good stead, and because of the strength of such organisation the Muslims faced the various crises in the time of Hadrat Abu Bakr and successfully overcame all crises. It is a matter of regret that because of the vicissitudes of history we have adopted the organisations obtaining in the secular west, and have disregarded our own heritage. It is necessary that we should resurrect our heritage, and adopt the pattern set by the Holy Prophet and successfully worked by Hadrat Umar. We may make such modifications as may be necessary to suit modern conditions, but we will not be true to ourselves if we disregard our own organisation and adopt the pattern of organisation obtaining in the secular west which is repugnant to the spirit of Islam.

16

MUSHAF, HADITH, TASAWWUF, FIQH AND POETRY

The Mushaf

The Holy Qur'an. The Holy Qur'an was revealed to the Holy Prophet in parts from time spread over a period of twenty three years. Whenever the Holy Prophet received the revelation, he would dictate it to some person who would record it on some piece of leather, date skin or even bones and stones. The principal scribe of the Holy Prophet was Zaid bin Thabit. Many companions committed the entire Qur'an to memory, and these "Huffaz" could recite the entire Qur'an from memory. The Holy Prophet kept all the piece of leather, date stones and other materials on which the verses of the Holy Qur'an were recorded in his custody.

The need for the compilation of the Holy Qur'an. During the life time of the Holy Prophet, revelation was a constant process, and there was no occasion for giving the various verses the form of a book. After the death of the Holy Prophet, the process of revelation came to close, and now the need for some sort of compilation was felt. In the battle of Yamamah, most of the "Huffaz" were martyred. It struck Hadrat Umar that if the "Huffaz" died, there was the danger that at one stage there would be no body who could be depended upon as the custodian of the Holy Qur'an.

The project compilation of the Holy Qur'an. Hadrat Umar suggested to Hadrat Abu Bakr that all the revelations of the Holy Qur'an should be collected, and compiled in the form of a book. Hadrat Abu Bakr was in the first instance reluctant to undertake the project for the reason that as the Holy Prophet had not felt the necessity of such compilation, it did not behove him, as the successor to the Holy Prophet, to take any initiative in the matter. Hadrat Umar, however, continued to press his proposal. He argued that as during the life-time of the Holy Prophet, the process of revelation was continuous, there was no occasion for stringing the various verses in the form of a compilation, but after the death of the Holy Prophet, and the cessation of the process of revelation, the position had changed, and it devolved on the successor of the Holy Prophet to suitably conserve the Holy Qur'an lest it might be lost or corrupted in the course of time. The argument appealed to Hadrat Abu Bakr, and on futher consideration, he agreed to undertake the project.

Zaid bin Thabit. Zaid bin Thabit was summoned by Hadrat Abu Bakr and entrusted with the task of collecting all the verses, and compiling them in a book form. Zaid's immediate reaction to proposal was that if he had been asked to remove a mountain from its original site, and place it elsewhere, he would have considered it easier than the task of compiling the Holy Qur'an. Hadrat Abu Bakr appreciated the difficulties of Zaid bin Thabit' but observed that the word of God had to be preserved for the guidance of the coming generations, and the task had to be undertaken, whatever the odds. Zaid accepted the commission, and after hard labour and in consultation with the various companions of the Holy Prophet produced a compilation. Hadrat Abu Bakr was himself a *Hafiz*. He, therefore, checked the compilation of Zaid very minutely, and after making whatever changes were necessary, he kept the finally approved copy in his personal custody. He gave the sacred compilation the name of "Mushaf".

Hadrat Abu Bakr and the Hadith

The Hadith. When companions of the Holy Prophet heard anything from him, or saw him doing an act, they faithfully preserved an account of what he had said or done.

When all such accounts were compiled and edited, the corpus became the Hadith, a source for the Muslims.

Items of the Hadith attributed to Hadrat Abu Bakr. Out of the entire collection of Hadith running into thousands of items, only 142 items are attributed to the authority of Hadrat Abu Bakr. Of all the companions of the Holy Prophet, Hadrat Abu Bakr was the closest to him, and one would expect Hadrat Abu Bakr to be a repository of a larger number of traditions. The comparitively smaller number of traditions owing their authority to the reporting of Hadrat Abu Bakr is attributed to the extraordinary care and caution exercised by Hadrat Abu Bakr in sifting the tradition.

Hadrat Ayesha's account of the preservation of traditions by Hadrat Abu Bakr. According to Hadrat Ayesha, Hadrat Abu Bakr had originally a collection of over five hundred traditions, and he deposited the compilation with her for custody. Hadrat Ayesha relates that one night she noticed that Hadrat Abu Bakr felt very restless. He tossed about in the bed, and could not sleep, Hadrat Ayesha got worried whether he was suffering or was worried. He made no reply, but remained restless throughout the night. The following morning he asked Hadrat Ayesha to bring him the collections that he had deposited with her. She brought the compilation and he set fire to it. On the enquiry of Hadrat Ayesha, Hadrat Abu Bakr explained his conduct thus: "The collection contained many traditions which I had heard from other people. I thought that if I died and left behind a traditions accepted by me as authentic, but really not so, then I would have to answer for that."

Traditions authenticated by Hadrat Abu Bakr. Some of the tradition authenticated by Hadrat Abu Bakr are as follows:

(1) If the water is flowing, any aquatic animal found dead therein would be *Halal.*

(2) He who cleanses his teeth pleases God.

(3) If a man is with *Wudu,* and then takes his meals, he need not have the *Wudu* again.

(4) He who offers the morning prayers comes under the protection of Allah.

(5) No prophet dies until he offers prayers behind some one of his followers.
(6) If any body sins, and then offers prayers of repentence, Allah pardons him.
(7) The prophet dies at the spot where he is to be buried.
(8) The Jews and the Christians have earned the displeasure of God for worshipping the graves of their prophets.
(9) The dead man suffers because of the mourning over his dead body.
(10) Give in charity, even though it may be a single date.
(11) Do your job yourself. Do not put yourself under the obligation of any person for doing anything for you.
(12) He who deceives a *Momin* (firm believer) is accursed.
(13) He who is bad tempered, dishonest, unjust and tyrannous has no place in paradise.
(14) Prophets of Allah leave nothing to be inherited.
(15) He who travels in the way of Allah has a claim to paradise.
(16) Wherever there are two Muslims, the third one among them is Allah.
(17) Do not speak a lie, for a falsehood poisons faith.
(18) A just ruler is the shadow of Allah on earth.
(19) He who helps a person in distress earns the protection of Allah.
(20) If the people of paradise were to trade in anything they would have traded in cloth.
(21) He who wants to escape from torture of hell should not be hard on the people.
(22) If you wish for the mercy of Allah, be kind to His people.
(23) The people who abandon Jihad will not prosper.
(24) He who builds a mosque for Allah, Allah will build a house for him in the paradise.
(25) Religion is the standard of Allah, hold it aloft.
(26) On the occasion of the pilgrimage, the most excellent actions are the raising of the voice in the

talbiyah, and the shedding of the blood of the animals brought for sacrifice.

(27) He whose feet becomes dusty in the service of Allah, Allah will preserve him from hell fire.

(28) Infidelity moves more steathily among my people than the creeping of an ant.

(29) There is no part of the body that complains not of the sharpness of the tongue.

(30) The thief must be put to death for the fifth theft.

(31) The Friday prayer is an atonement for all that occurs until the next Friday prayer, and ablution on a Friday is an atonement for ablutions until the next Friday.

(32) To every one who, has fought at Badr, is announced the tiding of paradise.

(33) He who condoles with a bereaved mother, Allah will cover him with His shadow.

(34) A slanderer will not enter paradise.

(35) Neglect not to invoke Allah against Satan.

(36) The Surah of *Hud* has made me (the Holy Prophet) grey.

Hadrat Abu Bakr and Tasawwuf

Tasawwuf. Tasawwuf stands for purification. According to the Holy Qur'an, the purpose of Islam is that:

> "Allah wishes to remove from you all uncleanliness, And He will purify you a complete purifying."

Hadrat Abu Bakr was a pure soul, and he had all the attributes which are the sine qua non of Tasawwuf.

Hadrat Junaid. Hadrat Abu Bakr was the first person to give instructions about the reciting of the sacred *Kalimah* as a means for purification of the heart. According to Hadrat Junaid, a prominent Sufi of Baghdad, the noblest saying about 'unification' is that of Hadrat Abu Bakr who said:

> "Glory to God who has not vouchsafed to His creatures any means of attaining knowledge of Him except through

impotence to attaining such knowledge". The implication is that *Ijz* or helplessness is the only way of attaining the knowledge of God. The test of learning is that one should have the feeling that he has yet much to learn.

Imam of the Sufis. Hadrat Ali Hajveri has stated in his classic work *Kashful Mahjub* that Hadrat Abu Bakr is the Imam of the Sufis. Most of the Sufi orders originate with Hadrat Ali, but the Naqshbandi order originates with Hadrat Abu Bakr who is regarded as the first person to percieve the truth about Sufism. The Sufis maintain that Hadrat Abu Bakr rose to the highest stage of Tasawwuf, and that he had some of the qualities that characterised the Prophet Abraham. The Holy Qur'an confers on Abraham the title of *Awwah*, one who sighs much, and this was the name by which Hadrat Abu Bakr was known among his companions. Hadrat Abu Bakr would often sigh and say "I wish I were a bird", or "I wish I were a tree', or again "I wish I were a hair on the body of a Momin". On seeing a bird perched on the branch of a tree, Hadrat Abu Bakr would heave a sigh and say, "O bird you are happy. You eat of the fruits of the tree, and live under its shadow. You have no fear of rendering accounts. How I wish I had been in a position similar to yours".

Sufic thought of Hadrat Abu Bakr. Hadrat Abu Bakr said: "Our abode in this world is transitory. Our life therein is but a loan. Our breaths are numbered, and our indolence is manifest."

According to Hadrat Abu Bakr's way of thinking, the world is too worthless to engage our thoughts for whenever you occupy yourself with what is perishable, you are made blind to what is eternal. This is obviously the thought of a Master Sufi.

Philosophy of the life of Hadrat Abu Bakr. According to Hadrat Ali Hajveri the approach of a Sufi is as follows:

> "O God give me plenty of the world, and make me desirous of renouncing it. First bestow on me goods that I may give thanks for them, and then help me to abstain from them for Your sake so that I may have the treble merit

of thanksgiving, liberality and abstinence, and that my poverty may be voluntary, not compulsory."

This was the basic approach of Hadrat Abu Bakr as well. By hard work and labour he amassed considerable wealth, and then spent it entirely in the way of Allah. Hadrat Abu Bakr led the life of a poor man, but he was not poor in the sense that he had no money; he was poor only in the sense that he had no desire for money. Poverty in his case was not compulsory it was voluntary. In the case of a person who has no resources, poverty is compulsory. On the other hand, a person who has enough of money but prefers to live like a poor man, takes over to poverty in a voluntary way. Hadrat Abu Bakr's life was a striking example of preferring voluntary poverty to compulsory poverty in the Sufi way.

Apogee of Tasawwuf. According to a well-known anecdote, the Holy Prophet invited contribution from the Muslims for financing the expedition to Tabuk. In response to the invitation Hadrat Umar brought a considerable portion of his wealth. As he came loaded with the contribution, Hadrat Umar thought that day he would surpass Hadrat Abu Bakr in the matter of service to Islam. The Holy Prophet was very happy to receive the contribution from Hadrat Umar. "Have you left anything for yourself" asked the Holy Prophet, and Hadrat Umar replied, "I have left one half for myself." Then Hadrat Abu Bakr came with his contribution, and when the Holy prophet put him the same question he promptly replied, "I have brought all I had, I have left Allah and His Prophet for myself and my dependents." This approach marks the apogee of Tasawwuf.

Fear of God. The main plank of Sufism is fear of God. Throughout his life, Hadrat Abu Bakr was guided by the principle of the fear of God . As the caliph, he enjoined all the functionaries of the State to fear God. It is on record that when offering prayers the fear of God would so overwhelm Hadrat Abu Bakr that he would look like a stick of dry wood.

Hadrat Abu Bakr's Prayer. The ususal prayer of Hadrat Abu Bakr was:

"O Allah You know me better than I do;
And I know myself better than the people;
O Allah make me better than what the people think of me,
And forgive me for the sins which the people do not know,
And do not call me to account for what the people say about me."

It is the typical prayer of a Sufi.

Equation between man and God. When the Holy Prophet died, and the people would not believe that he was dead, Hadrat Abu Bakr said:

"Whoever worshipped Muhammad, let him know that Muhammad is dead, but whoever worships the God of Muhammad, let him know that He lives and dies not."

This classic quotation which has passed into history is an embodiment of the highest values of Islam and Sufism. It sets an equation between man and God, and it cannot be put in more meaningful words than what Hadrat Abu Bakr did. That is the most consummate thought of a Sufi.

Hadrat Abu Bakr's way of Sufism. According to Hadrat Data Ganj Bakhsh, Hadrat Abu Bakr's way of Sufism was the contemplative way as compared to the purgative way of Hadrat Umar. When Hadrat Abu Bakr prayed he recited the Holy Qur'an in a low voice, while Hadrat Umar recited the Holy Qur'an in a loud voice. When the Holy Prophet asked Hadrat Umar the reason for his reciting the Holy Qur'an in a loud voice he said, "I wake the drowsy and drive away the devil." When Hadrat Abu Bakr was asked to explain why he recited the Holy Qur'an in a low voice, he said, "He with whom I converse will hear." With Hadrat Abu Bakr the recitation of the Holy Qur'an was the means of communion with God and that was the Sufi way.

Father of Tasawwuf. Tasawwuf is the way of truth. Tasawwuf implies that a Sufi should be assiduous in piety. It also means that one should give up all else for God's sake. The keynote of Tasawwuf is selfless devotion. If we study the attributes of Hadrat Abu Bakr, we are struck by the fact that all the attributes that go to make a Sufi were very conspicuous with Hadrat Abu Bakr. He was "Siddiq" endowed with the vision to perceive that truth. He was most assiduous in piety. He gave away all his wealth for God's sake. He was selfless. When he became the Caliph he stated on oath that he had never coveted the office. Hadrat Abu Bakr was the symbol of selflessness among the companions of the Holy Prophet. His devotion and dedication to Allah, His Prophet, and Islam were of the highest order, and no other companion of the Holy Prophet excelled him in that respect. No wonder Hadrat Abu Bakr is the "Father of Tasawwuf".

Hadrat Abu Bakr and Fiqh

Origin of Fiqh. The Holy Prophet got most of his knowledge directly from God through the process of revelation. Whenever the Holy Prophet had a difficult point to decide, he got the guidance from Allah. After the death of the Holy Prophet, the process of revelation ceased, and the task before the Muslims was to take decisions in the light of guidance that could be obtained from the Holy Qur'an and the Sunnah. That gave rise to Fiqh, the application of the principles of Islam to the day to day problems, and the settlement of disputes.

Father of Fiqh. The process of Fiqh began with Hadrat Abu Bakr, and he is regarded as the 'Father of Fiqh'. He was the first to frame the rules of *Ijtihad.* He laid down the principle that in deciding a case he would obtain guidance in the first instance from the Holy Qur'an. If the Holy Qur'an was silent in the matter, he would look for guidance to the traditions of the Holy Prophet as duly authenticated. If the traditions were also silent he was to decide the case according to his best judgment He held:

> "If my decision is just then it will be from God. If it is erroneous, it will be mine, and may God pardon me."

Primacy of Hadrat Abu Bakr in the matter of Fiqh. According to traditions, a woman came to the Holy Prophet in the last days of his life, and asked for his decision on a particular point. The Holy Prophet was unwell, and he asked her to come again. The woman said, "If I come next, and you are not there, to whom should I go?" The Holy Prophet said, in that case go to Abu Bakr." That established the primacy of Hadrat Abu Bakr in the matter of Fiqh.

Burial of the Holy Prophet. Immediately on the death of the Holy Prophet controversy arose as to the place where he Holy Prophet should be buried. Many different opinions were expressed in the matter. One view was that the Holy Prophet should be buried in the Prophet's mosque. Another view was that he should be buried in the common graveyard at Madina where his companions were buried. One view was that he should be buried at Jerusalem where others prophets lay buried. And yet another view was that he should be buried in the Holy Ka'aba at Makkah. As successor to the Holy Prophet, Hadrat Abu Bakr gave the decision that in accordance with a tradition of the Holy Prophet, the prophets are to be buried at the spot where they breathed their last, and as such he should be buried in the quarter of Hadrat Ayesha where he had breathed his last. This decision commanded the approval of all, and was duly carried into effect.

Property at Fidak. The Holy Prophet had some property at Fidak. The income from the property was utilized for the maintenance of the family of the Holy Prophet, and for other beneficial purposes. After the death of the Holy Prophet, Hadrat Fatima and some other members of the Holy Prophet's family lodged a claim for the inheritance of the property. Hadrat Abu Bakr ruled that, according to a tradition of the Holy Prophet, all that the prophets leave is for the community, and the usual laws of inheritance are not to apply to such property. Hadrat Abu Bakr accordingly did not accept the claim for inheritance. He ruled that the property would be state property, but the income therefrom would be utilised for the same purposes for which it was utilised during the lifetime of the Holy Prophet.

Exemption from Zakat. Immediately after the death of the Holy Prophet when the wave of apostasy spread over the land, some of the tribes demanded that they should be exempted from the payment of Zakat. The companions around Hadrat Abu Bakr advised that in view of danger that threatened the Muslims, the demand should be exempted. Hadrat Abu Bakr held that the payment of Zakat was a fundamental requirement of Islam, and it was not open to him to compromise on a fundamental injunction of Islam. He accordingly rejected the demand, and declared that if Zakat was not paid, he would fight for it.

Obedience to the orders of the Holy Prophet. During his lifetime the Holy Prophet had ordered that an expedition should be sent to Syria under the command of Usama b. Zaid. After the death of the Holy Prophet the general view of the companions was that in view of the danger that threatened Madina the expedition to Syria should be abandoned. It was further held that if the expedition was to be necessarily sent, a veteran commander should be appointed instead of Usama who was a young lad of nineteen only. Hadrat Abu Bakr held that as on these points the Holy Prophet had already given specific instructions, it was not open to him to amend or vary the orders of the Holy Prophet. He therefore ordered that the expedition to Syria was to be undertaken under the command of Usama as ordered by the Holy Prophet.

Murder of Malik b. Nuweira. When in the campaign against Bani Tamim, Khalid b. Walid killed Malik b. Nuweira, and married his beautiful wife Laila and it was alleged that Khalid was guilty of murdering a Muslim, Hadrat Abu Bakr held that as Commander in the field, Khalid had the authority to exercise his discretion, and if Malik had been killed it was, in the circumstances of the case, a lapse and not a wilful murder. Hadrat Abu Bakr settled the case by paying blood money to the heirs of Malik. When Hadrat Umar insisted on the punishment of Khalid Hadrat Abu Bakr declared that he could not sheathe the sword, which God had willed to be wielded against the infidels.

Al-Faja'a. Al-Faja'a, an adventurer posed to be a

Muslim, and got some arms from Hadrat Abu Bakr to fight against the apostates. Al-Faja'a betrayed the trust. Action was taken against him. He was taken captive, and brought to Madina where Hadrat Abu Bakr ordered him to be roasted alive. Later, Hadrat Abu Bakr regretted the decision. He wished he had pardoned him or killed him in some other way.

Father's share. Once a man complained before Hadrat Abu Bakr that his father wanted to appropriate all that he had. Hadrat Abu Bakr summoned the father, and asked him to take as sufficed for his maintenance, and leave the rest to his son.

A son disowned by the father. Once a man was brought before Hadrat Abu Bakr who had been disowned by his father. Hadrat Abu Bakr ordered:

"Smite him on his head for Satan is in his head."

Vow of silence. Once Hadrat Abu Bakr went to a woman of the tribe of Ahmas called Zaynab. She did not speak as she was under a vow of silence. Hadrat Abu Bakr said to her, "Speak, for silence is not lawful; it is one of the practices of the times of Ignorance."

Loss of an ear. Once in a quarrel a person had been deprived of an ear. Hadrat Abu Bakr awarded him fifteen camels. He said, "The hair and turban will conceal the disgrace of it."

Killing a man in anger. Once Hadrat Abu Bakr was enraged with a man and his anger became violent. One of the companions said, "O Caliph, shall I cut off his head ?" Hadrat Abu Bakr said, "Woe to you, this is not lawful."

Unlawful food. Once a slave of Hadrat Abu Bakr brought him some food which he ate. Later the slave told him that he had earned some money by telling fortune, and the food had been purchased with that money. Hadrat Abu Bakr held that such food was unlawful. He put his hand on his throat and vomited what was in his stomach.

Predestination. Once Hadrat Abu Bakr was asked,

"Do you think that fornication by a man is predestined?" He was next asked, "If it is predestined why should the man be punished ?" Hadrat Abu Bakr said, "The man is responsible for his act, but God knows before hand how a man would act".

Insulting the Holy Prophet and satirising the Muslims. In Yemen, a woman in her songs said nasty things against the Holy Prophet. Another woman recited verses satirising the Muslims. Muhajir b. Umayya, the Governor of Yemen cut off the hands of both the women. When the case was reported to Hadrat Abu Bakr he held that the women who had insulted the Holy Prophet should have been killed, while the other woman who had merely satirised the Muslims deserved a lenient treatment.

Asma bint Numan. In Yemen, Ikramah married a lady Asma bint Numan. The marriage became the subject of criticism because at one time Asma had been married to the Holy Prophet, and it was not lawful for a Muslim to marry a woman the Holy Prophet had married. Hadrat Abu Bakr decided that as in that case the Holy Prophet had returned the lady to the tribe without consummating the marriage, there was no objection to a Muslim marrying her.

Marriage to the first husband. Once a woman was divorced by a person, and she married another man. Before her second marriage was consummated she reconciled with her former husband, and wanted to return to him. Hadrat Abu Bakr ruled that she could not return to her first husband unless the second marriage was consummated, and she was properly divorced.

The case of Hadrat Umar's son Aasim. Hadrat Umar divorced one of his wives, and she took her young son Aasim with her. One day Hadrat Umar saw his son playing in the street. He lifted the boy, and brought him to his house. The mother applied to Hadrat Abu Bakr for the restoration of the child. Hadrat Umar resisted the suit, but Hadrat Abu Bakr decided the case against Hadrat Umar, and awarded the custody of the child to the mother.

Grandfather's share. In a case where the father was

not alive, but the grandfather was alive, Hadrat Abu Bakr awarded to the grandfather the share otherwise admissible to the father.

Share of the grandson. In a case where the son was not alive, Hadrat Abu Bakr awarded to the grandson the share otherwise admissible to the son.

Share of the grandmother. In a case, Hadrat Abu Bakr awarded the grandmother one-sixth share in the property left by the grandson.

Execution of the thief. Once a man came to Hadrat Abu Bakr from Yemen. His hands had been cut off for some act of theft. He stayed with Hadrat Abu Bakr for the night, and prayed for all the time. The man represented that the Governor of Yemen had cut off his hands in a high handed way. Hadrat Abu Bakr felt impressed with the piety of the man, and thought that perhaps the Governor of Yemen had been unfair to the man. In the morning, Asma the wife of Hadrat Abu Bakr complained that she had lost her locket. On enquiry it transpired that the man had stolen the locket, and sold it to goldsmith. Hadrat Abu Bakr ordered the man to be killed.

Mutilation. About awarding the punishment of mutilation, Hadrat Abu Bakr addressed a Governor as follows:

> "I have heard that you laid hands on a woman who had showered abuses on me, and you got her hands amputated. God has not sought vengeance even in the case of polytheism which is a great crime. He has not permitted mutilation even with regard to manifest infidelity. Try to be considerate and sympathetic in your attitude towards others in future. Never mutilate because it is a great offence. God purified Islam and the Muslims from rashness and excessive wrath. You are well aware of the fact that those enemies fell into the hands of the Messenger of Allah who had been recklessly abusing him, who had turned him out of his home, and who had fought against him but he never ordered their mutilation." *(Hadrat Abu Bakr ke Sarkari Khatut* by Khurshid Ahmad Fariq.)

Poetry in the Time of Hadrat Abu Bakr

Poetry. Hadrat Abu Bakr's caliphate lasted for some two years only. The period was occupied first by apostasy wars, and then by wars in Iraq and Syria. The Holy Qur'an dominated the intellectual scene, and there was accordingly not much of activity in the field of poetry. The Arabs had, however, an inherent taste for poetry, and the age did produce some eminent poets. Some of the events of the period were duly celebrated in poetry.

Hadrat Abu Bakr. There is some controversy on the point whether Hadrat Abu Bakr was or was not a poet. The Holy Qur'an did not talk of poets and poetry in favourable terms, and as such the early Muslims avoided poetry. Islam condemned frivolous poetry only; it allowed poetry of inspiring and ennobling character. A poem was written by Hadrat Abu Bakr on the occasion of the expedition of Ubayda bin Al-Harith. We have quoted these verses in an earlier part of this book in the Chapter entitled "Expedition of Ubayda bin Al-Harith".

Hadrat Fatima Zahra. Hadrat Fratima Zahra, the daughter of the Holy Prophet wrote an elegy on the death of the Holy Prophet. Some of the verses of the elegy are:

"It is not wondrous that whoever
Smells the fragrance of Muhammad's tomb
Will never smell another perfume.
Destiny hurt me with a bereavement so sad and so dark
That if it had fallen on the days,
They would have been turned into eternal nights."

Hadrat Ali. After the death of Hadrat Fatima, addressing her grave, Hadrat Ali said:

"O thou grave, to thee I resort
For paying homage unto thee,
O thou ! the repository of my beloved;
Ye answer me not,
O thou beloved tomb ! what ails you,
You respond not to the supplications.

Art thou out of humour, because of the
Love that I bore ye".

Khansa. Among the Arabian women who excelled in poetry, the place of honour is held by Khansa. She wrote elegies mourning the death of her brother Bakr. The following lines are well known:

Sunrise awakes in me the sad remembrance
Of Bakr, and I recall him at every sunset."

Mutamim bill Nuweira. Mutamim bin Nuweira mourned in elegiac verses the death of his brother Malik bin Nuweira. The death of Malik was also mourned by another poet Abu Namir Saadi. He wrote:

O ye man, tell the people of your tribe
That they should ride away from here forthwith;
For with the murder of Malik the night has become endless.
By his high handedness Khalid killed Malik
And married his wife Laila.

Hassan bin Thabit. Hassan bin Thabit was the poet laureate of Islam. He wrote some verses in the praise of Hadrat Abu Bakr. These verses are:

When thou rememberest the affliction of a faithful brother
Then remember too thy brother Abu Bakr and what he hath done,
The best of men, the most pious and just of them
Save the Prophet, and the most faithful in performing what he hath undertaken
The second, the follower, the place of whose witnessing is extolled
And the first among those who have borne witness to the Prophet.
He also said:
The second of the two in the glorious cave and verily,
The enemy went round about it when they ascended the mountain,

And verily they knew that he was the beloved of the
Apostle of God
Who hold no one his equal among the people.

Labid. Labid was another eminent poet of the age. Once he went to Hadrat Abu Bakr and recited the verse:

"Is not every thing but God unprofitable ?" Hadrat Abu Bakr said, "You have spoken truly".

Labid continued:

"And every joy is surely Meeting"

Hadrat Abu Bakr exclaimed, "Here you are wrong. There is with God a joy that never passes away."

After Labid had left, Hadrat Abu Bakr said, "Sometimes a poet speaks words of wisdom."

Afif bin Mandhar. Afif bin Mandhar celebrated the victory of the Muslims in Bahrain in the following terms:

"Did you not see that under the behest of God
The river became subservient to the Muslims;
We prayed to God and He in His bounty
Made the channel dry to make the way for the Muslims;
And like the communities of old we saw
The river split in two channels to make way for the
Muslims."

Qa'qa'. Qa'qa', a valiant commander or the army of Khalid composed the following verses with reference to the battle of Firaz in Iraq:

"We grarppled with the forces of Rome and Persia at
Firaz,
And the Muslim forces overpowered the enemy;
So violent was our charge
That the forces of the enemy could not withstand it
And they were scattered like the leaves of trees.
We captured them in large numbers,
And drove them before us like cattle."

'Atika. On the death of Abdullah a son of Hadrat Abu Bakr his wife 'Atika composed an elegy in the course of which she said:

> "Abdullah, I have sworn that my eyes shall never cease grieving for thee;
> And my body shall ever remain covered with dust."

Khufaf b. Nudbah. Khufaf b. Nudbah as Salami known as one of the poets of "Arab Chivalry" mourning the death of Hadrat Abu Bakr said:

> "Tell every living thing that there is no permanence for it:
> And for the whole universe its decree is destruction
> The goods of men are but as a trust,
> Borrowed on the condition of repayment,
> And a man strives, but there is one who]lies in wait for him,
> The eye mourneth for him with the severity of grief
> He groweth old, or is slain or subdued
> Sickness that hath no remedy makes him to lament,
> Verily, Abu Bakr was as the rain
> What time Orion causeth not the herbage to grow with moisture,
> Neither the youth that wears the Mizar nor one that wears the Rida
> He who strives to attain unto the excellence of his days
> Earnestly, is apart and solitary upon the earth."

NOTES

In this Chapter I have tried to give an account of Hadrat Abu Bakr's services to Islam in the matter of the Mushaf, Hadith, Tasawwuf and Fiqh. I have also referred to poetry during the times of Hadrat Abu Bakr.

The Holy Qur'an was revealed to the Holy Prophet, but was compiled by Hadrat Abu Bakr. In this respect too, Hadrat Abu Bakr was the "second of the two". The services of Hadrat Abu Bakr in the matter of the compilation of the "Mushaf" deserve the obligations of the Muslim community for all times to come. Hadrat Abu Bakr saved Islam on the political front by crushing apostasy and unifying Arabia. By leading forces to Iraq and Syria, Hadrat Abu Bakr made Islam a world force. On the spiritual plane, Hadrat Abu Bakr saved Islam by compiling the Mushaf, and preserving the Word of God in the original form.

In the second section I have referred to some of the 'Hadith' narrated on the authority of Hadrat Abu Bakr. Hadrat Abu Bakr was very particular about the truth and authenticity of the 'Hadith. Although he was the closest companion of the Holy Prophet, only 142 Hadith are attributed to Hadrat Abu Bakr. That speaks for the great care that he took in the matter of the narration of 'Hadith'. I have quoted some forty Hadith. This section is based on Jalaluddin Suyuti's *History of the Caliphs.*

In the third section 1 have tried to highlight the role of Hadrat Abu Bakr in the matter of ' "Tasawwuf". When we study the attributes of Hadrat Abu Bakr we are impressed by the fact that all the attributes that go to make a Sufi were very conspicuous with Hadrat Abu Bakr. He was ' Siddiq" endowed with the vision to perceive the truth. He was most assiduous in piety. He was a symbol of selflessness. His devotion, dedication and love for Islam, Allah and the Holy Prophet were of the highest order. No wonder Hadrat Abu Bakr is the "Father of Tasawwuf". In writing this section I have obtained guidance from Hadrat Data Ganj Bakhsh's *Kashful Mahjub.* I have profited from Nicholson's translation of *Kashful Mahjub.*

I have also obtained help from my book *Hadrat Data Ganj Baksh — A Spiritual Biography.*

In the fourth section I have referred to Hadrat Abu Bakr's services in the matter of Fiqh. Fiqh stands for the application of the principles of Islam to the day to day problems and the settlement of disputes. In making, his decisions, the Holy Prophet was guided by revelations. Hadrat Abu Bakr had to decide cases without any external help. The science of Fiqh began with Hadrat Abu Bakr, and he is recognised as the "Father of Fiqh". He was the first to sponsor Ijtihad. In this section I have referred to some of the well-known decisions of Hadrat Abu Bakr. In compiling this section 1 have obtained help from:

(1) *Hadrat Abu Bakr* by Syed Moinul Haq;
(2) *Abu Bakr* by Muhammad Hussain Haykal; and
(3) *History of the Caliphs* by Jalaluddin Suyuti.

In the fifth section I have referred to poetry in the time of Hadrat Abu Bakr. In writing this section I have obtained help from:

(1) *Literary History of the Arabs* by Nicholson; and
(2) *History of the Caliphs* by Jalaluddin Suyuti.

17

ANECDOTES, SAYINGS, SERMONS AND INTERPRETATION OF DREAMS

Anecdotes of Hadrat Abu Bakr

Anecdotes. In the various accounts about Hadrat Abu Bakr that have come down to us, we come across some anecdotes which illuminate certain aspects of the life of Hadrat Abu Bakr. We refer to some of these anecdotes in this Chapter.

Reaction to praise. Once, someone highly praised Hadrat Abu Bakr. After the man who praised him had left, Hadrat Abu Bakr prayed to God:

> "O Allah, You know me more than myself, and I know myself more than these people who praise me. Make me better than what they think of me, and forgive those sins of mine of which they have no knowledge, and do not hold me responsible for what they say."

Milking the goats. Before becoming the Caliph, Hadrat Abu Bakr used to milk the goats of the widows in the Mohalla. When he passed through the street after becoming the Caliph, one of the widows remarked, "Now, he would not milk the goats for us". Addressing the widows, Hadrat Abu Bakr said, "No, the Khilafat would make no change. I would continue to milk your goats."

The two lions. On an occasion when Hadrat Abu Bakr

was busy with the preparation of plans in connection with the campaigns in Syria and Iraq, a companion presented a case concerning his tribe for the decision of the caliph. That irritated Hadrat Abu Bakr, and he said:

> "I am busy considering plans to crush the two lions who are waiting for an opportunity to destroy the Muslims and you are diverting my attention to petty matters".

Revelations of Musailima. After the death of the false prophet Musailima; a deputation of Banu Hanifa waited on Hadrat Abu Bakr. He enquired of them what were the teachings of the false prophet. As a specimen of his teaching they recited the following verse which was alleged to have been revealed to him:

> "O frog ! holy are you. You do not prevent the drinker, nor do you make the water dirty. Half the world belongs to us, and half to the Quraish, but the Quraish are a cruel people."

On hearing this, Hadrat Abu Bakr remarked: "God be praised. Is this the divine word. It has no sublimity of divinity. To what depths he had dragged you".

Necklace of his sister. On the occasion of the conquest of Makkah, the necklace of his sister was wrenched from her neck by one of the horsemen. To the people assembled in the mosque, Hadrat Abu Bakr said, "I call for the necklace of my sister in the name of God." He repeated this three times, and when there was no response he said, "O sister, reckon upon your necklace as a present to God, for by Allah there is little of honesty among men now-a-days."

Veterans of the Bakr. On one occasion, Hadrat Abu Bakr was asked, "O Vicegerent of the Apostle of God, will you not employ in service those who fought at Badr ?" Hadrat Abu Bakr said, "I know their dignity, but I am loath to defile them with the world ? "

Doing things himself. Once when Hadrat Abu Bakr was riding a camel, the reins of the camel dropped from his hands. He came down from the camel to pick up the reins. He was asked why he had not asked other persons to pick up the reins for him. He said, "My Prophet has ordered me to do my things myself, and not beg anything from any human being."

No distinction. Once Hadrat Abu Bakr was sitting with a number of persons. A person came, and he said, "Peace be to you, O Caliph of the Prophet". Hadrat Abu Bakr felt irritated and said, "There is no distinction between the Caliph and other Muslims; why have you wished peace to the Caliph alone and not to the other members of the assembly ?

No train of followers. In the second year of his caliphate, Hadrat Abu Bakr went to Makkah on pilgrimage. On this occasion many persons gathered around him and began to follow in his train. Hadrat Abu Bakr wanted them to disperse for he did not want to be given any undue importance to himself.

Head of defeated enemy. Once a commander sent to Hadrat Abu Bakr the head of the defeated enemy. Hadrat Abu Bakr deprecated the practice as un-Islamic. He issued instructions to all concerned that in future the heads of the defeated enemy should not be cut for despatch to him. He urged that due respect should be shown to the dead, even though they were enemies.

Hunting of game. Once a hunter hunted a raven with large wings. It was presented to Hadrat Abu Bakr. He turned it over and said, " No game is hunted and no tree is felled, save it has neglected the praise of God".

Holding the tongue. Once in anger, Hadrat Abu Bakr said something which he later regretted. He held his tongue and said, "This it is which has brought me to that to which I have come".

More poisonous than poison. Hadrat Abu Bakr was critical of women's passion for gold and perfume. He said, "The most deadly of things, more poisonous than poison, are the two that are red, gold and saffron."

Unfulfilled hopes. When Abdullah a son of Hadrat Abu Bakr was on death bed, he kept looking towards the cushion.

When he was dead, the persons who were attending him said to Hadrat Abu Bakr that at the time of death, his son had been looking towards the cushion. When the cushion was moved, some dinars were found thereunder. Seeing them, Hadrat Abu Bakr wrung his hands and said, "Verily we belong to God, and to Him is our return". Thereafter he recited the verse:

> "You shall not cease to announce the death of a friend until you are as he is;
> And verily, the youth cherishes a hope and dies without attaining it."

His reputation and decorum. Once Hadrat Abu Bakr was asked whether he ever drank wine during the days of Ignorance. He replied, "God forbid, I never touched wine even in the days of Ignorance". He was asked "why"' and he said, "I sought to preserve my reputation and retain my decorum, and verily he who drinks wine destroys his reputation and his decorum".

Joy which is not fleeting. Once the poet Labid had a sitting with Hadrat Abu Bakr when he recited the verse "Is not everything but God unprofitable ?" Hadrat Abu Bakr said, "You have spoken truly". Then Labid recited, "And every joy is surely fleeting". Hadrat Abu Bakr said, "This is not correct. There is with God a joy which is not fleeting."

Freedom from accountability. Hadrat Abu Bakr used to say that accountability was a great challenge for man. Once he entered a garden where he saw a ring dove sitting on a tree. Seeing the bird, Hadrat Abu Bakr heaved a deep sigh, and said:

> "Happy you are O bird, that eats of the trees and seeks shelter beneath them, and are not called to account. Would that I were like you?"

His father's seat. Once Hadrat Abu Bakr was addressing the congregation in the mosque from the pulpit. Imam Hasan, the son of Hadrat Ali came to the pulpit and addressing Hadrat Abu Bakr said,' Come down from the seat of my father." Hadrat Abu Bakr said. "You speak the truth, this is your father's seat". He put up the child on his lap and wept. Hadrat Ali intervened to say, "This was not said at my instance". Hadrat Abu Bakr said, "I know that."

His love for the Holy Prophet. Once, addressing the Holy Prophet, Hadrat Abu Bakr said, "O Apostle of God, if you were to ask me to kill myself, I will do that." The Holy Prophet said, "Yes, I know that. I feel proud of you."

Distribution of the spoils of war. Whenever the spoils of war came, Hadrat Abu Bakr would distribute them equally among all the people. Some of the companions suggested that he should recognise precedence in faith as a ground for preference in distribution of spoils. Hadrat Abu Bakr said, "The recogoition of precedence in faith is for the Lord. It is for Him to reward the piety of such persons who have excelled in faith. These gifts which I distribute are but an accident of the present life."

Honour comes from Allah. In the second year of his caliphate, Hadrat Abu Bakr went to Makkah to perform the pilgrimage and stayed there with his father Abu Qahafa. On that occasion, the notables of the city came to wait on him. Referring to these notables, Abu Qahafa said, "They are the notables of our city. Make much of them, and honour them." Hadrat Abu Bakr said, "I will certainty make much of them, but as for honour there is none save that which comes from Allah."

Precedence for Islam. In the Battle of Badr, Abdul Rahman a son of Hadrat Abu Bakr who was yet a non-Muslim fought against the Muslims. Later Abdul Rahman became a Muslim. He told his father that at the battle there were occasions when he could strike at him, but then out of love for him he turned aside. Hadrat Abu Bakr said, "If I had such an occasion, you being an infidel, I would not have spared you."

He asked his son to divorce his wife. Abdullah another son of Hadrat Abu Bakr was so much lost in the love of his wife Atika that he did not participate in the battles against the non-Muslims. He even neglected his prayers. Thereupon

Hadrat Abu Bakr asked him to divorce his wife.

He was asked to sheathe his sword. At the Battle of Uhud, Abdul Rahman a son of Hadrat Abu Bakr again fought against the Muslim,. Before the battle began Abdul Rahman stepped forth from the ranks, and threw a challenge to the Muslims to let some one step forward and have a duel with him. Hadrat Abu Bakr accepted the challenge, and was about to fight a duel with his son, when the Holy Prophet commanded, 'Sheathe your sword and do not make us anxious about your person".

He slapped a Jew in the face. Finhas, a Jewish rabbi said: "We are rich but your Allah is poor. We are independent of Him but He needs us. Had He been independent of us, He would not have given us interest, which He has denied to you." Hadrat Abu Bakr felt outraged at this blasphemy. He slapped the Jew in the face and said, 'Were it not for the treaty between the Muslims and the Jews, I would have cut off your head O enemy of Allah."

Fight for the Prophet. When the Muslims encamped at Hudaibiya, Urwa b. Masud came to see the Holy Prophet on behalf of the Quraish. He insinuated that at the time of crisis, the followers of the Holy Prophet were likely to abandon him. Thereupon Hadrat Abu Bakr flared up and said, "May God curse you; how dare you think that we will abandon the Holy Prophet. Rest assured, we will fight to the last for him."

Hold fast to the stirrup of the Holy Prophet. Hadrat Umar regarded the treaty of Hudaibiya as humiliating to the Muslims. He saw Hadrat Abu Bakr, and wanted him to persuade the Holy Prophet to withdraw from the pact. Hadrat Abu Bakr said, "The Holy Prophet knows things more than we do. What the Holy Prophet has done is in the interests of the Muslims. Do not be critical. Hold fast to the stirrup of the Holy Prophet."

Judging what he did not know. In the case of the ordeal of falsehood, after God had revealed to the Holy Prophet the innocence of Hadrat Ayesha, she said to Hadrat Abu Bakr, "Father would you not have pardoned me if there had been no revelation." Hadrat Abu Bakr said, "What heaven would cover me, and what earth would carry me if I judged that which I did not know ?"

He wanted God to forgive him. Mistah was a relative of Hadrat Abu Bakr whom Hadrat Abu Bakr used to pay an allowance. Mistah took active part in spreading the calumny against Hadrat Ayesha. Thereupon Hadrat Abu Bakr swore that he would no longer help Mistah. Thereupon the verse descended on the Holy Prophet, "Let not those in affluence swear not to aid poor kinsmen. Let them forgive. Do you not wish that God should forgive you ?" Hearing this Hadrat Abu Bakr restored the allowance to Mistah saying, "Yes, I wish Allah to forgive me."

His feet became dusty in the service of God. When Usamah's army left for Syria, Hadrat Abu Bakr walked for some distance along with the army to see it depart. Usamah was riding on horseback, and he requested Hadrat Abu Bakr that he should be permitted to dismount or the Caliph should also ride on a horse. Hadrat Abu Bakr said, "No, neither shall you dismount nor shall I mount a horse, for according to a tradition of the Holy Prophet, he whose foot becomes dusty in the way of God will be preserved from hell fire."

He excelled all in the matter of generosity. For the financing of the expedition to Tabuk, the Holy Prophet invited contributions from all his followers. Hadrat Umar made a liberal contribution. When the Holy Prophet asked him, how much he had left for himself and his family, he said that he had given one half of his wealth for the cause of Allah and had left one half for himself and his family. Then Hadrat Abu Bakr came loaded with his contribution, and the Holy Prophet put him the same Question as to how much he had left for himself and his family. Hadrat Abu Bakr said, "I have brought all that I had. I have left Allah and His Prophet for myself and my family". Thus Hadrat Abu Bakr excelled every one in generosity.

He anticipated Hadrat Umar. It is related that a blind old woman lived in a suburb of Madina and had no one to support her. Hadrat Umar used to go in disguise to the house of the old woman, but was always surprised to find that someone else had anticipated him and had supplied the wants of the old woman. One night Hadrat Umar went to the house of the old woman earlier than usual and hid himself to watch as to who attended to the wants of the old lady. He had not to wait long for soon a man arrived who attended to the needs of the old woman, and this man was Hadrat Abu Bakr.

Foremost in breaking glad tidings. Once in the presence of Hadrat Abu Bakr and Hadrat Umar the Holy Prophet said that the recitation of the Holy Qur'an by Ibn Masud was the most perfect, and had been approved of by God. Later, Hadrat Umar went to the house of Ibn Masud to tell him of the approval of God. He thought that he would be the first man to give the glad tidings to Ibn Masud. When Hadrat Umar reached the house of Ibn Masud he found that Hadrat Abu Bakr had already been to the house of Ibn Masud and has informed him of the glad tidings.

Sweet dish. It is related that one of the wives of Hadrat Abu Bakr once wished for a sweet dish. The Caliph said that he had no money for such a luxury. She said, "Then permit me to save something daily, and then have a sweet dish when sufficient amount has been collected." This he permitted and in the course of a few days she saved some amount. Hadrat Abu Bakr deposited the amount in the treasury. He had his daily allowance reduced by the amount of the saving, holding that if something could be saved it meant that the allowance sanctioned in his favour was excessive to that extent.

The physician. During the course of his last sickness, some companions who visited him said, "O Caliph of the Prophet, should we call a physician to examine you?" He said "The physician has already examined me". What did he say, they asked. He said that the physician had said that he would do with the patient what he would will.

Encomium for the Prophet. During the course of his illness while looking at Hadrat Abu Bakr, Hadrat Ayesha recited:

"That bright face whose freshness gives water to the clouds,

Is affectionate towards the orphans,
And protects the honour of the widows."

Hadrat Abu Bakr opened his eyes and said, "No, the Holy Prophet alone deserves this encomium."

The Coffin. When at the point of death, Hadrat Abu Bakr desired that the two pieces of the cloth that he was wearing should be washed and used for his coffin, while the third piece could be purchased. Hadrat Ayesha said that they were not so poor as to be not able to purchase all the three pieces. He said, "New pieces of cloth can be better utilised for the living than for the dead. The cloth that covers the dead body is for absorbing blood and pus only."

Sayings of Hadrat Abu Bakr

Thus spoke Hadrat Abu Bakr. Hadrat Abu Bakr was of a contemplative bent of mind. He often expressed his thoughts in words conspicuous for their wisdom. A number of his sayings has come down to us, and these show the depths and dimensions of his thought and philosophy. Some of the sayings of Hadrat Abu Bakr which have assumed the character of proverbs are given hereunder:

Greatness. About greatness, Hadrat Abu Bakr said:

(1) Run away from greatness, and greatness will follow you.
(2) There is greatness in the fear of God, contentment in faith of God, and honour in humility.

Good actions. About good actions, Hadrat Abu Bakr said:

(1) Good actions are a guard against the blows of adversity.
(2) Be good to others, that will protect you against evil.

(3) If you expect the blessings of God, be good to His people.
(4) Every day, nay every moment , try to do some good deed.

Death. About death, he said:

(1) Have an earnestness for death, and you will have life.
(2) Death is the easiest of all things after it, and the hardest of all things before it.

Knowledge. About knowledge, he said:

(1) The more knowledge you have, the greater will be your fear of Allah.
(2) Without knowledge action is useless, and knowledge without action is futile.
(3) Knowledge is the life of the mind.
(4) When a noble man learns knowledge he becomes humble; when an ignoble person gains knowledge he gets conceited .
(5) When knowledge is limited, it leads to folly; when knowledge exceeds a certain limit, it leads to exploitation.

Advice. In the matter of advice, he said:

(1) When you seek advice, do not withhold any facts from the person whose advice you seek.
(2) When you advise any person you should be guided by the fear of God.
(3) If any body seeks your advice, offer right and since advice.
(4) He who is not impressed by sound advice lacks faith.

Kindness. About kindness he said:

(1) If you expect the blessings of God, be kind to His people.
(2) He who aspires to paradise should learn to deal wit the people with kindness.

(3) He who fears to weep should learn to be kind to those who weep.

Self-control. About self-control he said, "If you want to control other people, first control your self."

Patience and confidence. With regard to patience and confidence, he said:

"Patience is half faith, and confidence is full faith."

Society of evil persons. About the society of evil persons he held, "Solitude is better than the society of evil persons."

Honesty. About honesty he said, "The greatest truth is honesty, and the greatest falsehood is dishonesty."

Treatment of Muslims. About the treatment of Muslims he said, "Do not look down upon any Muslim, for even the most inferior believer is great in the eyes of God."

Help and cooperation. About help and cooperation, he said:

(1) "God blesses him who helps his brother."
(2) "Do not non-cooperate with one another, and have no grudge *of* jealousy."
(3) "Muslims should live like brothers."
(4) "God helps those who fear Him."
(5) "Allah will help him who moves in the way of Allah."

Jihad. About "Jihad", he said:

(1) "The people who abandon Jihad fall a victim to humility and degradation."
(2) "Jihad is obligatory for the Muslims."
(3) "To fight against the infidels is Jihad, but to fight against your evil self is greater Jihad."

Intentions. With regard to intentions, he said, "Intentions count in your actions."

Sadaqah. In the matter of the offering of "Sadaqah" he said, "When you offer any Sadaqah to a beggar, do it with humility and respect, for what you are offering is an offer to Allah".

Mosques. With regard to mosques he said: "He who builds a mosque in the way of Allah, God will build a house for him in the paradise."

Way of life. About the way of life he said, "Follow the way of life, which the Holy Prophet has shown you, for verily that is the right path."

Prayers. With regard to prayers, he said, "He who prays for five times a day is in the protection of God, and he who is protected by God cannot be harmed by anyone."

Neighbours. About neighbours, he said, "You should not quarrel with your neighbour, for he will remain where he is, but your high handedness will become the talk of the people."

Appearance of things. About the outward appearance of things he said:

(1) "Maybe a thing that you do not like is really in your interest."
(2) "It is possible that a thing that you may desire may be against your interest."

Love of God. About the love of God, and the love of the world, he said, "He who comes to take the love of God can have no taste for the love of the world."

Becoming a Muslim. About becoming a Muslim, he said, "He who becomes a Muslim does so in his own interest."

Falsehood. About falsehood, he said, "He who indulges in falsehood will find the paths of paradise shut to him."

Boasting. About boasting, he said, "He who boasts lowers himself."

Pride. About pride he said, "Pride in the case of a rice man is bad, but pride in the case of a poor man is worse."

Elation. In the matter of elation, he said, "Do not get elated at any victory, for all such victory is subject to the will of God."

Avoidance of complaints. With regard to the avoidance of complaints he said, He who avoids complaints invites happiness."

Attraction of the things of the world. About the attraction of the things of the world, he said, "If an ignorant person is attracted by the things of the world this is bad, but if a learned person is thus attracted, it is worse." He also said, "O man you are busy working for the world, and the world is busy trying to turn you out."

Justice. About justice, he said: "In the matter of justice, all should be equal in your eyes."

Deception and faithlessness. About deception and faithlessness he said, "Do not deceive or be faithless even with your enemy."

Measure. About the use of measure he said, "Use same measure for selling which you use for purchase."

Sin. About sin, he said: (1) It is good to repent from sin; it is better to avoid sin. (2) It is bad for a young man to sin, but it is worse for an old man to sin.

Evil. About evil he said, "Cursed is the man who dies himself, but the evil done by him survives."

Dyeing of hair. In the case of the dyeing of hair he said, "Youth is not restored by the dyeing of your hair."

Early rising. About early rising, he said, "It is a matter of shame that in the morning the birds should be awake earlier than you."

Piety. About Piety he said, "Piety is the most solid goodness, and the vilest of what is evil is vice."

Truth and falsehood. About truth and falsehood he said, "Truth is a trust, falsehood a treason."

Vain desires. About vain desires, he said, "Do not

follow vain desires for verily he prospers who is preserved from lust, greed and anger."

The best. Hadrat Abu Bakr prayed, "O Lord, render You the best of my life its close, the best of my deeds as the last, and the best of my days the day of Your meeting."

"O God verily I ask of You that which may be the best for me in the end. O God vouchsafe that the last good that You bestow upon me, is Your approbation."

Deadly things. Hadrat Abu Bakr said, "The most deadly of things are the two that are red, gold and saffron."

Reward of the believer. Hadrat Abu Bakr said, "The true believer is rewarded in every thing, even in affliction."

Life of the world. About the life of the world, Hadrat Abu Bakr said, "Our abode in this world is transitory. Our life therein is but a loan. Our breaths are numbered, and our indolence is manifest."

Condolence. While condoling the death of a companion, Hadrat Abu Bakr said to the bereaved family:

> "There is no harm in patience, and no profit in lamentation. Death is easiest to bear than that which precedes it, and more severe than that which comes after it. Remember the death of the Apostle of God, and your sorrow will be lessened."

Prayer for a dead man. When praying for a dead man Hadrat Abu Bakr said:

> "O God his people and his goods and his kindred have forsaken this servant of Yours. His sin was grievous, but You are Merciful and Compassionate."

Sermons of Hadrat Abu Bakr

Hadrat Abu Bakr's eloquence. Hadrat Abu Bakr was known for his eloquence and oratory. He used to address the faithful every week on Fridays. His sermons and addresses were the specimen of masterly eloquence, every word thereof vibrated with superb faith and appealed directly to the heart. All his sermons and addresses have not been preserved. Only a few of his sermons and addresses have come down to us, and these classical addresses which are veritable gems of literature evoke our admiration.

Inaugural address. On assuming office, he delivered the following address, which is a unique document for the guidance of all rulers:

> "Gentlemen, I have been placed in authority, though by Allah I was averse to the assumption of authority. I would have been pleased if any of you had taken over the office, and I would have assisted him. I have been made to rule over you though I am not the most worthy among you. If you expect me to act as did the Holy Prophet of God, know that I cannot do so, for the Apostle of God was a servant whom the Lord honoured with His inspiration and preserved him thereby from error. I am an ordinary mortal and not better than any of you. Therefore, watch over me. When you see that I am steadfast and obey Allah and His Prophet, then obey me. When you see that I turn aside from the right path do not obey me. Help me if I am in the right; set me right if I am in the wrong. Know that I have a devil that seizes upon me. Therefore, when you see me enraged avoid me for at that time I cannot be influenced by your counsels or glad salutations We have the Qur'an for our guidance. We have also with us the instructions of the Holy Prophet. These will be our unerring guides. Know O men that piety is the most solid goodness, and the vilest of what is evil is vice. Truth is a trust; falsehood a treason. The weak among you shall be strong with me till God willing his rights have been vindicated; and the strong among you shall be weak with me till, if the Lord wills, I have taken what is due from him."

Guidelines for the faithful. In the following sermon, Hadrat Abu Bakr set the guidelines for the conduct of the faithful:

> "Beware you of following vain desire, for verily he prospers who is preserved from lust, greed and anger; and beware you of pride for what pride belongs to him who is made of earth, and whom the worms devour after death. Today you are alive; tomorrow you may be dead. Therefore act uprightly from day to day and hour to hour. Be you patient for every work is accomplished through patience. Be you watchful for watchfulness is profitable. Act uprightly for a good act is acceptable to God. Refrain from things against which the Lord has warned you under pain of His wrath. Vie you with one another in hastening to obtain the things which the Lord has promised you in His mercy. Be heedful and in fear for the Lord has declared to you things for which He destroyed those that were before you and things through which He delivered those before you. Verily He has manifested to you in His book His commands and His prohibitions, the works He approves and that He abhors. God is He Whose assistance should be implored. There is no power or strength but in the Lord. Obey God, preserve your portion of excellence. Make your charitable donations even when you are poor. O Servants of God, think of your brethren and companions who have departed. Verily, the Lord has no co-partner, and between Him and any of His creatures there is no mediatory influence that can bestow good upon him or avert from him evil save in His worship and obedience to His commands for verily there is no good after which comes hell fire, and no evil after which comes heaven."

The light of the Book of God. In another sermon, Hadrat Abu Bakr said:

> "I commend to you piety to God. Praise Him as befits Him. Mingle desire with fear, for God praised Zikriya and the people of his house and said, "These strove to excel in good works and called upon Us with love and with fear and humbled themselves before Us." Therefore, know, O servants of God, that the Lord holds your lives as a pledge for what is due to Him, and has taken your compacts regarding it, and has purchased of you a little

that is perishable, in exchange for eternal abundance; and this Book of God is among you, whose light cannot be extinguished, nor its wonders end. Therefore, seek you illumination from its light, and accept counsel from His Book and seek light from it in the day of darkness. Verily He has created you for His worship and has appointed for you guardian angels honourable in the sight of God writing down actions, who know that which you do. And know O servants of God that you proceed and draw nigh to an appointed time, the knowledge of which, verily, is hidden from you. Vie you with one another in fulfilling the obligations of your appointed times before your appointed periods are completed, lest they cast you upon the evillest of your works, and verily there are some who have made over the obligations of their appointed times on others, and have taken no heed of themselves. Therefore, I forbid you to be like them. Then haste, flee, flee for behind you is a nimble pursuer, swift of deed. Where are the comely, beautiful of countenance, exulting in their youth ? Where are the monarchs who built cities and entrenched them round about ? Where are they who boasted of victories on fields of battle? Verily their pillars were overthrown when fortune betrayed them, and they went down into the darkness of the grave. Haste, flee, flee."

Hadrat Abu Bakr and the Interpretation of Dreams

Importance of dreams. Before the Holy Prophet was commissioned as the Messenger of God, the truth was generally revealed to him through dreams. His dreams were always true, and cast a shadow of the events to come. The Holy Prophet accordingly attached great importance to dreams. Dreams were regarded as a species of revelation, and the interpretation of dreams became a matter of spiritual exercise.

Hadrat Abu Bakr's expertise in the interpretation of dreams. According to a tradition, the Holy Prophet said that he was enjoined by God to relate his dreams to Hadrat

Abu Bakr. Whenever the Holy Prophet had a dream, he would relate it to Hadrat Abu Bakr. Whenever Hadrat Abu Bakr had a dream, he would likewise relate it to the Holy Prophet. They would then exchange views, and arrive at an agreed interpretation about the dream. In early Islam, interpretation of dreams was regarded as a spiritual exercise, and it was held that only those who had pure heats and possessed an inward vision could have meaningful dreams and interpret their significance. According to Ibn Sirin, who is regarded as the Imam of the science of the interpretation of dreams, Hadrat Abu Bakr was the best interpretor of dreams after the Holy Prophet.

Battle of Uhud. On the eve of the Battle of Uhud, the Holy Prophet saw in a dream that he was driving some cows, and some cows out of these were slaughtered. He also saw a dent on his sword. Hadrat Abu Bakr interpreted this dream to signify that some of the companions of the Holy Prophet would be martyred in the Battle of Uhud. The dent on the sword signified that one of the relatives of the Holy Prophet would be martyred.

Siege of Taff. When after the fall of Makkah, Taif was besieged, the Holy Prophet saw in a dream that he had with him a bowl of butter. A cock pecked at it and split it. Hadrat Abu Bakr interpreted the dream to mean that the siege of Taif would have to be raised without actual conquest.

Expedition against Banu Jadhima. When Khalid was sent on an expedition against Banu Jadhima of Kinana, the Holy Prophet saw in a dream that he swallowed a morsel of dates mixed with butter and enjoyed their taste. Some of them, however, stuck in his gullet when he tried to swallow them. Then Ali thrust in his hand and pulled them out. Hadrat Abu Bakr interpreted the dream to mean that something would happen in the campaign against Banu Jadhima at which the Holy Prophet would be happy as well as unhappy, and that he would send Hadrat Ali to put matters right. In the campaign against Banu Jadhima, the tribe was overpowered, and at this the Holy Prophet felt happy. The Holy Prophet, however, felt unhappy when he learnt that Khalid had killed some Muslims as well. The Holy Prophet said, "O God I am innocent before Thee of what Khalid has done". Ali was then sent to the tribe to pay blood money.

Herds of black and white sheep. On one occasion, the Holy Prophet saw in a dream that he was driving a herd of black sheep. Then he found himself driving a herd of white sheep. After some time the two herds were inextricably intermingled and all attempts to separate them were of no avail. Interpreting the dream, Hadrat Abu Bakr said that the black sheep signified the Arabs while the white sheep signified the people of other regions. The dream indicated that Islam would spread to other regions beyond considerations of colour and creed.

Hudaibiya treaty. On the occasion of the Hudaibiya treaty, the Holy Prophet saw in a dream that he was shaving his head after the pilgrimage. Hadrat Abu Bakr interpreted the dream to signify that the main Hajj would have to be deferred to the following year.

Two and a half steps. Once the Holy Prophet saw in a dream that he and Hadrat Abu Bakr were walking together side by side. Then the Holy Prophet outpaced Hadrat Abu Bakr by two and half steps. Hadrat Abu Bakr interpreted the dream to mean that the Holy Prophet would be the first to be summoned to God, and that Hadrat Abu Bakr would follow him after two and a half years.

Drawing water from a well. On another occasion, the Holy Prophet saw in a dream that he was drawing water from a well. Then he stepped aside and asked Hadrat Abu Bakr to draw water. Hadrat Abu Bakr was able to draw water for two to three rounds only, and then he showed signs of exhaustion. Hadrat Umar then took up the job, and he was able to complete ten rounds. Hadrat Abu Bakr interpreted the dream to signify that after the passing away of the Holy Prophet, the caliphate would vest in Hadrat Abu Bakr whose period of office would be two to three years only. He will be succeeded by Hadrat Umar whose period of office will be ten years.

Wading through night soil. Once Hadrat Abu Bakr saw in a dream that he was wading through the night soil of the people. He related the dream to the Holy Prophet who interpreted it to mean that after the death of the Holy Prophet, Hadrat Abu Bakr would be called upon to undertake apostasy campaigns.

Three moons. Once, Hadrat Ayesha saw in a dream three moons descend on her house. She related the dream to Hadrat Abu Bakr, and he interpreted it that her house would be the burial place of three luminaries of the world. Subsequently the Holy Prophet, Hadrat Abu Bakr, and Hadrat Umar were buried in her house.

Urinating blood. Once a person waited on Hadrat Abu Bakr and asked for the interpretation of his dream. In the dream he had seen himself urinating blood. Hadrat Abu Bakr addressing him said, "God curse you. It appears that you go to your wife even when she is with monthly course. Desist from that."

Opening of the sky. Mahrz b. Nuzlah, a companion saw in a dream that the sky had opened for him and that he had reached the seventh heaven. Hadrat Abu Bakr interpreted the dream to signify that he would meet the death of a martyr, and that his abode would be in paradise.

NOTES

In this Chapter I have made an attempt to assemble anecdotes, sayings and sermons of Hadrat Abu Bakr. I have also given an account of the interpretation of dreams by Hadrat Abu Bakr.

In the first section I have collected some forty anecdotes of Hadrat Abu Bakr. These anecdotes project the piety, faith, depth of insight, loftiness of character, shrewdness of judgment, and the wisdom of Hadrat Abu Bakr. I have collected these anecdotes from various sources, particularly:

(1) *History of the Caliphs* by Jalaluddin Suyuti;
(2) *Early Heroes of Islam* by G. A. Salik; and
(3) *Hadrat Abu Bakr by* Syed Moin-ul-Haq.

In the second section I have assembled some forty sayings of Hadrat Abu Bakr. Most of these sayings have the character of proverbs and can be quoted with advantage on various occasions. Ferozsons have published a book in Urdu entitled *Thus Spoke Hadrat Abu Bakr.* In compiling this section I have taken advantage of this compilation. I have also obtained help from:

(1) *History of the Caliphs* by Jalaluddin Suyuti; and
(2) *Hadrat Abu Bakr* by Syed Moin-ul-Haq.

In the third section I have referred to three sermons of Hadrat Abu Bakr. Hadrat Abu Bakr was a great preacher, and he must have delivered numerous sermons. Unfortunately these sermons have not been preserved. After a good deal of search I have been able to lay hands on the extracts of three sermons of Hadrat Abu Bakr. These sermons give an idea of the preachings of Hadrat Abu Bakr. These sermons vibrating which faith are most impressive, in structive, and inspiring. The first sermon which he delivered on the occasion of the assumption of office is found in almost every biography of Hadrat Abu Bakr. For the second sermon I am indebted to G. A. Salik's book *Early Heroes of Islam.* For the third sermon I am indebted to *History of the Caliphs* bv Jalaluddin Suyuti.

In the fourth section, I have assembled Hadrat Abu Bakr's interpretation of dreams in about a dozen cases. Hadrat Abu Bakr was conspicuous for his truthfulness and veracity, and because of these ennobling qualities, Hadrat Abu Bakr could give a correct interpretation of dreams. Hadrat Abu Bakr was not a prophet, but because of his lifelong devotion and attachment to the Holy Prophet, there was something of semi-prophethood about him. In the spiritual hierarchy he stands midway between the ordinary men and prophets. He was endowed with uncommon insight and foresight and sometimes he said things which had the characteristic of prophesies about them. On his death bed he foretold that his wife Habiba who was pregnant would give birth to a daughter. He also foretold that he would die on the same day as the Holy Prophet. Both these prophesies proved to be true. According to Suyuti we have it on the authority of Salman the Persian, an eminent companion that Hadrat Abu Bakr foretold victories for the Muslims in the near future.

18

DEATH OF HADRAT ABU BAKR

Passing away of Hadrat Abu Bakr

Illness of Hadrat Abu Bakr. On the 7th of Jamadi-ul-Akhir of the 13th A H. corresponding to the 8th of August 634 C.E., Hadrat Abu Bakr fell sick, and out of this sickness he never recovered. There are two accounts about the sickness of Hadrat Abu Bakr. One account is that the 8th of August 634 was a cold day, when Hadrat Abu Bakr took a bath and caught a chill. Another account is that about a year ago, along with some other companions Harith bin Kaladah, and Attab bin Usaid he had eaten some food which was poisoned, and which was to have its effect after a year. Harith b. Kaladah and Attab b Usaid died on the same day as Hadrat Abu Bakr, and that lends support to the theory that the death of Hadrat Abu Bakr was because of the effect of poison.

The physician. Hadrat Abu Bakr developed high fever, and was confined to bed. His illness prolonged, and when his condition worsened, he felt that his end was near. Some companions called on him to enquire about his welfare. They said, "O Vicegerent of the Apostle of God, may we call a physician to examine you". He said that the physician had already visited him. They enquired as to what had the physician said. Hadrat Abu Bakr said that the physician had said that he would do what he would do.

Refund of the amount drawn from the treasury. When Hadrat Abu Bakr felt that his end was near, he wanted to know what amount he had drawn from the State treasury as allowance for the office of the Caliph. He was told that this amount was six thousand dirhams. He directed that the plot of land which belonged to him should be sold, and from the sale proceeds, the amount of six thousand dirhams should be paid to the State treasury. He next took stock of the personal fortune that he had acquired since becoming the Caliph. These assets included a slave, a camel, and some cloth. He directed that these assets should be handed over to the new Caliph. When in pursuance of the will of Hadrat Abu Bakr, the amount of six thousand dirhams and other assets were handed over to the new Caliph, Hadrat Umar, the new Caliph wept and said, "O Abu Bakr, may God bless you; you have made the task of your successor most difficult."

Property bequeathed to Hadrat Ayesha. Hadrat Abu Bakr had bequeathed some property to Hadrat Ayesha. Now that he was on death bed he desired that the property should be divided among her two brothers and three sisters in accordance with the Islamic Law. Hadrat Ayesha said that they were two sisters, Asma and herself, and enquired as to who was the third sister ? Hadrat Abu Bakr said that his wife Habiba was pregnant, and he had a feeling that the child would be a girl. Indeed after the death of Hadrat Abu Bakr, a girl was born to Habiba, who was named Umm Kulthum. Hadrat Ayesha complied with the wish of her father and released the property in her charge for distribution among her brothers and sisters.

The Coffin. Hadrat Abu Bakr next asked Hadrat Ayesha as to how many pieces of cloth were used for the coffin of the Holy Prophet. Hadrat Ayesha said that three pieces had been used in the coffin of the Holy Prophet. Hadrat Abu Bakr thereupon desired that for his coffin as well, three pieces should be used. He wanted that the two sheets which he was wearing should be washed and used for his coffin, while the third piece might be purchased. Hadrat Ayesha said that they were not so poor as not to afford to purchase all the three pieces required for the coffin. Hadrat Abu Bakr said, "No, the new material will be of more use to the living than the dead. The cloth for the dead body is merely meant to absorb blood and pus, and it is not necessary that the cloth should be new."

The day of death. Hadrat Abu Bakr enquired of Hadrat Ayesha as to what was the day on which the Holy Prophet had died. She replied that the day was Monday. Hadrat Abu Bakr next enquired as to what was the day that day. She said that it was Monday. Hadrat Abu Bakr said that in that case he would die that day. He desired that if he died that day, he should be buried the same day.

Last moments of Hadrat Abu Bakr. As Hadrat Abu Bakr lay on the death bed, Hadrat Ayesha wailed:

> "And one so unsullied in honour that the cloud
> draws moisture from his face;
> The protection of orphans,
> the defence of widows."

Hadrat Abu Bakr said, "No, this encomium must be reserved for the Holy Prophet alone." Hadrat Ayesha said:

> "Wealth is of no avail to a man,
>
> On the day when the death-rattle is in his throat, and his breast is contracted by it."

Hadrat Abu Bakr uncovered his face and said, "It is not so. Say that the agony of death shall come in truth; this, O man, is what you sought to avoid." He swooned, and on regaining consciousness, he recited the verse of the Holy Qur'an:

> "Lord, let me die a true believer:
> And join me with the blessed ones on high who are virtuous."

With these words of the Holy Qur'an on his lips, Hadrat Abu Bakr expired. From God he had come and to God he returned. It was 22nd of Jamadi-ul-Akhir of 13 A.H. corresponding to 23rd of August, 534 C.E. The day was Monday. His death took place between the hours of the *Maghrib* and *Isha* prayers. He was 63 years at the time of his death. That was the exact age at which the Holy Prophet had died.

Burial. According to the will of Hadrat Abu Bakr, his dead body was prepared for burial by his wife Asma b. Umas. She was helped by his son Abdul Rahman. The funeral prayer was led by Hadrat Umar. He was buried the same night in the house of Hadrat Ayesha by the side of the grave of the Holy Prophet. In life, Hadrat Abu Bakr had the honour of being a bosom companion of the Holy Prophet, after death he had also the honour of resting by the side of the Master.

Abu Qahafa. When Hadrat Abu Bakr died, his father Abu Qahafa was at Makkah. It is reported that when Hadrat Abu Bakr died, the city of Makkah was convulsed by an earthquake. Abu Qahafa said that the earthquake was indicative of some calamity. Soon the sad news arrived of the death of Hadrat Abu Bakr. Abu Qahafa mourned the death of his son. Abu Qahafa died six months later at the age of ninety-seven.

Appointment of Hadrat Umar as his Successor

Nomination of successor. Realising that his end was drawing near, Hadrat Abu Bakr felt that he should nominate his successor so that the issue should not be a cause of dissension among the Muslims after his death. Hadrat Abu Bakr summoned Abdul Rahman bin Auf, and asked for his opinion about the nomination of Hadrat Umar as the Caliph, Abdul Rahman favoured the nomination. Some other companions were also consulted. The general consensus was that Hadrat Umar was the fittest person to be appoined as the Caliph. Usaid bin Hudai said, "After you, O Caliph, Umar is the most deserving person for the office of the Caliph. There is none more resolute than he among us. His inner self is better than his exterior." Hadrat Usman favoured the nomination and remarked, " What is hidden of Umar is better than what outwardly appears; there is not his equal amongst us." Sayeed bin Zaid supported the proposal emphatically.

The general consensus. The general consensus was that Hadrat Umar was the fittest person to be nominated as the Caliph. There was, however, an under current of feeling that Hadrat Umar had the fiery and irascible temper, and he might not be able to show moderation so necessary for the head of the community. Hadrat Abu Bakr observed that Hadrat Umar's display of severity was meant to counteract his (Hadrat Abu Bakr's) leniency. Hadrat Abu Bakr felt that when the full responsibility of government was devolved upon Hadrat Umar, he would become moderate in his opinion. Hadrat Abu Bakr said:

> "I can say from my personal experience that Hadrat Umar has always cooled me down whenever I have lost my temper with any one, just as whenever he felt me to be too lenient he counselled greater severity. For this reason I feel certain that with time, Hadrat Umar will achieve the moderation that you desire."

Objection of Talha. Talha who was related to Hadrat Abu Bakr, and perhaps coveted the caliphate for himself objected to the nomination of Hadrat Umar. He said:

> "O successor of the Prophet, you knew full well how harsh Hadrat Umar has been towards us all during your regime, and God only knows what he will meet to us when you are gone. You know that you are leaving us for ever, and yet you are content to leave us in the hands of a man whose fierce and ungovernable rages are well known to you. Think O Chief, what answer will you give to Your Lord for such a behest?"

At this objection of Talha, Hadrat Abu Bakr who was lying prostrate on his bed rose up with considerable effort and addressing Talha said:

> "Have you come to frighten me? I swear that when I meet my Lord, I will gladly tell Him that I appointed as ruler over His people, the man who was the best of them all."

Hadrat Ali. Thereupon Hadrat Ali who was present on the occasion rose to say that he would acknowledge no one as Caliph save Hadrat Umar. Hadrat Abu Bakr was much impressed with the integrity of Hadrat Ali for not pressing his own claim, and putting the interests, of the community above his personal interests. Turning to Hadrat Ali, Hadrat Abu Bakr said:

> "Ali, you are indeed a prince in the most exalted sense of the word, for others are mere men."

Hadrat Umar. Then Hadrat Abu Bakr sent for Hadrat Umar, and informed him that he had nominated him as his successor. Hadrat Umar said that he did not covet the office. Thereupon Hadrat Abu Bakr said, "But the office needs you. I have prayed to God to direct me rightly to the choice of my successor, and my choice is fundamental for the unity and concord of the Muslims."

The testament. Hadrat Umar acquiesced, and Hadrat Abu Bakr dictated the testament to Hadrat Usman in the following terms:

> "In the name of Most Merciful God. This is the last will and testament of Abu Bakr bin Abu Qahafa, when he is in the last hour of the world, and the first of the next; an hour in which the infidel must believe, the wicked be convinced of their evil ways, I nominate Umar bin al-Khattab as my successor. Therefore, hear to him and obey him. If he acts right, confirm his actions. My intentions are good, but I cannot see the future results. However, those who do ill shall render themselves liable to severe account hereafter. Fare you well. May you be ever attended by the Divine favour of blessing."

Approval of the people. The testament having been drawn up, Hadrat Abu Bakr supported by his wife Asma walked up to the door and addressed the people who had collected there. He told them that he had appointed Hadrat Umar as his successor. They said, "We approve." After obtaining the approval of the people in general terms, Hadrat Abu Bakr lay on the bed, and prayed to God:

> "O Lord ! I have made this testament for the welfare of the community in order to counteract discord among them. What my intentions are, You know full well. I have

> spared the pains in making the best selection, O God, I entrust the Muslims to Your care. O Allah, keep their ruler on the right path. O God, make my successor the most pious of rulers, and confer peace on the Muslims."

Counsel to Hadrat Umar. Addressing his successor, Hadrat Umar, Hadrat Abu Bakr said:

> "Let not sorrow for me divert you from the service of the Lord. You saw what I myself did when the Prophet died, and there could be no greater sorrow for mankind than that. Truly, if grief had stayed me then from girding my loins in the cause of the Lord and of His Prophet, and if, I swear by Allah, I had shown the slightest weakness in carrying out the command of Allah on that day. He would have punished us by bringing on us destruction. I expect you to do your duty against all odds. May God bless you."

Wishes and Regrets of Hadrat Abu Bakr

Wishes and regrets of Hadrat Abu Bakr. On his death bed, when reviewing the main events of his life, Hadrat Abu Bakr gave expression to certain wishes and regrets. He said that there were three things which he did and which he wished he should not have done. There were three things which he did not do and wished that he should have done them. There were three things which he did not enquire from the Holy Prophet, and which he should have enquired.

Things which he did, but should not have done. The first thing which he did but wished that he should not have done was that he should not have insisted on Hadrat Ali offering him allegiance as Caliph. The second thing was that when Faja'a Salmi was brought to him he should not have ordered him to be burnt alive, but should have killed him otherwise or let him free. The third thing was that he should not have accepted the caliphate, but should have seen that either Hadrat Umar or Abu Ubaida were declared as the Caliph, and he should become a Minister to the Caliph. When Hadrat Ali was asked to take the oath of allegiance to Hadrat Abu

Bakr, that annoyed Hadrat Fatima, and Hadrat Abu Bakr felt sorry for such annoyance. Faja'a was burnt to death, and that was against a tradition of the Holy Prophet which laid down that if a person professed to be a Muslim, he should not be burnt to death. Hadrat Abu Bakr had no personal interest in the Caliphate, and, therefore, he always longed that someone else from among the Quraish should have become the Caliph, and he could have helped him as his Minister.

Things which he did not do, and wished that he should have done them. The first thing which he did not do, but wished that he should have done it was that when Asha'as bin Qais was brought to him as a captive he should have ordered him to be killed, and should not have pardoned him. The second thing was that when he sent the forces against the apostates he should have remained at Zu Qissa, so that he could have proceeded to the help of the Muslim force fighting against the apostates. The third thing was that when he commissioned Khalid to proceed to the Syrian front, he should have sent Hadrat Umar to Iraq and in this way he should have spread both his hands in the way of Allah. Asha'as the Kinda chief was deceitful by nature, and Hadrat Abu Bakr not only pardoned him, but married his sister to him. Hadrat Abu Bakr felt that that was a mistake as Asha'as was a faithless person. Hadrat Abu Bakr directed the apostasy campaign from Madina. Hadrat Abu Bakr felt that a better base for such operations was Zu Qissa. When Khalid was withdrawn from the Iraq front, the Muslim position on this front became weak. It would have been a better course of action if reinforcement should have been sent to Iraq under the command of a leader like Hadrat Umar.

Things that he should have enquired from the Holy Prophet. The first thing which Hadrat Abu Bakr wished to have enquired from the Holy Prophet was as to who should be his successor. The second thing was what share should be allowed to the Ansar in the administration. The third thing was as to what part of the inheritance should be allowed to a niece or a paternal aunt. The caliphate issue has remained a source of great headache to the Muslims and Hadrat Abu Bakr felt that if there had been any definite instructions of the

Holy Prophet on the point that could have eased the situation. The question of the equation between the Ansars and the emigrants also involved considerable controversy, and it would have been in the fitness of things if some definite guidance from the Holy Prophet on the point was forthcoming. The question of giving share to a niece or a paternal aunt involved difficulty and if there had been a specific ruling from the Holy Prophet that would have solved the point.

Hadrat Ali's Oration on the Death of Hadrat Abu Bakr

Hadrat Ali's oration. When Hadrat Ali came to know of the death of Hadrat Abu Bakr, he rushed to his house, and standing outside the house wherein lay the dead body of Hadrat Abu Bakr, delivered an oration, which is a masterpiece of oratory, and is a beautiful summing up of the character and personality of Hadrat Abu Bakr.

Master of many virtues. Hadrat Ali said:

> "Mercy of God on you, O Abu Bakr. You were an affectionate companion and friend of the Prophet of Allah, a source of joy to him, and one who knew his secrets and enjoyed the privilege of being consulted by him. You were the first person to embrace Islam: you had the purest faith, and your belief in Islam was unshakable. Of all, you feared Allah most, and you were the source of the greatest advantage to His faith. You had been with the Prophet more than any one else and your love for Islam was superior to others. A blessing to the companions you were the best of associates. Master of many virtues, excelling others in accomplishments and superior to all in position, you resembled the Holy Prophet more than any other person in the uprightness of character and conduct and in kindness and excellence. Your rank was noble, and your position sublime, and you enjoyed the greatest confidence of the Prophet. May God reward you with goodness on behalf of Islam and the Prophet."

As-Siddiq. Hadrat Ali added:

> "For the Prophet of Allah you were like his very sight and hearing. You corroborated the truth of his message at a time when every body belied him, and so you were called As-Siddiq (the Veracious) by Allah in His revelations. He says, "The one who came with the Truth, and the one who corroborated the Truth. The one who came with the Truth was Muhammad (peace be on him), and one who corroborated the Truth was Abu Bakr. You supported him when others had deserted him, and you remained firm in helping him in misfortunes when others had withdrawn their support. In the days of hardship you were his best companion. You were "the second of the two", and his companion in the Cave. You were the person on whom God conferred tranquillity of mind. You were the only companion of the Prophet in his migration to Madina, and you were his Caliph among his followers and in the religion of Allah. You discharged the functions of the Khilafat in a most excellent manner at a moment when people had taken to apostasy, and you exhibited such firmness in enforcing the commands of Allah as had never been exhibited by the Khalifa of any other Prophet."

Firmness of Hadrat Abu Bakr. Talking about the firmness of Hadrat Abu Bakr, Hadrat Ali said:

> "You rose to the occasion when your colleagues showed lassitude, and you became bold when they were weak. You retained your adherence to the ways of the Prophet when others deviated from them. You were his true Caliph with no dispute or difference, although this gave offence to hypocrites and umbrage to the infidels, brought grief to those who were jealous and made the rebels wrathful. You stuck to the commands of Allah when others showed cowardice. You remained firm when others went astray. You passed through the Divine light while they remained behind. Afterwards they followed you and attained their goal."

Dignity of Hadrat Abu Bakr. About the dignity of Hadrat Abu Bakr, Hadrat Ali said:

> "You had the lowest voice but the highest distinction. Your conversation was most exemplary and your reasoning most just; your silence was longest in duration, and your speech was most eloquent. Bravest among men, and well informed about matters, your action was dignified."

Father to the believers. Hadrat Ali referred to Hadrat Abu Bakr as the 'Father of the Believers', in the following terms:

> "I swear by Allah, you were the leader of the believers. You came towards the Faith when others were away from it. You followed them when they turned towards it. Indeed you acted like a kind father to the believers till your filial affection made them your children. You bore the heavy burden which they could not and you professed to do what they had omitted. You preserved what they had ruined, and you taught them what they knew not. You took the risk when they were helpless, and you remained firm when they were impatient."

Hadrat Abu Bakr's equation between the believers and the infidels. Referring to Hadrat Abu Bakr's equation between the believers and the infidels, Hadrat Ali said:

> "You redressed the grievances of those who asked for justice; hence they turned to you for guidance and were therefore successful and got through you what they had never dreamt of. For infidels you were a source of terrible punishment and a burning fire, and for the believers kindness, affection and protection."

Righteousness, truth and benevolence of Hadrat Abu Bakr. Highlighting the virtues of righteousness, truth and benevolence of Hadrat Abu Bakr, Hadrat Ali said:

> "You flew in the atmosphere of piety, attained its noble reward and won in superiority. Your argument was never

weak, and your judgment was never faulty. You were never guilty of cowardice, and your heart was never crooked or misdirected. You were like a rock which stands firm in the face of hard blows and dashing winds. You were, as the Prophet of Allah has said, the most generous of men in friendship and in giving money. Again, as he says, you were weak in body, but strong in enforcing the commands of God. You were humble in your manners, but dignified in the estimation of God, great in the eyes of men and commanding respect with them. No one could even as much as wink at you, nor could any one taunt at you. You were not in a position to excite temptation and you were not partial to any body. The weak and the humble were strong with you as you secured their rights; and the strong were weak and humble with you, as you made them surrender the rights of others. In this matter those who were far from you were all equal. Those who obeyed and feared Allah most were nearest to you. Your dignity lay in righteousness, truth, and benevolence; your word was imperative and definite, your command mild and cautious, and your judgement wise and firm. Thus you extirpated evil and made the way for the Truth clear; difficulties were solved, and fires of evil and discord extinguished.

Hadrat Abu Bakr's high position in doing good. Speaking of Hadrat Abu Bakr's high position in doing good, Hadrat Ali said:

"You brought moderation to faith; strength to belief, firmness to Islam and the Muslims, and triumph to the command of Allah. Although it became a source of grief to infidels, yet I say it on oath that you made a great advance in this and placed in great difficulty those who came after you. Evidently you attained a high position in doing good."

Mourning on the death of Hadrat Abu Bakr. Mourning the death of Hadrat Abu Bakr, Hadrat Ali said:

"You are above lamentation; mourning for you is great in Heaven. Your death has broken the backbone of the people and we recite the verse 'From God you came and to God you have returned'. However we submit to what has been ordained by Allah and are ready to obey His commands. By Allah, never shall the Muslims suffer, after the death of the Prophet, a calamity greater than your death."

Conclusion. Concluding his oration Hadrat Ali said:

"You were a source of honour, protection and support to the Faith and for the believers you were like a group of men, a stronghold and a place of refuge; while for the hypocrites you were all strictness and terror. May Allah, in reward for these, take you near to your Prophet, and may He not deprive us of the fruits of your efforts and may He not mislead us after you. We recite once again 'From God you came, and to God you have returned."

Elegy on the Death of Hadrat Abu Bakr

Kufaf bin Umayr. On the death of Hadrat Abu Bakr, Khufaf b. Umayr wrote an elegy mourning the death of Hadrat Abu Bakr. He was a descendant of the famous Arab poet Imraul Qais. He was also known as Ibn Nudbah, the latter being his mother's name. He was present at the battle of Hunain. At the time of the conquest of Makkah he carried the standard of Banu Salim. He has the honour of being one of the greatest poets of Arab chivalry.

The Elegy. Mourning the death of Hadrat Abu Bakr, Kufaf said:

"Tell every living thing that there is no permanence for it;
And for the whole universe, its decree is destruction.
The goods of men are but as a trust;
Borrowed on the condition of repayment;
And a man strives, but there is one who lies in wait for him; The eye mourns for him, who is no more.

The man first in faith, without a peer.
Verily Abu Bakr was as the rain.
That brought verdure to the parched land.
When the young Muslim community was threatened with danger
He led the Muslims to victory
He was verily a great hero,
No one can attain the excellence of his days,
May God bless him, and
May his soul rest in peace."

Wives and Children of Hadrat Abu Bakr

Wives and Children of Hadrat Abu Bakr. Hadrat Abu Bakr married four wives in all. He had six children, three sons and three daughters.

Qutaila. His first wife was Qutaila. She belonged to the Bani Aamir tribe. She was the mother of two children, Asma and Abdullah. She did not accept Islam, and Hadrat Abu Bakr divorced her. Some time after 'Hijrat', Qutaila went to Madina to see her daughter Asma. Asma asked of the Holy Prophet whether she could see her mother, and whether she could stay with her. The Holy Prophet permitted Asma to play host to her mother.

Umm Ruman. Her second wife was Umm Ruman. She was the daughter of Aamir bin Umair. She was first married to Abdullah bin Harith. She had one son from Abdullah who was named Tufail. Abdullah was a friend of Hadrat Abu Bakr, and on his death, Hadrat Abu Bakr married Umn Ruman. She was the mother of two children of Hadrat Abu Bakr, namely Abdur Rahman and Hadrat Ayesha. When Hadrat Abu Bakr became a Muslim; Umm Ruman also accepted Islam. She died at Madina in 628 C.E. The Holy Prophet himself led her funeral prayers. The Holy Prophet is reported to have said, "If any one wishes to see a hour of the paradise, let hir see Umm Ruman".

Habiba. The third wife of Hadrat Abu Bakr was Habiba. She was the daughter of Zaid bin Kharijah Ansari, with whom

Hadrat Abu Bakr had the bond of brotherhood established by the Holy Prophet. While Umm Ruman lived at Madina, Hadrat Abu Bakr resided with Habiba in Sukh, a suburb of Madina. Habiba was the mother of Umm Kulsum who was born after the death of Hadrat Abu Bakr.

Asma. The fourth wife of Hadrat Abu Bakr was Asma. She was first married to Jafar bin Abu Talib, a brother of Hadrat Ali. She migrated with Jafar to Abyssinia in 615 C.E. She had three sons from Jafar, namely, Muhammad, Abdullah, and Aun. In 630 C.E., Jafar was martyred in the battle of Mauta. Six months later, Hadrat Abu Bakr married her. She had one son from Hadrat Abu Bakr who was also named Muhammad. She was a step sister of Umm Salma, wife of the Holy Prophet. Asma was a talented lady. She was well versed in the interpretation of dreams. According to the will of Hadrat Abu Bakr, Asma was authorised to prepare his dead body for the burial. After the death of Hadrat Abu Bakr, Asma married Hadrat Ali from whom she had a son Yahya.

Abdur Rahman. The eldest son of Hadrat Abu Bakr was Abdur Rahman. His mother was Umm Ruman, and he was the real brother of Hadrat Ayesha. When Hadrat Abu Bakr became a Muslim, and his other children were converted to Islam, Abdur Rahman refused to be converted to Islam. Hadrat Abu Bakr accordingly separated from him. In the battles of Badr and Uhud, Abdur Rahman fought on the side of the Quraish against the Muslims. He became a Muslim after the Pact of Hudaibiya. Thereafter he participated in the various battles fought by the Muslims. At the battle of Yamama, he killed Muhakkam al Yamama, the General Commanding the forces of Musailma. At the battle of Busra in Syria, he entered the city of Busra through a subterranean passage, and then dashing towards the city gates opened them for the main Muslim army to enter it. He died in 675 C.E., and buried at Makkah.

Abdullah. The second son of Hadrat Abu Bakr was Abdullah. He was born of Qutaila. He was mairied to Atika who was the daughter of Zaid bin Amr bin Naufal. She was a cousin of Hadrat Umar. She was extraordinarily beautiful, and Abdullah was so much lost in her love that he failed to participate in the various expeditions undertaken by the Muslims. He even neglected his prayers. Abdullah was so much overwhelmed with the love of Atika that he could not attend to other duties. Hadrat Abu Bakr gave vent to his anger, and told his son in plain words that his failings and shortcomings were too serious to be passed over. Abdullah placed himself at the mercy of his father. Hadrat Abu Bakr decreed that the penalty for such lapses was that Abdullah should divorce Atika within three days. Abdullah divorced Atika in pursuance of the command of his father. That, however, upset the mental equilibrium of Abdullah. He would neither eat nor drink. He would sob and sigh and sing heart rending verses giving expression to his grief over the loss of his beloved. When the Holy Prophet came to know of the matter, he annulled the divorce, and the lovers were reunited. Thereafter, Abdullah was very particular to take care that his love for Atika did not stand in the way of his duty to God. In all the campaigns that were undertaken by the Holy Prophet thereafter, Abdullah took active part and fought valiantly. Abdullah was wounded in the battle ot Taif, and later died of these wounds in 633 C.E. in the first year of the caliphate of Hadrat Abu Bakr. After the death of Abdullah, Hadrat Umar married Atika.

Muhammad. The third son of Hadrat Abu Bakr was Muhammad born of Asma bint Asma. He was hardly two or three years old at the time of the death of Hadrat Abu Bakr. Asma had two sons who both bore the name 'Muhammad'. One was the son of Jafar and the other was the son of Hadrat Abu Bakr. After the death of Hadrat Abu Bakr, Asma married Hadrat Ali, and Muhammad bin Abu Bakr was brought up under the care of Hadrat Ali. He was a great partisan of Hadrat Ali, and he was very active in the coup that led to the martyrdom of Hadrat Usman. During the caliphate of Hadrat Ali Muhammad became the Governor of Egypt. When Muawiyiah captured power, he had Muhammad killed.

Asma. The eldest daughter of Hadrat Abu Bakr was Asma. Her mother was Qutaila who did not become a Muslim and was divorced by Hadrat Abu Bakr. When the Holy Prophet and Hadrat Abu Bukr sought refuge in a cave outside Makkah on the occasion of Migration to Madina, Asma used to carry food to them under the cover of darkness. When the Holy Prophet and Hadrat Abu Bakr left the cave, Asma tore her apron and tied the goods with the two belts. For this ingenuity, she received from the Holy Prophet, the title "She of the two belts". She was married to Zubair, a cousin of the Holy Prophet. At Madina, soon after migration, Asma gave birth to Abdullah, who was the first Muslim child to be born after migration. After the tragedy of Kerbala, Abdullah declared himself as the Caliph at Makkah. When the Umayyads stormed the city of Makkah, Abdullah consulted Asma who was then eighty years old, as to what he should do. She advised "If you believe your cause to be right you should be ready to die for it; if on the other hand your object is merely worldly gain, then you may certainly compromise with your enemy". When Abdullah died and the Umayyads had his body hung at the city gate, Asma went to the dead body of her son, and she said pathetically, "The rider is still riding the horse".

Hadrat Ayesha. The second daughter of Hadrat Abu Bakr was Hadrat Ayesha, who had the unique honour of being the only virgin to be married to the Holy Prophet. She became a widow at a young age. During the caliphate of Hadrat Abu Bakr and Hadrat Umar she enjoyed great influence. When Hadrat Ali became the Caliph, she was involved in the battle against him. Thereafter she retired from politics, and lived a quiet life at Madina. She was very talented, and was an authority on theological and judicial matters.

Umm Kulsum. The third daughter of Hadrat Abn Bakr was Umm Kulsum. She was born of Habiba bint Zaid Ansari. Umm Kulsum was born after the death of Hadrat Abu Bakr. On coming of age, Umm Kulsum was married to Talha bin Ubaidullah. On the death of Talha, she married his brother Abdur Rahman bin Ubaidullah.

Notes

In this Chapter the first section deals with the passing away of Hadrat Abu Bakr. The account given in this section is based on the account given in all the biographies of Hadrat Abu Bakr.

I have obtained help from the following books :

(1) *Abu Bakr* by Muhammad Hussain Haikal;

(2) *Abu Bakr, The Caliph* by A.A. Aziz ; and

(3) *Hadrat Abu Bakr* by Syed Moinul Haq.

(1) He had perfect faith in God. When the companions said whether they should call a physician, he said that the physician had already visited him and said that he would do what he would do.

(2) He willed that the allownace that he had drawn from the state treasury should be refunded by selling a plot of land that belonged to him. This is something unique in the history of the world.

(3) He set the example that the coffin need not be new.

(4) On the eve of death he developed prophetic vision. He foretold that his wife Habiba who was pregnant would give birth to a daughter. He also foretold that he would die the same day as the Holy Prophet.

(5) He died exactly at the age at which the Holy Prophet had died. Thus he followed in the footsteps of the Holy Prophet not only when alive, but even in the matter of death.

The second section deals with the appointment of Hadrat Umar as his successor. In that Hadrat aby Bakr set up new standards of selflessness. He had a son Abdul Rahman who was qualified in every way to succeed him, but he did not nominate him as his successor. Instead he nominated Hadrat Umar as his successor whom he considered to be the best choice. When we read his testament, and ponder over his counsel to his successor, or reflect over the contents of his prayers to God we cannot help but wonder at the greatness of Hadrat Abu Bakr. Verily in the history of the world any example of selflessness is to be given, that would be the example of Hadrat Aby Bakr.

In the third section I have given an account of the wishes and regrets of Hadrat Abu Bakr. At the time of death every person is apt to have some wishes and regrets. The character of the wishes and regrets of Hadrat Abu Bakr is different. There is nothing personal about his wishes and regrets. These are motivated by his love for Islam attachment for the Holy Prophet and devotion of God.

In the fourth section I have given what Hadrat Ali said on the occassion of the death of Hadrat Abu Bakr. I have adopted this address from Syed Moinul Haq's book *Hadrat Abu Bakr.* It will be seen that hadrat Ali paid a tribute to Hadrat Abu Bakr in the most glowing terms. This shows that what certain sects said about Hadrat Abu Bakr later did not command the approval of Hadrat Ali. It is regrettable that such sectarion differences should have arisen among the Muslims because of partisan considerations.

In the fifith section I have given some of the elegiac verses written by the poet Khafaf at the death of Hadrat Abu Bakr. I have quoted these from Jalaluddin Suyuti's *History of the Caliphs.*

In the last section I have given an account of the wives and children of Hadrat Abu Bakr. I would have liked to give some particulars about some other kinsmen of Hadrat Abu Bakr. But for his father Abu Qahafa we get no particuolars about the other relatives of Hadrat Abu Bakr in the sources that have come down to us.

19

HADRAT ABU BAKR, THE MAN

Distinctions of Hadrat Abu Bakr

Distinctions of Hadrat Abu Bakr. Hadrat Abu Bakr was a man of many distinctions. A study of his life reveals that in many respects he had the unique distinction of being the first or the topmost person. Hereunder we attempt to catalogue the main distinctions of Hadrat Abu Bakr.

Acceptance of Islam. Outside the family of the Holy Prophet, Hadrat Abu Bakr was the first person to accept Islam. While other persons always indulged in some argument in accepting Islam. Hadrat Abu Bakr was the only person who accepted Islam without any reluctance or hesitation, and without any argument.

Liberation of slaves. He was the first person to liberate slaves in the way of God.

First public address. When God ordered that the teaching of Islam should be made public, the first public address calling the people to God and His Prophet was delivered by Hadrat Abu Bakr.

The first mosque. Hadrat Abu Bakr was the first person to build a mosque in the history of Islam.

His titles. He had the unique distinction of being given the titles of 'Siddiq', and 'Atiq' by the Holy Prophet.

Companionship of the Holy Prophet. Of all the

companions, Hadrat Abu Bakr was the closest and the dearest to the Holy Prophet. He had the unique distinction of being the companion of the Holy Prophet in the cave in Mt. Thaur on the occasion of the Holy Prophet's migration from Makkah to Madina.

Masjid-i-Nabvi. The land for Masjid-i-Nabvi at Madina was purchased with the money of Hadrat Abu Bakr.

Wealth of Hadrat Abu Bakr. When Hadrat Abu Bakr accepted Islam, he had 40,000 dirhams with him. He spent the whole of this amount in the cause of Islam. The Holy Prophet acknowledged that he had utilised the wealth of Hadrat Abu Bakr more than the wealth of any other person. When the Holy Prophet invited contributions to finance the Tabuk expedition, Hadrat Abu Bakr had the unique distinction of contributing all that he had.

The Holy Prophet's regard for Hadrat Abu Bakr. The Holy Prophet was pleased to appoint Hadrat Abu Bakr as the first "Amirul Hajj" in the history of Islam. Hadrat Abu Bakr had the distinction to be appointed as the Imam to lead the prayers in the lifetime of the Holy Prophet. In his last address at Masjid-i-Nabvi, the Holy Prophet ordered that all doors opening into the mosque should be closed except the door leading to the house of Hadrat Abu Bakr.

Caliphate. Hadrat Abu Bakr had the distinction of being the first Caliph in the history of Islam. He was the first Caliph to nominate a successor. He was the only Caliph in the history of Islam who refunded to the state treasury at the time of his death the entire amount of the allowance that he had drawn during the period of his caliphate.

As a ruler. He was the first Muslim ruler to establish Baitul Mal. He was the first Muslim ruler to establish crown pasture. He was the first Muslim ruler to establish 'Ijtihad'.

His virtues. In the matter of virtue, Hadrat Abu Bakr excelled all other companions of the Holy Prophet.

Fiqh and Tasawuff. He is the Father of Fiqh. He is the

Imam of Sufis. After the Holy Prophet, he was the best interpretor of dreams.

Companionship of the Holy Prophet. Hadrat Abu Bakr had the distinction of being the closest and the dearest companion of the Holy Prophet. Four generations of the family of Hadrat Abu Bakr had the distinction of being the companions of the Holy Prophet, namely Abu Qahafa the father of Hadrat Abu Bakr; Hadrat Abu Bakr himself: Abdur Rahman the son of Hadrat Abu Bakr, and Abu Atiq Muhammad, a grandson of Hadrat Abu Bakr. No other family had such distinction. Hadrat Abu Bakr was the only ruler who became the Caliph during the lifetime of his father.

Conquests. When after the death of the Holy Prophet, most of the tribes of Arabia apostatised, it was Hadrat Abu Bakr who reconquered Arabia for Islam. He was the first Muslim ruler to conquer Iraq. He was the first Muslim ruler to conquer Syria.

Compilation of the Holy Qur'an. *He* was the first person to compile the Holy Qur'an and called it "Mashaf".

After death. After death, Hadrat Abu Bakr had the distinction of being buried by the side of the Holy Prophet.

Hadrat Abu Bakr in the Holy Qur'an

References in the Holy Qur'an. Hadrat Abu Bakr has the unique distinction of being referred to in the Holy Qur'an in several verses.

Al-Bara'at. In Sura "Al-Bara'at", there is a reference to Hadrat Abu Bakr in the following verse:

"He being the second of the two,
When they were in the cave
And when Muhammad said to his companion
'Grieve not, surely God is with us,
Then God came to their help,
And protected them with an army
Which they saw not". (IX : 40)

Al-Lail. The following verses in the Sura "Al-Lail" refer to Hadrat Abu Bakr:

"Those who spend their wealth for increase in self-purification
And have in their minds no favour from any one,
For which a reward is expected in return,
But only the desire,
To seek the countenance of their Lord, Most High
And soon will they attain complete satisfaction."
(XCII : 18-21)

"He who gives in charity, and fears Allah
And in all sincerity testifies to the best,
We will indeed, make smooth for him,
The path to bliss". (XCII : 1-7)

Al-Ahzab. When the verse "Surely Allah and His angels bless the Prophet" (XXXIII : 56) was revealed, Hadrat Abu Bakr enquired of the Holy Prophet whether he was included in the divine grace which was bestowed on the Holy Prophet. It was on this that the following verse was revealed which contains an implied reference to Hadrat Abu Bakr:

"He it is,
Who sends His blessings on him,
And so do His angels
That He may bring him forth
Out of utter darkness into light,
And He is merciful to the believers". (XXXIII : 43).

Al-Imran. The commentators are agreed that the following verse of Sura "Al-Imran" refers to Hadrat Abu Bakr, and Hadrat Umar:

"And take counsel with them in the affair". (III : 158)

Al-Waqiah. Shah Wali Ullah and other commentators hold that in the following verse of Sura "Al-Waqiah", the "believers that are good "refers to Hadrat Abu Bakr and Hadrat Umar:

"And if you back up each other against him,

Then surely Allah it is
Who is his Guardian,
And Gabriel, and the believers that do good,
And the angels will be his helpers." (LXVI: 4).

Ar-Rahman. According to commentators the following verse in Sura "Ar-Rahman" refers to Hadrat Abu Bakr:

"And for him
Who fears to stand before his Lord,
Are two gardens", (LV : 46)

Al-Imran. The following verse in Sura "Al-Imran" with reference to the Jews has an implied reference to Hadrat Abu Bakr:

"And you will certainly hear from those
Who received the Book before you
And from the polytheists much that is wrong,
But if you preserve and fear God,
That is the steadfastness of things."

An-Nur. In Sura "An-Nur", the following verse refers to Hadrat Abu Bakr:

"And let not those of you
Who possess grace and abundance
Swear against giving to the near of kin and the poor
And those who have migrated in the way of Allah,
And they should pardon and turn away.
Do you not like that God should forgive you ?" (XVIII. 24)

Holy Prophet's Estimate of Hadrat Abu Bakr

Most virtuous. The Holy Prophet said that if all the virtues were catalogued these would be three sixty in number and Hadrat Abu Bakr possessed all the three sixty virtues. Among the Companions Hadrat Abu Bakr was the most virtuous.

Special way. The Holy Prophet said, "Allah will; show His glory to the people in a general way, but He will show it to Hadrat Abu Bakr in a special way."

Greatness of Hadrat Abu Bakr. About the greatness of Hadrat Abu Bakr, the Holy Prophet said:

> "Never has the sun risen or set on an person, except a Prophet, greater than Abu Bakr."

Best of human beings. The Holy Prophet said, "Verily, Abu Bakr is the best of human beings, except the Prophets."

Companionship of Hadrat Abu Bakr. About the companionship of Hadrat Abu Bakr, the Holy Prophet said:

> "Abu Bakr, you were my companion in the cave, and you will be my companion in Heaven on the spring of Kausar."

Kindliest of Persons. Hadrat Abu Bakr was a kind hearted person and he freely spent his money for the relief of the Muslims in distress. For this attribute, Hadrat Abu Bakr earned the following remarks from the Holy Prophet:

> "The kindliest of my followers towards the believers in faith is Abu Bakr."

Truthful and veracious. About the truth and veracity of Hadrat Abu Bakr, the Holy Prophet said:

> "Never did I invite any person to accept Islam who did not doubt and hesitate and express anxiety save only Abu Bakr who embraced it without the slightest hesitation when I spoke to him of the faith."

The Holy Prophet's confidence in Hadrat Abu Bakr. The Holy Prophet said:

> "Never was anything revealed to me that I did not pour in Abu Bakr's ears."

Glad tidings of paradise. The Holy Prophet gave glad tidings of paradise to ten of his companions, Hadrat Abu Bakr headed this list. Addressing Hadrat Abu Bakr, the Holy Prophet said:

> "Abu Bakr, you will be the first of my people to enter paradise."

Place for Hadrat Abu Bakr in the paradise. The Holy Prophet even beseeched God to recognise the merits of Hadrat Abu Bakr:

> "Almighty God, give, I beseech You, a place to Abu Bakr like that of mine in paradise on the Day of Judgment."

The Holy Prophet's obligations to Hadrat Abu Bakr. The Holy Prophet said:

> "There is none whom I owe obligation and I did not repay it except Abu Bakr, for I owe him much for which Allah will compensate him on the Day of Judgment."

Obligations of the people to Hadrat Abu Bakr. The Holy Prophet enjoined the Muslims as follows:

> "The love of Abu Bakr and gratitude towards him is incumbent upon every one of my people."

Hadrat Abu Bakr, The Man

Personal description. According to Waqidi, Abu Bakr in personal appearance was a man having a fair colour and a slender body. His waist was slightly bent so that the cloth that he wore round it often slipped down. He had a thin face with deeply set eyes and broad forehead. He had no flesh on his finger joints. His height was in proportion to his body. He had curled hair. His voice was sweet. He dyed his beard. Indeed he had the look of a patriarch.

Virtues of Hadrat Abu Bakr. Hadrat Abu Bakr was a paragon of virtues. According to a tradition the Holy Prophet addressing his companions one day asked who out of them had attended a funeral; who had paid alms; who had visited a sick person; who had visited a graveyard; and who had kept a fast. Hadrat Abu Bakr alone answered to all these requirements. The Holy Prophet said that if all the virtues were catalogued these would be three hundred and sixty in number. The Holy Prophet was pleased to observe that Hadrat Abu Bakr possessed all these three hundred and sixty virtues.

Siddiq. The Holy Prophet conferred on Hadrat Abu Bakr the honorific title of *Siddiq*. There may not be much in a name, but there is much in a surname. If we were to sum the qualities of Hadrat Abu Bakr in one word, that word would be *Siddiq*. The word *Siddiq* may be rendered as 'truthful, faithful and veracious". Hadrat Abu Bakr was truthful. He always spoke the truth. He was a man of strong views. His faith had the strength of rocks. He was a man of iron resolution and when once he formed an opinion, no body could influence him. He was a man of great devotion and dedication. He was a man of great and deep insight and extraordinary judgment. He had a highly developed faculty of perceiving the truth, and arriving at unerring judgment. When the Holy Prophet declared his mission Hadrat Abu Bakr accepted the call without any hesitation, reluctance or argument. That was because Hadrat Abu Bakr could perceive where the truth lay. When the Holy Prophet declared that the previous night he had ascended the Heaven, Hadrat Abu Bakr forthwith believed in such ascension.

Intelligence of Hadrat Abu Bakr. Hadrat Abu Bakr was highly intelligent. When men like Hadrat Umar felt unhappy over the terms of the Hudaibiya Pact, Hadrat Abu Bakr felt that the Pact was in fact in the interests of the Muslims. When on the occassion of the Farewell Pilgrimage the Holy Prophet declared that God had perfected the religion for them that day and other persons felt happy, Hadrat Abu Bakr felt sorry for this implied that having completed his mission the Holy Prophet was about to pass away. When during his illness the Holy Prophet delivered that God had given his servant the choice between immortality or a return to Him, and he had accepted the latter course, Hadrat Abu Bakr wept for this implied than the Holy Prophet was not going to survive his illness.

Memory of Hadrat Abu Bakr. Hadrat Abu Bakr blessed with extraordinary memory. He had but to listen to any verses once, and he could thereafter repeat them accurately. He memorised the Holy Qur'an. He was most eloquent. His addresses were always characterised by deep thinking which impressed the listeners. He could quote the traditions with authority.

Judgment and scholarship of Hadrat Abu Bakr. About the judgment and scholarship of Hadrat Abu Bakr, Shah Wali Ullah of Delhi has made the following observations:

> "He was just like other scholars among the Companions in his knowledge of the Qur'an and the Sunnah. In what he excelled others was that whenever he was faced with a difficult problem, he would exercise his judgment and deeply ponder over it. The Almighty would cast a ray of enlightenment on his heart and would reveal to him the truth. As the manifestation of this enlightenment was connected with the excellence of the heart it impressed itself in the form of determination and not a mere idea".

Steadfastness of Hadrat Abu Bakr. Because of his inner insight and conviction, Hadrat Abu Bakr was always steadfast in his actions. When the Holy Prophet died and the people would not believe that he was dead, Hadrat Abu Bakr made them realise the grim reality, and advised them to be steadfast. When some of the tribes offered to remain Muslims provided they were exempted from the payment of Zakat, and the Companions around him advised him to accept the offer, he remained steadfast and refused to compromise. When Usama's army was to be sent to Syria, many persons advised that it was not the proper time to send the expedition. He remained steadfast in the decision, and decided that the expedition to Syria would be undertaken, whatever the consequences.

Courage of Hadrat Abu Bakr. Because of his faith and resolution he was very courageous. It is stated that once Hadrat Ali asked his companions as to whom they considered to be the bravest person. They said that he (Hadrat Ali) was such a person. Hadrat Ali said, "No. Hadrat Abu Bakr was the bravest. On the day of the battle of Badr, when no one was forthcoming to stand guard at the pavilion where the Holy Prophet prayed, Hadrat Abu Bakr stood with his sword, and did not allow the enemy come near the site."

Hadrat Abu Bakr's love for Islam. Hadrat Abu Bakr's love for Islam was of great depth. Islam in fact became the end all and be all of his existence. In the battle of Badr, Abdur Rahman a son of Hadrat Abu Bakr who had by that time not accepted Islam fought on the side of the Quraish. When Abdur Rahman became a Muslim he told his father that on the day of the battle of Badr, he had on several occasions come within a striking distance, but he went the other way. Hadrat Abu Bakr said that if he had such an opportunity, he would not have spared him. Hadrat Abu Bakr was a loving father, but when his son Abdullah in his love for his wife Atika neglected his prayers, and did not participate in some expeditions, Hadrat Abu Bakr took him to task and asked him to divorce his wife.

Generosity of Hadrat Abu Bakr. Hadrat Abu Bakr was very generous. When he became a Muslim he had an amount of 40,000 dirhams. The entire amount was spent by him in the cause of Islam. He paid for the liberation of slaves. He financed the journey of the Holy Prophet from Makkah to Madina on the occasion of emigration. He paid for the land acquired for the construction of the Prophet's mosque at Madina. When the Holy Prophet invited contributions for financing the Tabuk expedition, Hadrat Abu Bakr contributed all his assets for the purpose, and when the Holy Prophet enquired as to what he had kept for himself and his dependents, he said that for himself and his dependents he had left Allah and His Prophet.

Selflessness of Hadrat Abu Bakr. He was an embodiment of selflessness. When he became the Caliph he was paid a meagre allowance from the treasury. On his death bed he sold a plot of his land and repaid the entire amount to the treasury. He lived a simple unostentatious life. One of his wives once expressed the wish to have a sweet dish. Hadrat Abu Bakr deposited the amount in the public treasury and had his allowance reduced to the extent of the saving made by his wife, on the ground that such amount was surplus to his genuine needs.

Humility of Hadrat Abu Bakr. Hadrat Abu Bakr was very humble. When he would see a bird he would sigh that he were like such a bird. He would often say that he would prefer to be a hair on the body of a Muslim. When he went to perform the 'Hajj', and some people walked in his train, he asked them not to follow him, but to go their own way. Before becoming the Caliph he used to milk the goats in the Mohalla. After becoming the Caliph when Hadrat Abu Bakr passed the street, one of the girls said that as he had become the Caliph he would no longer milk the goats for them. Hadrat Abu Bakr heard these remarks and said that the caliphate made no difference to him, and that he would continue to milk their goats. If any one praised him, he would say, "O Allah, You know me more than myself, and I know myself more than these people who praise me. Make me better than what they think of me, and forgive those sins of mine of which they have no knowledge, and do not hold me responsible for what they say."

His avoidance of obligation to others. He took particular care to avoid obligation to others. He would do all the work for himself with his own hands, and would not allow other people to oblige him. Even if he happened to drop the reins of the camel from his hands he would alight from the camel, and pick up the reins himself, instead of asking some one else to help him. Once the people around him asked why he did not let other persons do the petty jobs for him. He said, "My beloved Prophet has ordered me not to seek the obligation of any human being, for I want to remain obliged to God-alone."

His regard for the poor. Hadrat Abu Bakr looked after the wants of all the poor people. During the winter he would distribute clothes and blankets among the poor. There is a story that in an out of the way street in Madina there was a blind old woman. Hadrat Umar would go to her house every morning, but he always found that some one else had anticipated his visit and supplied all the wants of the old lady. One day Hadrat Umar went to the house of the lady earlier than usual and found that the man who visited the old lady every morning was none other than Hadrat Abu Bakr.

Greatness of Hadrat Abu Bakr. Hadrat Abu Bakr lived a devoted and dedicated life, and he was particular to follow in the footsteps of the Holy Prophet. Love for the Holy Prophet was a passion with him. The Holy Prophet was pleased to acknowledge that while he had been able to repay all the obligations that he owned to others, he had not been able to repay the obligations that he owed to Hadrat Abu Bakr. During the lifetime of the Holy Prophet, Hadrat Abu Bakr was only the "second of the two", and he played a supporting and corroborative role. After the death of the Holy Prophet, he rose to his full stature, and he verily proved to be a giant among men. He had to face many crises, but with his wise handling of the situations, all such crises were successfully overcome and Islam was launched on the road to destiny. The Holy Prophet had lit the lamp, and though after the death of the Holy Prophet, a furious storm raged Hadrat Abu Bakr guarded the lamp with great care, and saw to it that no blowings could extinguish the flame.

Hadrat Abu Bakr as seen by Western Writers

Western writers. Some of the western writers have paid glowing tributes to Hadrat Abu Bakr. The assessments made by non-Muslim writers give objective view of the greatness of Hadrat Abu Bakr.

Encyclopaedia of Islam. In the *Encyclopaedia of Islam*, it is stated about Hadrat Abu Bakr:

> "His was a gentle character. During recitation of the Qur'an he shed tears, a thing that made great impression on many, but especially on the women; and as his daughter related, he wept with joy at the news that he would accompany Muhammad as companion on emigration.... No sacrifice was too great in his eyes for the sake of the new faith. Thus it came about that of his considerable fortune estimated at 40,000 dirhams, he brought to Madina the small sum of 5,000 dirhams".

Von Kremer. In his book *The Orient under the Caliphs*, Von Kremer says:

> "Abu Bakr the successor and representative of the Prophet in the highest affairs of the Muslim community was a simple man of the old Arabian fashion, and when summoned to the caliphate he was changed in no respect...His household remained as unpretentious as ever. He had only one slave who after finishing the domestic work, made himself useful by cleaning the swords of the faithful."

H. G. Wells. In his *History of the World*, H. G. Wells writes:

> "...There can be little doubt that if Muhammad was the mind and imagination of primitive mind. Abu Bakr was its conscience and its will. Throughout their life together it was Muhammad who said the thing, but it was Abu Bakr who believed the thing."

Sir William Muir. In his book *The Caliphate, its Rise, Decline and Fall*, Sir William Muir has made the following assessment of the character of Hadrat Abu Bakr:

> "Abu Bakr had no thought of personal aggrandisement. Endowed with the sovereign and irresponsible power, he used it simply for the interests of Islam, and the people's good. But the grand secret of his strength was faith in Muhammad. "Call me not the Caliph of Allah" he would say, "I am but the Caliph of the Prophet of Allah'. The question with him ever was what did Muhammad command, or what now would he have done? From this he never swerved a hair's breadth. And so it was that he crushed apostasy and laid secure the foundations of Islam. His reign was short, but after Muhammad himself there is no one to whom the faith is more beholden."

Stanley Lanepole. In his book *Studies in a Mosque*, Stanley Lanepole has observed:

> "Abu Bakr's calm judgment and quick sagacity joined to a gentle and compassionate heart, were of incalculable service to the faith of Islam."

Andre Servier. About the qualities of Hadrat Abu Bakr, Andre Servier has observed as follows in his book *Islam and the Psychology of the Mussalmans:*

> "He was a man of simple manners, and in spite of his unexpected elevation lived in poverty. When he died, he left behind a worn out garment, a slave, and a camel. A true partriach, after Madina's own heart, he had one great quality—energy; and he possessed what had given victory to Muhammad, and what was lacking ill his enemies, an unshakable conviction. He was the right man in the right place."

Dr. Weil. In his work *A History of the Islamic Peoples,* Dr. Weil writes as follows:

> "Abu's Bakr's private life was as irreproachable as was his public life. He used the treasures which his Generals sent to him out of the booty, for the purposes of the State and State alone. He himself remained as poor as before. He was kind, simple and pious. As the first collector of the Qur'an, to him belonged the credit of its complete preservation. As a law giver he set an excellent example for his successor, for in cases unprovided for in the Qur'an and the traditions of the Prophet, he gave decisions in consultation with the jurists, decisions which with few exceptions became binding authorities."

Edward Gibbon. In his *History of the Saracens,* Edward Gibbon writes:

> "When Abu Bakr assumed the office of the Caliph, he enjoined on his daughter Ayesha to take a strict account of his patrimony, that it might be evident whether he were enriched or impoverished by three pieces of gold only, but on the Friday of each week, he distributed the residue of his own and the public money first to the most worthy, and then to the most indigent of the

> Muslims. The remains of his wealth, a coarse garment and five pieces of gold were delivered to his successor, who lamented with a modest sigh of his own inability to equal such an admirable model."

Simon Ockley. In his book *History of Saracens,* Simon Ockley writes:

> "He never saved any money in the public treasury, but every Friday night distributed what there was among persons of merit. His chastity, temperance, and neglect of the things of this life was exemplary. He desired Ayesha to take an account of all that he had gotten since he was Caliph, and distributed it among the Mussalmans, being resolved not to be enriched by his preferment. His whole inventory amounted to no more than five dirhams which when Umar heard, he said that Abu Bakr had left his successor a hard pattern."

NOTES

In the Chapter entitled "Hadrat Abu Bakr, The Man" I have made an attempt to spotlight the qualities of the head and heart of Hadrat Abu Bakr. Verily the Holy Prophet was a superman. Hadrat Abu Bakr was a man, but he was the best of men. Indeed Hadrat Abu Bakr set the pattern of what a model Muslim be. In the life of Hadrat Abu Bakr we find a standing demonstration of the change that Islam can make in a man. If we seek a model Muslim, then verily such a Muslim is Hadrat Abu Bakr. A character study of Hadrat Abu Bakr is thus the study of Islam as a character building force.

Hadrat Abu Bakr was a man of many distinctions. In the first section of this Chapter I have summed up the various distinctions of Hadrat Abu Bakr. He was the first or the foremost in many things, and I have made an attempt to catalogue all such things which make for his precedence. If one studies the life of Hadrat Abu Bakr carefully, the distinctions of Hadrat Abu Bakr would become manifest to him. By analysing the various aspects of the character of Hadrat Abu Bakr I have drawn up a list of the distinctions of Hadrat Abu Bakr on my awn account. I have in this connection obtained help from the following books:

(1) *Hadrat Abu Bakr* by Muhammad Hussain Haikal.
(2) *Hadrat Abu Bakr* by Syed Moinul Haq.
(3) *History of the Caliphs* by Jalaluddin Suyuti.
(4) *"Abu Bakr, the Caliph"* by A. A. Aziz.

The list of the distinctions of Hadrat Abu Bakr is not exhaustive; it is mainly illustrative.

Hadrat Abu Bakr was not popular with men alone; even Allah approved of his conduct on more than one occasion. There are implied references to Hadrat Abu Bakr in several verses of the Holy Qur'an. In the second section of this chapter I have referred to the verses of the Holy Qur'an which according to commentators have an implied reference to Hadrat Abu Bakr. In writing this section I have obtained help from the following books:

(1) *Commentary of the Holy Qur'an* by Allama Yusuf Ali.
(2) *Commentary of the Holy Qur'an* by Maulana Maududi
(3) My book *Digest of the Holy Qur'an.*
(4) *History of the Caliphs* by Jalaluddin Suyuti.

In the third section I have summarised what the Holy Prophet said of Hadrat Abu Bakr. In compiling this section I have mostly relied on Suyuti's *History of the Caliphs.* This assessment of the character and virtues of Hadrat Abu Bakr leaves no doubt that after the Holy Prophet, Hadrat Abu Bakr is the most distinguished person among the Muslims.

In the fourth section I have projected some aspects of the lofty character of Hadrat Abu Bakr. According to the Holy Prophet there are three sixty virtues and Hadrat Abu Bakr possessed all the virtues. If something were to be said about each virtue of Hadrat Abu Bakr that would need the dimensions of a book. This section is therefore not exhaustive, and does not sum up all the qualities of Hadrat Abu Bakr. It is illustrative in character and affords some glimpses of the eminence of Hadrat Abu Bakr as a man.

In the fifth section I have referred to the assessment of Hadrat Abu Bakr made by some of the western writers. In compiling this section, I have taken help from the following books:

(1) *Encyclopaedia of Islam;*
(2) *The Orient under the Caliphs* by Von Kremer;
(3) *History of the World* by H. G. Wells;
(4) *The Caliphate, Its Rise, Fall, and Decline* by Sir William Muir;
(5) *Studies in a Mosque* by Stanley Lanepole;
(6) *Islam and the Psychology of the Mussalmans* by Andre Servier;
(7) *History of the Islamic People* by Dr. Weil;
(8 *History of the Saracens* by Edward Gibbon; and
(9) *History of the Saracens* by Simon Ockley.

It will be seen that the qualities of Hadrat Abu Bakr are not praised by Muslims alone; these are recognised by non-Muslims as well.

20
HADRAT ABU BAKR IN HISTORY

Role of Hadrat Abu Bakr

Hadrat Abu Bakr's place in history. Hadrat Abu Bakr became the Caliph on the 8th of June 632 C.E., and he died on 23rd August 634 C E. The period of his caliphate covers two years, two months and fifteen days only. Judged by the usual standards this period was too short to make an impact on history. Surprisingly enough, however, the caliphate of Hadrat Abu Bakr did not merely make an impact on history; it changed the very course of history. The suppression of apostasy, the unification of Arabia, and the conquests of greater parts of Iraq and Syria within the space of two years are the extraordinary marvels of history. The speed, the magnitude, the extent and the permanence of these campaigns excite our wonder and evoke our admiration. For these achievements, Hadrat Abu Bakr holds a unique position in the history of the world in general and the history of Islam in particular.

Dynamics of the leadership of Hadrat Abu Bakr. Hadrat Abu Bakr came to power in the midst of a crisis-loaded situation. The crises which he was called upon to encounter were multi-dimensional in character, being psychological, religious, political and international. Islam stood at the brink of a precipice, and any wrong step on the part of Hadrat Abu Bakr at that stage would have led to the disintegration of

Islam. That he not only averted the process of disintegration, but made Islam a world force which could successfully contend against the giant empires of Byzantium and Persia speaks for the dynamics of his leadership.

Historic role of Hadrat Abu Bakr. The historic role of Hadrat Abu Bakr comprehends the following achievements:

(1) His supporting role of Islam,
(2) His suppression of apostasy and unification of Arabia; and
(3) His confrontation with the giant empires of Byzantium and Persia and conquests of parts of great Iraq and Syria.

Supporting role of Islam

Conversion to Islam. He accepted Islam without any hesitation, argument or reluctance. His conversion to Islam became a landmark in the history of Islam. His conversion according to Muir proved to be the greatest guarantee of the sincerity of Muhammad (peace be on him).

Missionary of Islam. He was the greatest missionary of Islam after the Holy Prophet. Through his efforts many young men among the Quraish joined the fold of Islam.

Liberation of slaves. When the slaves who had accepted Islam were tortured by the Quraish, Hadrat Abu Bakr purchased these slaves from their masters and set them free.

Persecutions of the Quraish. Whenever the Quraish maltreated the Holy Prophet and did him violence, Hadrat Abu Bakr always intervened to protect the Holy Prophet.

Ascension. When the Holy Prophet gave an account of his ascension and some of the Muslims, even, were overcome by doubts, Hadrat Abu Bakr declared in unequivocal terms that what the Holy Prophet said was the truth. Hadrat Abu Bakr became a witness to the truth.

Migration. When the Holy Prophet migrated from

Makkah to Madina, Hadrat Abu Bakr was his companion. Hadrat Abu Bakr looked after the Holy Prophet with the affection and tenderness of a true friend. He met the entire expenses of the journey,

Masjid-i-Nabvi. When the Holy Prophet purchased a plot of land for constructing a mosque at Madina, Hadrat Abu Bakr paid the price.

Battles. In the battle of Badr, Hadrat Abu Bakr acted as a bodyguard of the Holy Prophet. In the battle of Uhud when there was confusion and other companions dispersed, Hadrat Abu Bakr was the first to join the Holy Prophet. In the battle of Hunain when the other companions dispersed, Hadrat Abu Bakr continued to attend the Holy Prophet.

Hudaibiya pact. When the Hudaibiya pact was executed and some of the companions, including Hadrat Umar were critical of the terms of the Pact, Hadrat Abu Bakr supported the Holy Prophet, and held that it was in the best interests of the Muslims.

Liberal contribution. When the Holy Prophet invited contributions for the financing of the Tabuk expedition, Hadrat Abu Bakr donated all that he had, saying that for him and his family Allah and the Holy Prophet were enough.

Psychological crisis. When the Holy Prophet died the entire Muslim community was in the throes of a psychological crisis, and even such a man as Hadrat Umar declared, "Who says that the Holy Prophet is dead ? Moses like he has gone to meet the Lord, and would return to us after some time". At this juncture, Hadrat Abu Bakr perceived the grim reality and said, 'He who worships Muhammad let him know that Muhammad (peace be on him) being a mortal is dead. But he who worships the God of Muhammad (peace be on him), let him know that He being immortal lives and would live for ever".

Support for the Holy Prophet. Hadrat Abu Bakr did not support the Holy Prophet in his lifetime alone; he supported him even after his death. When it was suggested to him that

Usama's expedition should not be despatched or at least Usama should be replaced by a veteran commander, Hadrat Abu Bakr rejected the demands on the ground that the orders of the Holy Prophet had to be followed at all costs, and could not be reversed.

Zakat. When some tribes sought exemption from Zakat, Hadrat Abu Bakr refused the demand on the ground that with regard to a fundamental injunction of Islam there could be no compromise.

Caliphate. When a political crisis threatened the Muslim community in the matter of the successor to the Holy Prophet, Hadrat Abu Bakr was able to persuade the Ansar to relinquish the caliphate in favour of the Quraish.

Saviour of Islam. When after the death of the Holy Prophet the Muslim community came to be threatened with danger from all sides. Hadrat Abu Bakr piloted the crisis with consummate skill. He did not merely save Islam in Arabia; he made Islam a world force which successfully confronted the empires of Persia and Byzantium. Abu Huraira, an eminent companion declared that but for Hadrat Abu Bakr, Islam would have disintegrated Hadrat Abu Bakr, verily, played the role of the saviour of Islam.

Preservation of the Holy Qur'an. Hadrat Abu Bakr sponsored the compilation of the *Mushaf*, and in this way the Word of God was preserved for all times for the guidance of mankind.

Apostasy Campaigns

Apostasy campaigns. When after the death of the Holy Prophet, the storm of apostasy burst in the country and most of the tribes transferred their allegiance to false prophets, things for Islam appeared to be very dark. Hadrat Abu Bakr faced the crisis with strong determination that knew no wavering. Apostasy campaigns began in August 632 C.E. and by February 633 C.E., apostasy was totally suppressed; Arabia stood unified, and all people in Arabia joined the fold of Islam. That was a remarkable achievement which changed the course of history. One shudders to think what would have been the fate of Islam, if Hadrat Abu Bakr had, God forbid, failed in suppressing apostasy.

Riddah campaigns. These campaigns are labelled by the Muslim historians as *Riddah* campaigns, i.e. campaigns against apostasy. Some western writers have found fault with this approach.

J. Wellhausen, a German scholar has advanced the view that the *Riddah* was a break with the leadership in Madina and not with Islam qua religion. Caetni, a French author has advanced the view that certain tribes regarded Islam as an agreement with Muhammad (peace be on him), and considered the election of Hadrat Abu Bakr as a private affair in Madina with which they were not concerned. Becker an English writer has held that the majority of those who seceded had never adopted Islam, and as such the campaigns against them could not be regarded as apostasy campaigns. Dr. Elias S. Shoufani, a Jewish scholar has held that contrary to what Muslim historians have claimed, the *Riddah* was not a religious movement; it was the Nejd tribes' repudiation of their fiscal obligations to Madina. Dr. Shoufani argues that in fact Arabia was far from being unified at the time of the death of the Holy Prophet. In the words of Dr. Shoufani:

> "The appellation of *Riddah* was carelessly expended by early story tellers to cover all movements in Arabia which were antagonistic to Madina. Later, the Muslim jurist adopted the facts to fit in their legal discourse, thus giving their accounts, a religious turn; and after that, historian embraced the early jurists' interpretation".

Implications of the view-points of western writers. In the ultimate analysis the implications of the view-points of western writers work out as follows:

(1) By holding that Arabia was far from being unified at the time of the death of the Holy Prophet, the point sought to be made out is that the Holy Prophet

in spite of his claim had not succeeded in completing his mission.

(2) By holding that the *Riddah* was a break with the leadership in Madina, and not with Islam qua religion, the point sought to be made out is that Hadrat Abu Bakr was guilty of waging war against the Muslim for political and selfish ends.

(3) By holding that the majority of the people had not accepted Islam and as such there was no question of their apostasy, the point sought to be made out is that Hadrat Abu Bakr was guilty of war of aggression against the people of Arabia and forcing Islam through the sword.

(4) By holding that the Muslim jurists adopted the facts to fit in their legal discourse, the point sought to be made out is that both the Muslim jurists and historians have distorted and perverted history.

All these are wild allegations and baseless accusations which do not stand the test of any analysis of the course of history.

Unification of Arabia under the Holy Prophet. Dr. Shoufani's thesis is that, at the time of the death of the Holy Prophet, Arabia was far from being unified, and many people had not accepted Islam. It is accordingly argued that where the people had not accepted Islam, the question of apostasy did not arise. There is fallacy in this thesis as the following arguments would show:

(1) The society in Arabia was tribal in character. The tribes sent representative delegations to Madina, and these delegations accepted Islam for their tribes. Regular agreements were drawn up, and it cannot be said that only some persons accepted Islam, and most of them did not. As a matter of fact all the tribes who sent delegations accepted Islam. It is on record that all tribes had sent their delegations. It, therefore, follows that all the people in Arabia, other than those like the Christians of

Najran with whom there was an agreement to the contrary, had accepted Islam.

(2) When the Sura "Al-Bara'ah" was proclaimed on the occasion of the pilgrimage in 631 C.E. the "declaration of discharge" signified in specific terms that Arabia had been unified under Islam, for unless there was unification there could be no discharge.

(3) When in 632 C.E. over one lakh Muslims assembled on the occasion of the Farewell Pilgrimage, it was a proof positive of the unification of Arabia. On this occasion the Holy Prophet declared in unequivocal terms that two religions were not to be tolerated in Arabia, and that Islam alone was to prevail. How could the Holy Prophet make such a declaration, if Arabia was not unified ?

(4) On the occasion of the Farewell Pilgrimage God revealed that God had completed the religion and chosen Islam for them. That clearly means that by the time of the revelation Arabia had been unified under Islam.

In view of the testimony of the Holy Qur'an, the view of the western writers that Arabia had not been unified under Islam during the lifetime of the Holy Prophet cannot be accepted.

Leadership in Madina. The view that the *Riddah* was a break with the leadership in Madina, and not with Islam qua religion is fallacious and cannot be accepted for the following reasons:

(1) There is no authority in support of the point that any tribe ever raised the issue of non-recognising the leadership of Madina.

(2) The western scholars are apt to view things in the light of the separation of the church and the state, and have failed to realise that there is no such separation in Islam and as such any defiance of

the authority at Madina which was the custodian of Islam had a religious connotation.

(3) The western scholars are under the impression that Zakat is a tax. Zakat is in fact not a tax; it is a religious obligation. Any refusal to pay Zakat was the refusal to follow a basic injunction of Islam, and as such this refusal was not a mere repudiation of a fiscal obligation; it meant refusal to accept a fundamental injunction of Islam. Any attempt to enforce such obligation was religious and not merely political in character.

(4) It is on record that Hadrat Abu Bakr laid down in specific terms that before fighting any tribe, it was to be given the option to accept Islam, and where it accepted Islam, no action was to be taken against it. It was further laid down that where a tribe responded by calling the "Adhan" it was to be presumed that the tribe followed Islam. No *Riddah* war was fought against any party which responded by; Adhan" and professed to be Muslim.

(5) The tribes against whom punitive action was taken definitely repudiated Islam. It is therefore absolutely wrong to hold that the *Riddah* was a break with the leadership in Madina, and not with Islam qua religion.

Significance of apostasy. The question that has been posed is that where the majority of the people did not accept Islam, the question of their apostasy did not arise, and hence, any campaign undertaken against them could not be an apostasy campaign. In the first instance it is not correct that the majority of the people had not accepted Islam. When delegations went to Makkah, and undertook to accept Islam on behalf of their tribes this implied that by agreement the entire tribe had accepted Islam. The position on the ground was that these tribes had accepted Islam, but when false prophets rose in their midst they transferred allegiance to them. The very process of offering allegiance to false prophets was apostasy pure and simple, and when the Muslims took action against the false prophets and their followers, such campaign was an apostasy campaign even though any of the followers might not have formally accepted Islam previously. After the revelation of Sura al-Bara'ah it was proclaimed that no religion other than Islam was to be tolerated in Arabia. This meant that if any attempt was made to enforce any new religion the Muslims could take up arms to suppress such religion and such a campaign taken in the name of religion would be an apostasy campaign .

Analysis of Montgomery Watt. Among the western scholars, Montgomery Watt has understood the position correctly. His analysis of the situation is as follows:

> "Moreover, as in the movement towards Islam, so in the *Riddah*, religion and political factors were inseparably mixed with one another. The Muslim historians were therefore right in regarding it as a religious movement; it was European scholars who erred by taking religion in a European, and not in an Arabic sense. The *Riddah* was a movement away from the religious, social, economic, and political system of Islam, and so was anti-Islamic".

Confrontation with Byzantium and Persia

International background. When Islam appeared on the world stage, the then world was dominated by two powers, Byazntium in the east and Persia in the west. There were spells of war as well as peace between these two powers. During the sixth century, Justinian (527—565 C.E.) was the emperor of Byzantium, while Anaushirwan (531—565 C.E.) was the emperor of Persia. Both of them were contemporaries and great rulers of all world fame. In Byzantium, Justinian was succeeded by Maurice, and in Persia, Anaushirwan was succeeded by Khusro Perwez (Chosroes II). Cbosroes II was overthrown in a military coup in 590, and he had to seek refuge with Maurice, the Byzantine emperor. With the Byzantine help, Chosroes II was restored to the Persian throne.

Maurice regarded Khusro as a son and during the last decade of the sixth century the two countries forged strong links of friendship. In 602 C.E. there was a revolt against Maurice. Maurice was killed, and Phocas became the emperor. There was another revolt in 610 C.E. when Heraclius became the Byzantine emperor. After the death of Maurice, the friendship between the two countries was over. In the second decade of the seventh century, Chosroes II invaded the Byzantine territories. Syria and Jerusalem fell to the Persians in 614 C.E. The Persians carried away the Holy Cross from Jerusalem. The Persians next marched to Egypt and annexed it in 616 C.E. For some time, the Byzantines lay low, but by 622 C.E. the Byzantines were strong enough to launch an attack against Persia. In the battle of Issus in 622 C.E,, the Persians suffered a defeat. Other battles were fought during 623-625 C.E, which were not conclusive. The decisive battle was fought on the banks of the Tigris near the city of Mosul in 625 C.E. when Persia surrendered and asked for terms. As a result of this reverse, there was a revolt against Chosroes II in 628 C.E., when he was killed by his own son Sheroyah. Sheroyah who ascended the Persian throne as Kobad II made peace with Heraclius. By the terms of the peace treaty Persia abandoned all the conquests that it had made earlier in the second decade of the seventh century. Sheroyah died within a year. After him there was complete anarchy in the Sassanian empire and during the next four years, there were a dozen kings including two women. The Byzantine empire on the other hand enjoyed a measure of stability under Heraclius.

Arab buffer stares. When the two empires of Persia and Byzantium expanded, these came to include territories populated by Arabs. As a matter of policy both the empires found it expedient to set up Arab buffer states at the periphery of their empires, In the sixth century, a Ghassanid Arab state was set up in Syria under Al-Harith b. Jabala. This state acknowledged the suzerainty of Byzantium. In the Persian empire a Lakhmid state was set up in Iraq with the capital at Hira. The Lakhmids acknowledged the suzerainty of Persia. The Ghassanids and the Lakhmids were often at war with each other. When Islam appeared on the world stage, the position about these buffer Arab states was changed. In Syria after the death of their king Al-Harith b. Jabala the Ghassanid state split into fifteen principalities. In Persia Chosroes II did away with the Lakhmid state, and took over the territory under the direct rule of Persia. The policy of the Holy Prophet was to win over the border Arab tribes to Islam. It was with a view to this end that the campaigns of Muta and Tabuk were undertaken during the lifetime of the Holy Prophet. When Hadrat Abu Bakr insisted on sending Usama's expedition to Syria, it was in continuation of the policy laid down by the Holy Prophet. With the disintegration of the Persian rule, there was a power vacuum in the coastal areas of east and south Arabia. Islam succeeded in filling up this vacuum. In Iraq, Islam had yet to make headway.

Campaigns of Hadrat Abu Bakr. When Hadrat Abu Bakr became the Caliph in 632 C.E., Islam was threatened with disintegration. Within a year, Hadrat Abu Bakr was strong enough to attack the Persian empire on the north east, and the Byzantine empire in the north west. These were giant empires with history extending over hundreds of years. They had large resources at their disposal. But yet against the Arab hordes the Persian and the Byzantine forces were not able to take a stand. In Iraq the Muslim forces gave blows after blows to the Persian armies. In Syria the same story was repeated, and the Byzantine forces in spite of the superiority in strength and vastness of resources could not withstand the Muslim forces. The story of the History of the Muslim armies in Iraq and Syria reads very much like a tale of the Arabian Nights, too difficult to believe, but yet an established fact of history. In this respect, Professor Hitti observes as follows in his *History of the Arabs:*

> "If some one in the first third of the seventh Christian century had the audacity to prophesy that within a decade some unheralded, unforeseen power from the hitherto barbarians and little known land of Arabia was to make its appearance, hurl itself against the only two powers of the age, fall heir to the one—the Sassanids, and strip the other, the Byzantine of its fairest provinces,

he would undoubtedly be declared a lunatic. Yet that was what happened.

Causes of Muslim success. How the Muslims were able to overpower the gigantic empires of Persia and Byzantium is one of the great mysteries of history. Various western writers have tried to discover in their own way the causes of the astounding success of the Muslims. They have referred to four main causes, namely racial, political, economic and moral.

Racial affinity. Von Kremer has observed as follows in his book *The Orient under Caliphs:*

> "Instead of fighting their powerful kinsmen the people of the frontier towns who were in the play either of the Byzantine or the Persian empire found it much more to their advantage to make common cause with the Arabs. It was thus that a comparitively smaller army which penetrated Syria and Iraq quickly grew like an avalanche, and crushed down all obstacles that stood in its way."

In his book *The age of Faith,* Will Durant has held that the racial factor was an important cause of the success of the Muslims, as both Syria and Iraq contained Arab tribes who had much in common with the Muslims.

In their book *World History* Flenley and Welch have held that the racial affinity of the people made the extension of the Muslim rule easier.

When Hadrat Abu Bakr undertook campaigns in Iraq and these campaigns were really not directed against the Byzantine or Persian empires; these were really directed to bring the Arabs living in Iraq and Syria to the fold of Islam. In the wars in Iraq and Syria many Christian Arabs fought against the Muslims, but many of them sided with the Muslims as well. We can thus concede that in the success of the Muslim arms in Iraq and Syria, Arab nationalism played its part.

Political cause. Will Durant has held, in his book *The Age of Faith,* the political cause of the success of the Muslims was that both Byzantium and Persia exhausted by war and mutual devastation were in a state of decline.

In his book *The History of the World* H. G. Wells has observed as follows:

> "It (Islam) prevailed because every where it found politically apathetic people, robbed, oppressed, bullied uneducated and unorganised and it found selfish and unsound governments out of touch with the people." In their *World History*, Flenley and Welch have also held that the political cause of the success of Muslims was that the Persian and Byzantine empires stood exhausted by mutual wars.

This analysis of the political situation is basically correct, and we can very well hold that when Islam appeared on the scene, these old empires were in the process of decline.

Economic causes. In his book *The History of Syria*, Professor P. K. Hitti has expressed the following views with regard to the economic causes about the success of the Muslims in Iraq and Syria:

> Viewed in its proper perspective the Islamic expansion was one in a series of migration waves carrying a surplus population from a barren peninsula to a border fertile region with a more abundant life. It was in fact the last stage in the age long process of infitration which had begun with the Babylonians some four thousand years before the Islamic movement. The Islamic movement, however, did possess one distinctive feature—the religious impulse. Combined with the economic factor this made the movement irresistible and carried it far beyond the confines of any preceding one. Islam admittedly provided a battle cry, a slogan comparable to that provided by democracy as a cohesive agency cementing tribes heterogeneous masses never united before. But while the desire to spread the new faith or to go to paradise may have been the motivating force in the lives of some of the Bedouin warriors the desire for the comforts and luxuries of settled life in the fertile

> Crescent was the driving force in the case of may of them."

The analysis of Professor Hitti is at the most partially correct. In the context of the events that led to campaigns in Iraq and Syria, there is nothing to show that such campaigns were undertaken because of any economic considerations. As a matter of fact economic considerations were a consequence and not a cause of the wars in Iraq and Syria.

Religious and moral courses. About the religious cause, Will Durant observes as follows in his book *The age of Faith:*

> "The Muslim leaders were passionate disciples of Muhammad; prayed even more than they fought, and in time inspired with a fanaticism that accepted death in a holy war as an open sesame to paradise.

About the moral factors, Will Durant observes as follows in his aforesaid book:

> "Christian ethics and monasticism had reduced in the Near East that readiness for war which characterised Arab custom and Muslim teaching. The Arab troops were more rigorously disciplined and more ably led; they were used to hardships and could fight on empty stomachs.

In their *World History*, Flenley and Welch have observed that new religion Islam provided the necessary unity, leadership and driving force for the Arabian expansion. They also hold that the Arabs were brave and determined fighters, and were more mobile than the Persians or the Byzantines.

Whether Islam was spread through sword ? Some western writers have taken pains to build up the thesis that Islam was spread at the point of sword. It is preposterous to hold that the Muslims won in Iraq and Syria because of their military strength. In the matter of military power and material resources the Arabs could never be a match for the empires of Byzantium and Syria with sophisticated military power and great economic resources. Under these circumstances there was no question of a great power asserting its faith backed by military strength. Islam was on the other hand a revolt against power, a militarily weak people contended against mightier people, and surprisingly enough they won. In the conquered territories the Muslims did not insist on the people becoming Muslims. They were allowed to follow their religion subject to the payment of 'Jizya'. As such there is absolutely no weight in the argument that Islam was at any stage spread through sword.

Fulfilment of history. Whatever the causes that led to the success of the Muslims when they emerged on the international horizon, so much is certain that the astounding success of the Muslim forces in Iraq and Syria reads very much like a tale from the Arabian Nights. Truth is said to be stranger than fiction, and it was certainly so in the case of the Muslim conquests of Iraq and Syria. It appears that the Muslims were merely an instrument for the fulfilment of history. Iraq and Syria fell to the Muslims just as a ripe apple would fall to the ground under the law of gravitation. It is an undeniable fact that by overpowering the empires of Persia and Byzantium, Hadrat Abu Bakr changed the course of history. The story of Hadrat Abu Bakr is the Story of faith that moved mountains.

NOTES

In the Chapter entitled Hadrat Abu Bakr in History" I have made an attempt to study the achievements of Hadrat Abu Bakr from the histographic point of view. It is the task histography to study the causes that led to certain historical events. The main historical events of the time of Harat Abu Bakr are: suppression of apostasy and unification of Arabia under Islam; and conquests of greater parts of Iraq and Syria. Hadrat Abu Bakr did not merely make an impact on history, he changed the very course of history. Under him the Arabs emerged on the international scene, and overpowered the giant empires of Persia in the east, and Byzantium in the west. The success of Hadrat Abu Bakr is a great marvel of history. It is the task of a student of history to analyse the causes that led to such unique achievement.

Western scholars have to study these phenomena in their own way. Most of the western scholars have taken the view that what the Muslims call the *Riddah* or Apostasy wars, were in fact not the wars of apostasy. I have discussed these views at length, and have exposed the fallacy in the approach of the western writers.

The western writers have spelled out the causes of the success of the Muslims in the campaigns against Iraq and Syria. I have referred to the findings of the western scholars, and given my comments.

In writing this Chapter, I have consulted the following books:

(1) *Ar Riddah and the Muslim Conquest of Arabia* by Dr. Elias Shoufani.
(2) *Chronologia Islamica* by Leone Caetani.
(3) *Annals* by Leone Caetani.
(4) *The Caliphate: Its Rise, Decline and Fall* by Sir William Muir.
(5) *The Arabs in History* by Bernard Lewis.
(6) *Cambridge Medieval History:* C. H. Becker.
(7) *History of the Arabs* by Philip Hitti.

(8) *The Caliphate* by Thomas Arnold.
(9) *An Interpretation of Islamic History* by H. A. R. Gibb.
(10) *History of the Islamic People* by Carl Brockelmann
(11) *The Arabs* by Arnold Hottingir.
(12) *A History of Muslim Historigraphy* by F. Rosenthal.
(13) *Muhammad at Makkah* by Montgomery Watt.
(14) *Muhammad at Madina* by Montgomery Watt.

My conclusion is that God chose the Muslims as an instrument for the unfolding of destiny and the fulfilment of history. Iraq and Syria fell to the Muslims just as a ripe apple would fall to the gound under the law of gravitation. It was the faith in Islam which was responsible for the success of the Muslims. Hadrat Abu Bakr who led the Muslims at this stage was an embodiment of faith, the faith that can move mountains, and verily such faith changed the course of history. In the writings of the western scholars howsoever sympathetic to Islam they may outwardly appear to be, there is always some undercurrent of thought motivated with the desire to belittle the achievements of Islam, and distort history. I wish the Muslim schloars should resurrect the history of Islam and project it in proper perspective.

APPENDICES

CHRONOLOGY

573 C.E.	Birth of Hadrat Abu Bakr.
582 C.E.	Travelled with a caravan to Syria and met th monk Bahira at Busra.
590 C.E.	Adopted the business of cloth merchant
591-600 C.E.	Married first Qutaila and then Umm Ruman.
595-609 C.E.	Birth of his children Abdul Rahman, Hadrat Asma, Abdullah and Hadrat Ayesha.
610 C.E.	Conversion to Islam.
613 C.E.	Islam began to be preached openly when Hadrat Abu Bakr gave the first address calling the people to Islam.
616 C.E.	Migration of the first batch of the Muslims to Abyssinia.
617 C.E.	The Quraish impose a ban on Banu Hashim. Hadrat Abu Bakr leaves Makkah for migration to Madina, but returns to Makkah at the instance of Al-Dughunna.
618 C.E.	Abandons the protection of Al-Dughunna.
619 C.E.	End Of the boycott against Banu Hashim, Death of Abu Talib, and Hadrat Khadija.
620 C.E.	Ascension of the Holy Prophet. Hadrat Abu Bakr becomes a witness to the Truth and is awarded, by the Holy Prophet, the title of As-Siddiq.
621 C.E.	The Holy Prophet is engaged to Hadrat Ayesha a daughter of Hadrat Abu Bakr.
622 C.E.	Hadrat Abu Bakr migrates to Madina in the company of the Holy Prophet.
623 C.E.	Hadrat Ayesha is married to the Holy Prophet.
624 C.E.	Battle of Badr.
625 C.E.	Battle of Uhud.

626 C.E.	Campaigns against the Jews.
627 C.E.	Battle of the Ditch.
628 C.E.	Hudaibiya Pact. Campaign against the Jews of Khyber.
629 C.E.	Makkah revisited. Death of his wife Umm Ruman. His marriage to Asma the widow of Jafar b. Abu Talib.
630 C.E.	Conquest of Makkah. Battles of Hunain and Taif.
631 C.E.	Campaign against Tabuk, Campaign against Dhatus Salasil. Acts as Amir-ul-Hajj, his third visit to Makkah.
632 C.E.	Death of the Holy Prophet. Farewell pilgrimage. His fourth visit to Makkah. His election as Caliph. Usamah's army leave for Syria in the last of June. Some of the tribes attack Madina in July but are repulsed. Battles of Zul Qissa and Abraq (August). Battle of Buzakha (September). Battle of Zafar (October). Battle of Daba in Bahrain (November). Battle of Yamama (December).
633 C.E.	Battle of Hajira in Bahrain (January). Campaign in Mahra (January); operations in Yemen and Hadramawt (January); battle of Kazims (April); battle of Mazar (April); battle of Walaja (April); battle of Ulleis (May); battle of Amgheeshiya (May); conquest of Al-Hira (June): battle of Anbar (July); battle of Ein-ut-Tamr (July); battle of Daumatul Jandal (August), death of his son Abdullah (September); battle of Huseid (October); Battles of Muzayyah, Saniyy and Zumeil (November); battle of Firaz (December).
634 C.E.	Muslim forces leave for Syria (April): Khalid marches from Iraq to Syria (June); battle of Busra (July); battle of Ajnadein (August); battle of Babylon (August); Death of Hadrat Abu Bakr 23rd August 634 C.E.

Bibliography

(1) *Abu Bakr, Siddiqi-i-Akbar* by Muhammad Hussain Haykal.

(2) *Seerat-i-Abu Bakr,* Taj Co.

(3) *Abu Bakr, the Caliph* by A. A. Aziz.

(4) *Hadrat Abu Bakr* by Syed Moinul Haq.

(5) *Al-Riddah and the Muslim Conquest of Arabia* by Elias Shoufani.

(6) *The Sword of Allah* by Lt. General A. I. Akram.

(7) *The Book of the Battles* by Al-Waqidi.

(8) *Tabaqat* by Ibn Saad.

(9) *The Book of Conquests* by Al-Baladhuri.

(10) *History of Islam* by Tabari.

(11) *History of Islam* by Ibn Khaldun.

(12) *History of the Time* by Masudi.

(13) *The Lions of the Forests* by Ibn al-Athir.

(14) *The Demise of the Prominent People* by Ibn Khallikan.

(15) *The Book of Examples* by Ibn Khallikan.

(16) *History of the Caliphs* by Jalaluddin Suyuti (Translated by Jarret).

(17) *Al-Ma'arif* by Ibn Quteiba.

(18) *Tarikh-i-Yaqubi* by Yaqubi.

(19) *Al-Buldan by* Yaqubi.

(20) *Alaqun Nafeesa* by Ibn Rusta.

(21) *Al-Aghani* by Isfahani.

(22) *Mujam-ul-Buldan* by Yaquti.

(23) *Decline and Fall of the Roman Empire* by Edward Gibbon.

(24) *Life of Muhammad* by Guillamme.

(25) *Life of Muhammad* by Sir William Muir.

(26) *Annals of the Early Caliphate* by Sir William Muir.

(27) *The Early Caliphate* by Maulana Muhammad Ali.

(28) *Successors of Muhammad* by Washington Irving.

(29) *Mohammadanism* by C.S. Huroronje.

(30) *Muhammad the Holy Prophet* by Hafiz Ghulam Sarwar.

(31) *The Arabs in History* by Bernard Lewis.

(32) *History of the Arabs* by P. K. Hitti.

(33) *Short History of the Saracens* by Syed Ameer Ali.

(34) *Outline of History* by H. G. Wells.

(35) *Studies of the Civilisation of Islam* by H. A. R. Gibbs.

(36) *Muhammad the Ideal Prophet* by Sulaiman Nawi.

(37) *Muhammad at Makkah* by Montgomery Watt.

(38) *Muhammad at Madina* by Montgomery Watt.

(39) *The Glorious Caliphate* by Athar Hussain.

(40) *The Caliphate* by Sir Thomas W. Arnold.

(41) *Kitabul Khilafa al-Islamia* by Rashid Rida.

(42) *Muhammad and Muhammadanism* by Bosworth Smith.

(43) *Muhammad: Prophet and Statesman* by Montgomery Watt.

(44) *Muhammad and the Rise of Islam* by D. S. Margoliuth.

(45) *Muhammad the Man and his Faith* by T. Andrae.

(46) *Muhammad and His Power* by P. De Lacy Johnstone.

(47) *Muhammad the Prophet* by Sardar Iqbal Ali Shah.

(48) *The Prophet of Islam* by Stanley Lanepoole.

(49) *Prophet of the Desert* by K. L. Gauba.

(50) *The Messenger* by R. T. C. Bodley.

(51) *The Greatness of Muhammad* by S. D. Kudsey.

(52) *The Great Prophet* by F. K. Durrani.

(53) *Essays on the life of Muhammad* by Sir Syed Ahmad.

(54) *Islam and the Arabs* by R. Landau.

(55) *The Ideal World Prophet* by Fazal Karim.

(56) *Wives of Muhammad* by Malik Fida Hussain.

(57) *Muhammad the Prophet* by Mohammad Ali.

(58) *The Life of Muhammad the Prophet of Allah* by E. Dinet and Sulaiman b. Ibrahim.

(59) *Hayat-i-Muhammad* by Muhammad Hussain Haykal.

(60) *History of Syria* by P. K. Hitti.

(61) The Arabs by Maxime Rodinson.

(62) *World History* by Flenley and Welch.

(63) *The Age of Faith* by Will Durant,

(64) *Apology for Muhammad* by John Davenport,

(65) *Muhammad Rasul Ullah* by Muhammad Hamidullah.

(66) *Early Heroes of Islam* by G. A. Salik.

(67) *Abu Bakr Siddiq and Farooq Azam* by Taha Hussain.

(68) *The Empire of the Arabs* by John Bagot Glubb.

(69) *Literary History of the Arabs* by Nicholson.

(70) *Call of the Minaret* by Kenneth Cragg.

(71) *Origin of Muhammadan Jurisprudence* by Joseph Schacht.

(72) *Studies in Early Hadith Literature* by Dr. Muhammad Mustafa Azmi.

(73) *Ashab-i-Rasul aur unke karname* by Nabi Ahmad Suha.

(74) *Cambridge History of Islam.*

(75) *History of the Saracens* by S. Ockley.

(76) *Short History of the Saracens* by Amir Ali

(77) *History of Muhammadanism* by C. Mills.

(78) *History of Muhammadanism* by W. C. Taylor.

(79) *History of the Islamic Peoples* by Dr. Well.

(80) *History of the Islamic People* by Brockelman.

(81) *A Short History of Islam* by S. F. Mahmud.

(82) *The Arab Kingdom and its Fall* by Wellhausen.

(83) *Encyclopaedia of Islam.*

(84) *Encyclopaedia Britannica.*